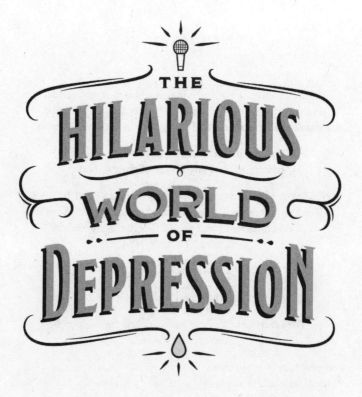

THE HILARIOUS WORLD OF DEPRESSION

JOHN MOE

ST. MARTIN'S GRIFFIN
NEW YORK

Published in the United States by St. Martin's Griffin, an imprint of St. Martin's Publishing Group

THE HILARIOUS WORLD OF DEPRESSION. Copyright © 2020 by John Moe. All rights reserved. Printed in the United States of America. For information, address St. Martin's Publishing Group, 120 Broadway, New York, NY 10271.

www.stmartins.com

Designed by Meryl Sussman Levavi

The Library of Congress has cataloged the hardcover edition as follows:

Names: Moe, John, author.
Title: The hilarious world of depression / John Moe.
Description: First [edition]. | New York : St. Martin's Press, [2020]
Identifiers: LCCN 2019058396 | ISBN 9781250209283 (hardcover) | ISBN 9781250270924 (ebook)
Subjects: LCSH: Depression, Mental.
Classification: LCC RC537 .M626 2020 | DDC 616.85/27—dc23
LC record available at https://lccn.loc.gov/2019058396

ISBN 978-1-250-20956-6 (trade paperback)

Our books may be purchased in bulk for promotional, educational, or business use. Please contact your local bookseller or the Macmillan Corporate and Premium Sales Department at 1-800-221-7945, extension 5442, or by email at MacmillanSpecialMarkets@macmillan.com.

First St. Martin's Griffin Edition: 2022

10 9 8 7 6 5 4 3 2 1

"A laughably relatable (and at times bittersweet) read . . . Uplifting."
—*Mandatory*

"More than once I woke my husband up shouting, 'Oh my God, THIS. IT IS *EXACTLY* THIS,' while reading this book. He was concerned but no more than usual."
—Jenny Lawson

For you and someone you know

CONTENTS

THE BIG SEXY CELEBRITY LASER FIGHT: A PREFACE

I don't always read book prefaces, so I figured I'd name mine something exciting to get you to check it out.

I've got this illness that I've been living with for decades. It's very serious, and it has caused significant damage to me and to those I love. The illness has negatively affected my physical health, my social skills, my moods, my self-image, and my outlook on the future. It is shapeless, colorless, and invisible. Though I am still alive, somehow, it is a potentially fatal condition, and lots of people die from it every year.

I am speaking, of course, about disco fever.

No, no, it's depression! I was vaccinated against disco fever years ago.

Here's the weird part: even when I was in the darkest and most despairing times of my depression, I still found depression funny. It was funny to me that the illness distorted my view of the real world like a funhouse mirror. It was funny that I could be immobilized by something that had no basis in a broken bone or bacteria or any tangible factor. And when other people, especially comedians and writers, shared their experiences with depression and those experiences were resonant with my own, I could laugh because we were all getting fooled together. I laughed in the same way an audience laughs at a particularly good trick pulled off by a magician. "We've all been deceived, but we don't know how!" I don't really yell that at magic shows. Maybe I'll start.

I created the podcast *The Hilarious World of Depression* to share the laughs and hope and human compassion that come from people talking to people about this traditionally dark topic. I've interviewed dozens of comics, musicians, writers, and public figures who have dealt with depression, and I've noticed a lot of things that come up again and again. Certain symptoms, distorted mindsets, and thought patterns recur in people from all walks of life who are facing off against this thing. And I often recognize what they're saying because it matches what depression has placed in my own head over the course of my life.

With this book, I'm putting it all together. This is my memoir and my illness's biography. It's stories of how I've been tortured by this thing but also found the absurd humor in it. It's the tale of how my illness might have gotten started, how it emerged, how it morphed and evolved over time, and, of course, how it keeps trying to kill me. Like a close friend who keeps trying to kill you. There's what I've learned from my own story, a story I don't talk about much on the show, and there are lots of contributions from *THWoD* guests. There's more here than I could ever get into a podcast.

I'm writing this book because books are sacred objects to me. My walls are lined with books I've read that remain there despite my wife's strongest hints that perhaps it is time they moved along. There will be some things in here—hopefully a lot of things—that resonate for you, either as a person dealing with depression or just as a citizen in a world filled with people doing so. With this book, I want to share with you both what I've learned and what my friends, the celebrities, have learned so you can think about the book, go back to it, bookmark parts, highlight or underline parts, and lend it to your friends. If you're reading this on a phone or an e-book reader, find those features, but don't draw all over the screen with a Sharpie. If you're listening to the audiobook, go ahead and draw all over my mouth and throat with the Sharpie and then lend my mouth to your friends.

I want to share all this in one place because if we talk, things get better, and more people we love might stick around so we can love them more.

THE
HILARIOUS
WORLD
OF
DEPRESSION

1

IN WHICH I
FINALLY GET BETTER

It was summer outside, bright and humid, and I was inside, sitting in a big poofy chair, ready to get into it with a new therapist.

"I'll probably make jokes," I said to begin our first appointment. "It's part of the way I talk. I like to make jokes about grim and grisly stuff as a way of facing it. The jokes, the laughs, that's oxygen for me. Maybe it's deflection. I'm not sure. I don't think so. You tell me."

"Okay," Julie said.

This was the intake session, where you tell the therapist your story and include descriptions of family of origin, traumas, any occurrence of mental illness on your family tree, current life, health habits, and the reason you made the appointment that put you in the poofy chair.

"I've been depressed my whole life, but I only found out about twelve years ago. I've been kind of faking my way through since childhood. I've managed to stop getting worse. I want to be better."

"Well, let's see if we can do something about that," said Julie.

I liked her. Finding a therapist is a bit like dating. You might have to have some very boring or weird or tense meetings before you find someone you connect with. I was fortunate that this felt good right away. For various reasons, I had mostly had short-term relationships with therapists in the past. Just flings. Even a few one-session stands. I had never been able to make much of a commitment. My mind was a wild stallion that demanded to run free.

I continued, "I have to say, though, I have a lot of reasons to think this won't work. And, yes, I know that might be the depression talking, but it's also the only evidence I've got. It's never gotten better before, really, so how could it? But yes, I'm ready to try. I hope it works. I doubt it will."

Julie was a bit younger than me but old enough to have lived a life; she had probably experienced hardship, probably had someone close to her die, so I felt like she would know what I was talking about. She was cheerful but reserved, reminding me of someone I might have known in college who was in a sorority but also kind of knew how silly sororities were.

"What's really, I guess, dumb? About this? Is that I've got this show I host. It's a podcast about depression, so I spend all day at work thinking about this stuff and a lot of time outside work talking about this stuff. I travel places to give speeches about this stuff. Right now, I'm working on a book about this stuff, too. But it all came out of this podcast."

"I know the podcast well," she said. "You emailed me about it, but I already knew it."

I *had* emailed her but figured she wouldn't read the email or remember it if she had because I'm dumb and worthless and everyone hates me. This didn't make me sad; it's the way I understood the world to be.

I kept talking, like I do. "But the thing about that show is that it's mostly about other people's depression. I feel like I understand other people's depression pretty well, actually. I can quickly figure out what their issues are and draw information and stories out of them. Make connections they hadn't thought of. The thing is, I don't know what is going on with me. It's hard to see a skyscraper from inside the skyscraper."

My first appointment with Julie took place after two full seasons of *The Hilarious World of Depression*. By the time I talked to her, I had conducted a couple of years' worth of deep and lengthy interviews with comedians, musicians, and writers who had dealt with clinical depression, or "Clinny D" as we had taken to calling it on the show. I'd also spent a lot of time with my public radio colleagues discussing those interviews and how best to present them in order to inform, enlighten, and entertain our audience. This moment, here with Julie, was really the first time I had attempted to do anything to improve my own mental health, which had ranged from "getting by" to "disastrous" for most of my life. I had spent years exhorting people to get help and to believe that they could get better while never believing that about myself.

Instead of attempting to actually improve the health of my mind, I had always looked for ways to just hold on for a while longer. Essentially, it was as if I were living in a house that kept catching on fire but all I had ever tried to do was douse the flames. From there, I guess, the plan was to sit in this charred, smoke-damaged house and say, "Well, now everything is okay!" without having any intention of fixing the walls, patching the roof, or figuring out where the goddamn flames kept coming from in the first place. Friends, that's just bad property management.

I had ended up believing that it was just too late for me. I was never going to do any better with my mental health, so the best-case scenario was to do no worse. I wasn't thrilled about that, but I accepted it. The notion of improving seemed a lot like getting your arm bitten off by a shark and then waiting for a new arm to grow back. What you really need to do then is stop the bleeding and launch a podcast about shark bite wounds. Okay, for real though, there are going to be a lot of metaphors and similes in this book. I can't even define depression. I've never found anyone who could. That's part of the problem. So, reader, it'll be analogy-a-go-go from here on; strap in.

I was in Julie's office because there was finally a critical mass of significant events in my life that made seeking help seem viable and sort of urgent in a prevention-of-dying kind of way. One was that I was turning fifty, which is only still middle age if you plan to be a hundred. Frankly, the sands of my mortal life were falling into the bottom part of the hourglass. I was on deadline before my dead line.

Also, lately, I kept wanting to . . . not so much die as simply not be alive anymore. I didn't want to kill myself—God, no, far from it—I just kept thinking about how nothingness, a nothingness in which I am not even aware of nothingness, would be sort of delicious. This, even though the world has wonderful stuff to offer, like my family and ice cream and the NBA playoffs. I'd be driving in to work or cleaning the kitchen or trying to sleep and boom! there came the thoughts of longing for the void, a void that I fully understood I would not perceive because that's the thing about voids. This feeling was morbid and, yes, depressing, but it was also just pesky. What it really was, of course, was a mind that wanted to rest but kept whirring along and pushing me to dark places.

My unique brand of depression responds to stress; specifically, it blows up under stress. When the going gets tough, I don't get amped up, I get despondent. I turn into a human version of a song by the Smiths. By the time I reached for the phone to call Julie for an appointment, I was basically Morrissey crooning alone in a darkened basement. Stressors included my soon-to-be high school senior son, Charlie, getting ready to apply to colleges, booking the next season of our show, and trying to do a good job writing the book you're reading right now.

And yes, there's always stress in life, we all go through stuff, but the rate at which I metabolized stress into depression had gone through the roof. It was a brutally efficient machine.

"What do you have to be stressed about?" the normies might have said, if I ever talked about these things with normal people. "You have a family, a house, a car, a good job. Just deal with it!"

As if I could simply do that. As if I chose this. As if I looked at the options available to me and they were clearly labeled "Perseverance" and "Freaking the Fuck Out All the Time" and calmly said, "Mmm, yes, I select option B."

Normies and saddies are different, you see. Let's say there's a long bridge going over a high canyon and there are two cars on it, one for the normies and one for the saddies. The normies are in a big land yacht of a Buick, weighs a ton, low to the ground. When a stiff wind blows, the normies feel a mild push but continue driving, perhaps casually noting that it's "gettin' windy out there!" Then they go back to listening to, I don't know, Foo Fighters. The saddies are piled into a Model T with a sail on top of it for some reason. They see the wind coming, and it's all they can do to keep from being blown off the road and plunging into the canyon. The normies see the saddies struggle and wonder what the problem is because, to them, the wind doesn't seem that bad. "Try being more positive!" the normies shout as the saddies' Model T goes tumbling off the side and the saddies deploy the parachutes they've gotten used to wearing.

I'd had good therapists in the past, briefly, but all I ever took away from therapy was a somewhat clearer understanding of how messed up I was. That's helpful, sure, but it's not really progress. Like knowing the brand of refrigerator you're locked in. And this was not the fault of the therapists I had seen, who were all trained pros and good at their jobs. It was my fault, or Clinny D's fault. I never wanted to go all that deep in therapy because that's where the monsters were. I'm talking about the really *really* bad memories, the deep bruises, the scars, the events that significantly shape a person through injury. Trauma. Rather than tackle the past, I was willing to settle for a tense ceasefire with it, letting my life be like Middle East countries that hate each other. There would be car bombings, but a homeland is a homeland.

I had gone through life with the belief, often heard in simpleminded quarters of popular psychology, that the past is the past and you just have to move on. "Let it go," the simple-minded say, again, as if no one had ever tried that before. Don Henley and Glenn Frey wrote a song along these lines called "Get Over It" (my response song would be called "Fuck Off, Don Henley and Glenn Frey, You Don't Know What You're Talking About"). I suspect most people who choose the willfully simplistic Henley method are people who've never had much unpleasant stuff in their past to begin with, because this notion is some bullshit. If you can't understand your past, then you don't really know how your mind got to where it is now, because you simply don't know yourself.

Making matters worse, depression causes the saddie to lose hope. It inserts despair where hope should go, and you're left at least suspecting, if not believing in your heart, that nothing will or even could get better. So to figure things out? I mean, depression doesn't even want you to get up, take a shower, and brush your teeth, so something like figuring out how your own mind works feels about as easy as taking a bus to Mars.

Over and over in interviews I conducted for the show, I heard about CBT, cognitive behavioral therapy. It's a practical method of psychological counseling that's built around retraining one's thought patterns so that everyday stimuli aren't converted into toxic thoughts. You tear down the old roads that always go to the bad parts of town, and you build strong new highways to prosperous neighborhoods. On the show, it was the guests who had gone through CBT who seemed to be doing the best. So when I went to find a new therapist, I limited my search. They had to offer this specific approach, they had to be relatively close to my house so I couldn't talk my way out of going, and they couldn't be, like, twenty-three and / or named Kristi.

In that first session, I only got about halfway through my biography. I think most therapists and patients can get this all done in one session, but we had to schedule a second to fully describe all the ick. I recall Julie's mouth actually dropping open during one description of family behaving in a not-at-all-nurturing manner. When you've shocked a professional therapist, you've accomplished something.

At the end of the second half of intake, Julie paused, collected some thoughts, and said, "You've been through more than most other people." I gave myself a little mental high five for being the trauma champ, quickly imagining a lavish yet morose award ceremony.

The longest road a person with depression travels can often be the one between where they are at present and where they can get help to improve. Seeking that out, making that appointment, and keeping that appointment can be a Herculean task. And yes, that sounds, well, crazy. If you can get better, why wouldn't you want to do that as soon as possible? It's like being super hungry but reluctant to go to the Free Pizza Store located ten feet away. (I don't know how the Free Pizza Store stays in business, honestly.)

(Also, now I imagine a depressed Hercules trying to figure out what therapist is in his insurance network and wishing he had some pizza.)

What keeps people away is a fear, one that depression itself is delighted to stoke, that as long as you don't find out you have mental health problems, then you somehow don't have mental health problems. If you never get a good look at the monster, then there's no need to fight the monster. The problem there is that yeah, that monster is real, and if you opt out of fighting it, the monster simply beats the crap out of you all the time.

While I had the monster pretty well contained, I wanted to start throwing some punches. I wanted to feel better.

So we got to work unpacking it all.

2

JUNIOR HIGH SCHOOL
AND DEPRESSION
BEING SOMEHOW CONNECTED

K a-whompo.

I got hit by a car on the way to school in seventh grade. Predawn haze at 7:25 a.m., darker due to the usual Pacific Northwest cloud cover. Right by the big roadside sign that read MARINE HILLS, denoting our middle-class housing development, there was an intersection that wasn't marked as a crosswalk but that kids used every day anyway, skittering across when there seemed to be a break in traffic. Frankly, it's a miracle that pubescent corpses didn't litter that road on a daily basis. It was a recipe for disaster, and I followed that recipe. As I crossed, failing to account for a car's acceleration based on its widening headlights, the driver was failing to account for children darting out when and where they shouldn't. Yes, I'm blaming myself for getting hit by a car. Habit. Sorry. The screeching of brakes got my attention so that I turned to face the midsize sedan coming at me, got clipped at the knees, flattened my torso across the hood and head-banged it, lost consciousness, rolled across the hood, and was deposited on the roadside, where I woke up.

No apparent damage. I could move everything, and nothing felt broken. The woman who hit me was freaked out but very kind. She gave me a ride home, where my mom looked me over and sent the woman on her way. I didn't have to go to school that day; Mom went to work. That was it. I stayed home, watching Bob Barker on *The Price Is Right* and thinking being hit by a car should be a bigger deal than this to other people. I was terrified.

The incident turned into a story to tell people at school, a few days of popularity, and an empty promise by the school to do something to make that stretch of road safer. Since I was physically fine, I regarded this as merely an odd thing that happened. But the older I get, the more I think about it and what long-term effect that trauma (and it was trauma) had. Trauma occurs when something happens that's too horrible for your brain to deal with, so you just store it away. Over time, the horrible thing, which is still there, starts coming out in a variety of ugly ways, causing mental problems that you don't even associate with the trauma because it happened so long ago.

Trauma is a wolf and your mind is a house and it's like, "Oh, I'm safe from that wolf because I trapped it in my house before it could hurt me." But then a while later, it's "Oh no! What happened to my house? My furniture is shredded and there's wolf poop everywhere! How did THAT happen? Oh hey, I'm being mauled."

A few years before being hit by a car, I had caught a BB from a BB gun in my chest. My friend Dean and I were messing around with one of the BB guns my family always seemed to have in the house. It wasn't loaded, so we were pumping air into the gun and then shooting each other to find out what compressed air felt like. Smart kids! When we took a break, my brother Rick dropped an actual BB in there. When Dean fired point-blank at me, the BB that he and I didn't think existed entered my chest and a trickle of blood made its way down my white T-shirt. Before I could comprehend what was happening, I was hurled into our family's Chevy van and my mom was rushing me to the hospital. We were told that the little metal pellet had missed my heart by an inch. It's still there, and I forget about it for years at a time until something like an MRI happens and the technician becomes very confused. It would be nice if I could feel as if surviving that and the car whomping made me invincible, but instead it has always made me feel like I could be killed at any moment. I don't know why Rick put that BB in there.

By junior high, boys and girls were coupling up, heavy metal and its attendant Satanism became crucially important, and everyone was suddenly talking about and consuming drugs. Federal Way, my hometown, is a working-class suburb, so while we didn't have expensive drugs, pot and amphetamines were cheap and plentiful.

About half of our class seemed to switch from being children to burnout headbangers over the summer before seventh grade. Kelly, a very sweet and kind girl from down the street who talked like a cartoon fawn, pulled out a joint as we walked to school one day, drastically changing my view of her, drugs, school, and, I suppose, cartoon fawns.

Sacajawea Junior High was made up of a series of small buildings, the covered outdoor paths between them serving as hallways. I assume the architects had in mind that this open outdoor plan would allow for a comfortable and less restrictive environment than anxiety-producing indoor hallways. If that was their intention, it was sabotaged by the bright yellow lines painted on the concrete pathways that surrounded the buildings. The yellow lines, abundant throughout the campus, were not to be crossed. A student absentmindedly wandering across a yellow line was to be gently corrected by any nearby teacher, whereas a student flagrantly crossing the yellow line in order to cause a ruckus was to be sent to the principal's office for punishment commensurate with their wanton yellow-line crossing.

In practice, none of it happened. The teachers couldn't remember the rules of the goddamn yellow lines and were always stressed out about them. Some of my happiest memories of junior high are of kids jumping on and over the lines and teachers shaking their heads and walking away while the administration's dream of a student body disciplined navy-brig-style shattered and we laughed as the adults' spirits broke. Good times.

Depression has no yellow warning lines. In my case, I was already carrying the trauma of two close calls with death. I also had a genetic predisposition, judging by the suicides and bleak life trajectories of various Norwegian ancestors, a low thrum of trauma that just kept getting passed down like a lefse recipe. Then there was just plain ol' hormone-squirting puberty, which must have had some degree of culpability.

This is why much of the conversation about the origins of major depressive disorder is so often off base. The emotion of being down, unhappy, or despairing as a response to negative circumstances can be excruciating, but it is not technically a disorder. In fact, it's logical and even healthy. A disorder is when you can't recover from that feeling. A disorder is when you feel that way even when devastating events are not taking place or when you can't hold down a job or relationships or take care of your responsibilities.

I will never know exactly why I started to go bonkers in junior high, but bonkers I went. I was sad, yes. Also agitated. Also gloomy. Sad, Agitated, and Gloomy are all dwarf characters from my goth remake of Snow White.

When it started to happen, I had no idea that these were symptoms of a treatable illness, that this was a health condition.

Junior high health class was no help. Sure, the resentful gym teacher running the "welcome to adulthood" orientation covered things like puberty, gonorrhea, syphilis, and unexpected body hair, but he never mentioned screaming brains or morbid thoughts. And if it wasn't discussed there, that meant there was no path from what was happening to "health." It meant that what I was going through was not normal, and if it wasn't normal, it was obviously bad. So I kept quiet, as millions of adolescents do every day.

None of the preparation I'd had for junior high ever involved the idea that I would be increasingly unable to concentrate in class, at home, anywhere, really. It was never mentioned that I would routinely fail to remember what a teacher had said a few minutes earlier or what they were saying right in the moment. None of this had been a problem before. I had considered myself to be a bright kid until that point. I was proud of me. But no longer.

At some point in seventh grade I moved into what I now know to have been obsessive compulsive disorder and what I then knew as I Am Going Crazy. It started small. When I turned around to my right I would have to make sure to turn back around to my left, coming back to my starting position, before walking forward. If I attempted to walk forward without reorienting myself, it would eat at me, my brain screaming, *"Fix this!"* until I stopped, respun, and moved on in temporary peace.

There's a misconception around OCD that all people who have it are delusional, that they live in a different world where life and death are determined by whether they tap the doorknob an odd or even number of times. But for me, and for a lot of other folks with OCD, that's not how it works. They know how stupid this whole thing is; they fully realize how silly it is to have to go through these patterns all the goddamn time. They know it's making them late for work, and like anyone else with a mental illness, they would love to make the whole thing stop, but they just cannot.

Looking back on it, this was all about control. When school seemed like chaos and home felt like chaos, a calibration of body turns was something over which I had domain.

My friend Dean, my almost-BB-assassin, at whose house I spent a good deal of time, had two dogs: Punkin and Buffy. Punkin, fluffier and more relaxed and confident than Buffy, was my favorite of the two. When I realized I had a preference, I was mortified; I felt as if I had committed a great crime. As if the dogs or anyone would care that I had a favorite. (Punkin was factually a better dog. Fuck Buffy.) If I patted Punkin, I'd have to make sure to pat Buffy. I'm not sure what would happen if I didn't, but it would be bad. Eventually, I'd count the number of pats I'd give Punkin so Buffy would receive the exact same amount. From that point on, I'd dread even seeing those dogs because they represented a mountain of compulsory math.

It would happen at home, too, even during the most calm and mindless times. Channel 13 had *The Groovie Goolies* reruns on in the afternoon. It was a 1970 cartoon about hipster monsters because, hey, sure, why not. I didn't get the cultural references or what I can only assume were thinly veiled LSD allusions, but I would sometimes watch it, sprawled on the couch, trying to relax after school. During one episode, I was struck with a wave of guilt about watching such bad TV and decided to turn it off and go outside. I did so just as the announcer introduced a cartoon band called the Mummies & the Puppies, which was supposed to be a riff on the Mamas & the Papas, except, and follow the joke here, with mummies and puppies. I went outside, and after a few minutes I began to wonder what song this band was performing. "It doesn't matter," I thought.

But it mattered. This is the D part of OCD, the disorder that interfered with my basic ability to control my own brain. I didn't know what the song was on *Groovie Goolies*, I had been outside long enough that it was over, and now I would never know it. There was no YouTube. Television happened in the moment and then it was gone forever. I would never know. I WOULD NEVER KNOW. Intellectually, of course, it didn't matter, but my mind had been petting Punkin and would never see Buffy again. And so I kept going fucking crazy.

For months after that, every day out of nowhere my mind would scream a reminder that I would never know what the Mummies & the Puppies sang. The thought, the terrible incompleteness of the experience, would then torment me all over again. Oh, my mind knew what a stupid thing this was to get obsessed about, but that didn't stop it; it only cranked up a roar of self-loathing to go with the OCD. "I could call channel 13," I thought, "and ask them who made *Groovie Goolies*, then write a letter to those people and ask them." But I didn't do that, because that's what a crazy person would do, and I didn't want to be locked in a padded room. I figured the padded room and the straitjacket were the inevitable terminus of any ride aboard the crazy train.

(Just now, I typed "groovie goolies mummies puppies" into Google and was instantly presented with numerous YouTubes of the Mummies & the Puppies performing various different songs. So there is no way of knowing which one was aired that day. I'll never know. But that's fine! Ha ha. I don't care. Ha ha! Ha.)

This recurrent spiraling thought was impossible to shake and soon led to other unknowns upon which to fixate. Which kid was the first one to leave Math at the end of the period when I wasn't looking? What did they play on the radio that afternoon after Blondie's "Call Me"? I took small comfort from the fact that none of these other fixations would last more than a few days, whereas the Mummies & the Puppies looked to be there, as far as I could tell, for the rest of my life. Today, I know that my intrusive or recurring thoughts were common and linked to OCD and anxiety.

Okay, so if you're obsessing over cartoon bands and unable to concentrate in class or have a measure of peace, you should get some help because you have a mental disorder. I never even considered it.

In my family, when things went wrong, you carried on as if they hadn't. My father drank, a lot, alone, and persistently. He was never abusive; he just checked out from the world most nights, and you couldn't get anything resembling intelligent conversation out of him after dinnertime. It was a problem. It was compulsive behavior. It was an illness. It was addiction. It was alcoholism. We pretty much stayed silent about it. If there's a big furry animal in your family and it has big claws and hibernates in the winter and can swat salmon out of a stream, but no one ever calls it a bear, you can go through many years not knowing you have a bear living in your house. Eventually, you'll think you must have been scratching yourself with your own razor-sharp claws.

My elementary school, Nautilus Elementary, was one of a few that fed into Sacajawea, so seventh grade included a bunch of kids I'd never met, some of whom appeared to be fully operational adults. Rob Stone, for instance, was packed with muscles, six feet tall, and had a glazed seen-it-all or possibly super-stoned facial expression that made it hard to believe he was twelve. One would think he was crashing our classes while on break from managing a Jiffy Lube. He may have had children of his own. We instinctively gave Rob plenty of space and regarded him as our alpha male. It's very possible that Rob was aware of none of this. He might have actually been stoned. Many people were. Rob and I were in Language Arts together.

In the spring of seventh grade, there was a school fundraiser that involved selling magazine subscriptions. I sold some to my mother. This success entitled me to a long red licorice rope as incentive to sell more. When this red licorice rope was delivered to me in Language Arts, Rob Stone asked if he could see it. He was Rob, so I said okay and passed it to him just as class was getting started. He proceeded to tear off bits of the licorice rope and eat them until the rope was gone. Mr. Gabrio was going on and on about prepositions, and I didn't want to interrupt him with my licorice accusations or receive the beating from Rob that might follow.

Instead, I cried. I didn't want to, but I couldn't help it. Sure, most people would rather have a licorice rope than not have one, especially if you had earned one by getting your mother to buy a *Sports Illustrated* subscription from you for you. So I was a little sad. But it's not like a waxy candy rope was an exquisite treat; I could get one at the 7-Eleven next door to the school for a quarter. What got me more was the tone it seemed to set along these first steps to adulthood: the Rob Stones of the world could simply take licorice ropes from the Me's of the world, and the Me's couldn't do anything about it. It's Darwin. The strong take from the weak, and thus the strong get stronger and the weak wither. The strong will also get mates and make more strongs while specimens such as myself get systematically eliminated from the gene pool. It should be noted that in my junior high I was one of the only people who believed in Darwinian evolution.

The problem was that once I started crying, I could not stop. This had been the case for months. Something upsetting would happen and the tears would start to flow and then I had to cover for it, pretending to rub my eyes, wiping them on my shirt while appearing to scratch an itch. The tears were indeed coming from a place of emotion, but they were coming out in a stupidly disproportionate volume, as if there was something wrong with my ducts. It was like a nosebleed. I'd cry so much I'd get dizzy and disoriented.

I need to pause briefly here to add that I was elected vice president of my seventh-grade class and president of my eighth-grade class, both times after very well-received speeches at school assemblies. I was regarded as a leader and selected by the school to attend a prestigious theater camp and participate in a cultural program that involved Native American tribes. I am typing this paragraph long after I wrote the original draft of this chapter because I simply forgot that these things happened. Depression has painted these good, happy, proud moments as inconsequential. Depression (who is a real dick) hides these memories from me so that when I think of junior high I think of pain and humiliation instead of being elected president of the eighth grade. To give depression some credit, I was a really awful eighth-grade president. I didn't do anything; I should have been impeached, or resigned my position to the much more competent vice president, Mary Ann Luce.

Beyond Rob Stone's brilliant licorice rope con game, I was not short of things to cry about. My older brother Rick was in his senior year at Federal Way High School, although never necessarily *at* Federal Way High School. This made home feel not so much like an active crisis but like an ominous potential one. Home felt like a Coen brothers movie where someone gets an idea for a robbery and you know it's going to go horribly wrong. Home felt like a place where Steve Buscemi would end up in a wood chipper.

John Lennon was shot and killed in December that year, the event made more surreal by my finding out about it from Howard Cosell on *Monday Night Football*. A few months before that, Mount St. Helens had erupted 150 miles away, and people who had been on the news the day before were now dead, killed by the earth itself. I was terrified that Mount Rainier, a mere forty-five miles away, would be next, burying us all in ash or lava before we even knew what was happening. The thing about "active" volcanos is that they might erupt in two hundred years or tomorrow, making them sub-ideal things for emotionally crumbly kids to live adjacent to.

Speaking of fireballs descending from the sky to kill us all, Ronald Reagan had been elected president. From everything I had heard, which was always filtered first through anxiety and only later through reality, time permitting, nuclear war was more imminent than ever. Reagan was either going to launch a nuke at Moscow before they launched nukes at us or he would be so belligerent as to force them into firing off the first missile just so he could retaliate.

And here, I need to make one thing abundantly clear: our generation knew we were going to die in a nuclear war. It was a fact. It wasn't something we feared, it was something we expected as sure as the tide rolling in and the sun coming up. A kid can't understand brinkmanship or grasp the history of the Cold War. A kid is unable to spell "détente," let alone know what it means. To a kid, owning a bunch of missiles and pointing them at something means that those missiles will go off at some point. Like the bottle rockets we bought every summer.

Jimmy Carter always seemed a bit too willowy and indecisive to hit the launch button, but Reagan was just bold and possibly senile enough to do it, and with his election the end of the world was going to happen soon. Maybe I'd make it to high school before being vaporized, but probably not. I'd find myself daydreaming or worrying about college, usually worrying, or thinking about what kind of job I'd have as an adult, and I'd stop myself and shut the daydream/worry down. There wasn't going to be a college or an adulthood. I had fleeting hopes of having sex before the world was destroyed, but from what I could tell, this was going to be more of a desperate shot from midcourt at the buzzer.

Our only hope was that it would be an instant flash and evaporation rather than radiation, mutation, and a Mad Max world where we'd kill or be killed for water. In my town, wedged against the freeway, south of Seattle and north of Tacoma, it was openly discussed and commonly known that we were shoo-ins for the evaporation scenario since we were located very near the Boeing plant. The Soviets, we told each other in ghoulishly reassuring tones, would want to knock out Boeing first so as to cripple America's air capabilities.

I mentioned this to my wife, Jill, many years later, well into my (miraculously achieved) adulthood, and she said no, she would have died first, not me. Everyone knew that her Chicago suburb hometown of River Forest would be the recipient of missile number one because if they hit Chicago itself, half the blast would go into Lake Michigan. By hitting River Forest, specifically Wieboldt's department store at the corner of Lake and Harlem, the blast radius would achieve maximum lethality. Why Wieboldt's? "I don't know," she said. Jill had a plan in high school: if the missiles are heading for Wieboldt's, try to have sex with the cutest guy available very quickly. Now we've been married going on twenty-five years and we have three kids, proving we've had sex at least three times, so it all worked out.

In my non-obliterated adulthood, I learned that kids everywhere comforted themselves by telling each other they'd die quick. My friend John Roderick is from Alaska, which he knew would be hit first because they're so close to Russia. Another friend, Katie Sisneros, who grew up in Nebraska, believed she'd be first to die because of the old air force base in Omaha. I believe that nearly every American around my age grew up resolute in the belief that the Soviets wanted to kill them first and do it quickly.

And now, today, no one ever talks about this! We all lived on death row, but the executioner never showed up, and eventually the cell doors were opened, we walked out, and no one ever spoke of it again. As a generation, as a society, we never talk about the shit that went down with the fear of nuclear war. Not really. We'll laugh about how scary *The Day After* was, but we never recognize that we were raised in despair and probably handed it down to our kids and to later versions of ourselves.

If there had been a checklist of depression symptoms back then, I could have filled in a whole lot of squares on it:

- Despair—Certainty of nuclear war
- Recurring thoughts—*The Groovie Goolies*
- Crying—The Rob Stone incident
- Anxiousness/restlessness—All the time

Frogs, contrary to the oft-used analogy, will indeed hop out of a pot of water being brought to a boil. Of course they will. All surviving frogs are from a lineage of the specimens best equipped for survival. They are the Rob Stones of the amphibian world. I was more like a frog handcuffed inside the pot of soon-to-be-boiling water. A kid can't hop out of his own life. It's not like I could get a job and relocate to a new city. How would I even get there? My bike? Kids just have to take it, and do so without any knowledge that some bad times in life are temporary. Just as pubes had arrived and would be there forever, I figured all these mental troubles would be as well.

By my eighth-grade year, my presidency year, we had not yet been blasted out of existence in a nuclear war, but everything else had gotten worse. I had all the despair, the persistent crying, and the obsessive looping spiraling thoughts, as well as the restless anxiety, which by this point was blasting into pretty profound agitation. Seeing me as an increasingly withdrawn kid perpetually on the verge of tears, my beloved classmates were always kind and supportive. Ha! No. They bullied me incessantly. Kids I had been sure I was ahead of in terms of status were now threatening to beat me up. Boys who had been my friends, at whose houses I had played Dungeons & Dragons, were cackling with glee that they could push me around, because better me than them. In rage and fear, I would then turn on Don, the kid who never talked to anyone and was always dirty, who wore the same clothes every day, and cruelly mock him, thinking I could transfer this awful feeling down the line. I am sorry, Don.

It was too much to take, and way too much to take in Price's US history class. No one ever called him Mr. Price; it was always just Price, and he, in turn, called students by their last names as well. In this way, it was as if everyone played on the junior high football team he coached. He shared a classroom wall with (Mr.) Thurston, the track coach, who also taught history. They were good friends and ran their classes with a towel-snapping toxic masculinity where boys who played football were lionized while boys who didn't, and all girls, were scoped out for signs of weakness and vulnerability so that the ridicule could commence.

Since we lived only a short walk and perhaps an automotive collision away from school, I always went home for lunch to make myself soup and take a mental break. During one particularly awful class, Price casually mentioned giving me a lunchroom detention for some minor infraction. Days went by and he never followed up on it because it had merely been some idle punitive threat to entertain himself and the football players at the expense of my dignity and peace of mind. But some of my classmates remembered and threatened to remind him of this to see how upset I would get. I got a lot upset and begged them not to follow through on their threat, which only made them heighten the drama to see me suffer more. Understand: they were not threatening me with violence, just inconvenience while eating a sandwich, but the idea of not getting my daily break from people like them was unimaginably awful. Finally, I offered them money not to remind Price, which was such a pathetic act of self-abasement that they laid off, embarrassed for me and perhaps finally ashamed. They've all apologized since, the latest apology one month before I typed this, from a guy who found out I was writing a memoir.

At home, there was never any open talk about Dad's problem with alcohol or my brother Rick's growing marijuana habit. In both cases, we denied it or silently accepted it as a thing we couldn't do anything about, got dressed, and kept going. That's the model of Norwegian culture anyway, and it seems likely to me now that if you've lived through a Nazi occupation, as my parents had as children, the best way to survive is to keep walking and not think too much. Stands to reason also that if you've had an armed Nazi soldier in your house, drinking a few (or more than a few) extra vodkas pales by comparison. In many ways, we got away with denying the problems, too. There was love in our house. There was always food in the fridge, there were inside jokes and wonderful and lengthy camping trips where we all slept side by side in the tent. We had lazy afternoons on our little boat on Puget Sound, fishing for salmon and cod. College tuition got paid. But working around the issues doesn't mean they go away.

One day in eighth grade I simply couldn't handle my growing and unspecified mental menace any longer. Instead of walking into Price's class, I headed straight for the office and asked to see a counselor. I cannot recall if the school secretary knew me well enough to be alarmed by the tears welling in my eyes, but she waved me through. The counselor, Mr. Gish, worked out of a tiny office in the back and usually handled things like schedule changes rather than counseling in the psychological sense. Gamely, he asked what was going on and why I was so upset.

I had no idea why I was so upset. I lacked even the vocabulary to describe the things my brain was doing. Depression does its damage and then it hides, covering its tracks, making you think that it is not an illness, that you're just bad and weird.

I tried, though. "I . . . hate school" was the best I could offer, and only after a long silence. His office was mercifully stocked with Kleenex, and I used a lot of them. "I just hate school." I knew I had to go to school no matter what, and I also knew things weren't ever going to get better there. I had lost hope.

Arguably, Mr. Gish could be considered my first therapist. He said I should talk to my mom about what was going on. It was an option I had never considered.

According to *THWoD*:
Junior High Is a Time People Get
Ka-whompoed

Depression is an illness. And it tends to follow a similar pathology in all its patients. Certain characteristics, events, and responses occur over and over again among humans because we're really not all that different from one another. I'm sorry if you thought you were a special, unique, one-of-a-kind shining star, but you're not. Hard as it may seem to believe, nothing you're going through hasn't happened to other people. And that's good news because tested treatment, or at the very least fellowship, is readily available. Hi. Welcome.

Occasionally, in this book, I'll take a step out to share some stories from the fellowship of the depressed.

In making *THWoD*, I found that my experiences at Sacajawea weren't unique at all. If I had a nickel for every person I've talked with who got smacked by depression in junior high, then, friends, I'd have a tall stack of nickels. It makes sense when you think about the confluence of puberty hormones, stress from academics, and the emergence of primitive and appalling forms of dating. Back then, it would have been helpful to know that in a few decades I'd host a show where lots of celebrities talked about that era as the one when they got whomped by Clinny D. I'd have a word for what happened next instead of the word I used, which was "AAAAUUUUUGGGHHHH!"

From kindergarten on, Jeff Tweedy, the future front man of the band Wilco, was a big-time crier at school, and it continued well into junior high. Jeff was easily provoked to gushes of tears that proved difficult or sometimes impossible to turn off. "Kids in my generation, if we were crying, the response was 'I'll give you something to cry about.' It meant you were weak," he told me. He also suffered severe migraines that could make him vomit thirty times in a row. He's convinced, though he admits he has no science to back it up, that the migraines were caused by his body trying to make his psychic pain into something more real so that he could be nurtured and taken care of.

Between the migraines and the weeping, Jeff's head and his mind made school a nightmare. "From my earliest ages, I could remember going to school and panicking," he said. "About my mom dying or feeling like I couldn't stay at school. So I was a crybaby. I was a mama's boy. That was the explanation, that I was too close to my mother."

By our present-day understanding of mental health, by my estimation, Jeff was probably depressed or had an anxiety disorder, and that illness presented itself in a variety of behaviors that he was way too young to manage. He couldn't explain that behavior then and can't completely explain it now. There's no logic to it. A broken leg makes sense. You fall out of a tree, there's a snapping sound, there's a bone shard protruding from your skin, you need to get to the hospital where they will fix it. A mind? Not so much.

These middle grades, whether you start in sixth grade or seventh, whether you call it middle school or junior high, usually mark the emergence of an awareness that, hey, I'm going to be an adult at some point here. As I mentioned, there's dating, drugs, Satanic music, all the stuff that we adults enjoy daily. But among the grown-up role models kids look to, there's historically been very little openness about mental health, and what talk there is tends to be terrifying. I've spoken with a lot of people whose aunts or grandmothers had been institutionalized and remained locked away for years. Thus a kid grows up associating mental illness with being taken from your family and put in a building with scary people, probably forever.

When comedian Jen Kirkman was on the podcast, she remembered being in middle school and feeling that something was terribly and indescribably wrong. "'Don't tell Mom the symptoms,'" she told herself, "because something in me knew this is psychological. It has to do more on the crazy spectrum. 'Tell her something physical.' And I would say, 'I feel dizzy.'"

When Jen finally did open up to her mom about how she was feeling, her mom said, "Nana has it, I have it, you have it now. And we just call it stress." That was the end of the conversation.

In hosting *The Hilarious World of Depression*, I have found that a lot of people in the broadly defined Generation X demographic had the same sense of impending annihilation as I did. And it absolutely messed them up.

Jen Kirkman recalls being made to watch *The Day After* with her parents, because apparently a child needs to see nuclear devastation either to get used to it or to use their pubescent powers to avert it. Soon after, she was on a field trip to Plymouth Plantation in Massachusetts, where actors dressed up and pretended to be from the 1600s. "I heard a plane fly by really low—I think there was some kind of naval air force thing in the neighborhood. Nothing dangerous, just a plane," she says. "And I did a duck and cover. I hit the ground. And then I had that feeling of I can't breathe, my heart's racing, feelings of unreality where you feel like you're fainting. And it feels like you're dying, even though I'm sure dying feels nothing like this. It's just terror. It's an immediate terror. And I took to the ground and then I yelled at one of the pilgrims, like 'Drop your act, we're under attack!'"

Jen had to go sit on the bus for the rest of the field trip, too traumatized to taunt the actors like the rest of the kids, asking the 1600s costumed characters if they had VCRs at home.

Margaret Cho, who is roughly my age, told me that when *The Day After* came out, it gave her budding depression plenty of reason to believe that since we're all doomed, nothing means anything. "[There was a] consciousness that we could possibly blow ourselves up, and then we'd have to deal with the radiation, and you can't eat anything, your hair's falling out, and everybody's bleeding out of their butt."

Very recently, after meeting many more of my generation who had grown up certain their hometown would be the first hit in a nuclear war, I finally looked into it. It turns out my friend Katie was right. Omaha was one of the first targets, along with Washington, DC.

I'm sure the boomers and other generations would assure me that the certainty of nuclear destruction dangled over everybody. The young people of today see that same doom coming not from Soviet generals but from the planet itself, and it likely seems no less hopeless to them.

3

CAROL BURNETT AS COPING
MECHANISM

My family didn't avoid talking about problems *by* watching *The Carol Burnett Show*; we avoided talking about problems *and* watched *The Carol Burnett Show*.

It was the best, funniest, most delightful hour of television available on our broadcast schedule, and it felt like a window into the greatest place in the world. In Carol's world you didn't have to read between the lines to get at what someone really meant. If somebody was drunk, it was just for a sketch. The bad stuff was swiftly resolved and all pretend anyway.

This was before streaming or DVR or even videotapes, so if you wanted to watch Carol, you had to be there for Carol, and I was always there for Carol.

Now, memory always paints a scene to match the mood you remember. It's unlikely the whole family, all six of us, sat on a single sofa together, piled on laps and armrests, to laugh uproariously at Carol and company, but that's the warmth I felt in that hour, and that's how I remember it. We were all very different people, but we all loved comedy. I loved it because it was funny, and in order to exist more fully in that pocket of family warmth.

I was the youngest of four kids, and in a situation like that, you have to have an angle. Metteline, ten years older than me, was born in Norway a couple of years before our parents decided to hit the reset button on their lives and try America. She was our leader, and she had her political platform, which she would expound on regularly: don't be conformist, don't be sexist, and listen to punk and New Wave music. I would be the only kid in fifth grade listening to Kate Bush and X-Ray Spex albums, and that made me feel like I had secret superpowers of coolness. I had just turned eight when she went off to college and majored in psychology.

Rick was four years behind Metteline and the first born in the United States. In terms of archetype, he'd be considered the "black sheep" or the "rebel" or the "one who has a variety of learning disabilities and nascent mental problems leading to a frustrating time in school and a tendency to pursue interests outside the traditional rules of a society that rejected him." Rick got bad grades but read all about science and space in *Omni* magazine. He was the first in the family to ride a motorized minibike and the first to crash a motorized minibike. He was funny, but in such a deadpan way that you never quite knew when he was joking, a trait he got from our dad and a trait I could never master. When he was offered pot, he greeted it like Harry Potter being given his first wand, and it led to him becoming his own Voldemort. He was the coolest guy imaginable and my hero.

Elisabeth, or Lisbet, was between Rick and me, older than me by two and a half years. She turned sharply in the other direction from Rick. Got perfect grades, kept an even temper, got along with everyone in the family, and listened sympathetically to everyone's complaints about everyone else. She was academically driven and a high achiever at sports. For all this, we teased her mercilessly as being the perfect child, mocking her lack of flaws. To this day, I have an innate belief that Lisbet is better than me at all things, and I will probably not manage to kick that before I die. Baked into me is hard knowledge that the areas where I surpassed her are areas that don't matter, and the areas where she surpassed me, I unshakably know, are the areas that count. HOW DO YOU LIKE THE BOOK SO FAR, LISBET?

As for me, I quickly glommed onto the "funny one" label. Everyone needs a Ringo. All members of the family enjoyed comedy, sure, but I lived it. It wasn't just about laughs for me, it was about structure. There's a premise, a setup, and a punchline. And at the punchline, as the audience laughs, a little burst of happiness gets delivered to the brain. A hit of dopamine.

Being the funny one was shrewd, too, because all four of us kids were comedy nerds. My older siblings understood shows like *Monty Python* and *Saturday Night Live* and I watched too, smiling, laughing when they laughed, and usually falling asleep. By going as hard as I could into something everyone liked, I thought, I would therefore be loved. Solid logic, confused little boy! When my own jokes went over well, I felt like I had earned a place in the family, which was thrilling but made each day a high-stakes standup appearance. Only by being useful or talented, and receiving external recognition, would I achieve personhood. I couldn't imagine a world where I was a worthwhile person by dint of mere existence; I felt like I needed to earn it and prove it every day. Don't worry, this feeling went away after only several decades.

One year Rick received a tape recorder for Christmas, and he wanted stuff to put on the drugstore cassettes that came with it. Metteline corralled the four of us into the rec room, a floor and a door away from our parents, to participate in semi-improvised skits to perform into the single small, spiral-cord-bound microphone. Generally, these were our versions of fractured fairy tales like on the Bullwinkle show or sketches crudely derived from *Laugh-In* or *Carol Burnett*.

Metteline assumed her natural perch as director, coming up with the scenes and assigning roles. If we needed a narrator, she would step in to ensure the scene went as she wanted it to go. Rick, owner of the equipment, was primarily the engineer and had the envied job of getting to hold the microphone. He did a bit of acting, usually if a scene required a generic male voice, and he was happy to provide sound effects like foghorns and haunted forests. But mostly he was interested in the gear.

Lisbet would be assigned the female protagonist parts—Goldilocks, Little Red Riding Hood, assorted princesses—and would be instructed to play them in the most prim and proper way possible. These reworked fairy tales inevitably resulted in the death of the central character, aka her. She played these roles with a hint of spite, always ceding the punchlines to others.

All of this cleared the path for me to step into character parts. Little Bunny Foo-Foo (the one hopping through the forest), Baby Bear, the Big Bad Wolf. There was something genuinely funny about a six-year-old attempting to convey an air of menace when said child did not even particularly understand the story in which he was participating. In the recordings, one could often hear Metteline feeding me lines, followed by me blasting into the scene, doing an untraceable accent, and diving for whatever laughs could be found.

Reader, I got those laughs. And I stored them in my heart. And then everyone else moved on with the rest of their evening. They had all just done a fun thing (except maybe Lisbet, who rightfully seemed a little stung and tricked by the whole deal), and that was all. But to me, those recording sessions were everything. We had been together, even the older kids, who were spending more and more time with their friends out of the house. In that time together, we had laughed a lot and I had proven myself as someone capable of providing value instead of being the underage burden on the rest of the family. I badgered my siblings, "Can we record tonight? PLEASE?"

"I'm going out."

"How about tomorrow night?" I implored.

"I'll be busy then, too. Maybe some other time."

It took me a long time to take a hint, even after some of the tapes went missing and were later found to have music on them. "I taped over them," Rick said dismissively. "I don't see what the big deal is," as my eyes filled with tears. The happiest moment of my life had been replaced by Bad Company or the Electric Light Orchestra.

Taping had given me two things: closeness to my siblings and laughs. With the former now fading away, I threw myself into the latter, which was becoming a more solitary pursuit. I could never get enough comedy and spent years consuming it constantly, to the detriment of everyday life functions like school and friendships. Why face the vagaries and humiliations of the world when there are *Hogan's Heroes* reruns every single day?

There's an awkward period in a suburban kid's life between about age twelve and age sixteen when you can't do much. You're too old to go "play" and yet too young to get a job or drive a car. And you're in the suburbs, where you need a car to do anything. Entire malls were built for the purpose of giving suburban pubescents a place to shamble around, browsing records at Musicland but never buying any, scoping teeny humor sections at B. Dalton Bookseller for any new arrivals, blowing the five bucks your parents had invested in your absence at the arcade. Malls are places you can look at things while time passes, but even the mall required either a ride or a terrifying bike trek across seas of parking lots.

While I was in this nothing-to-do phase one long dull summer, Mom decided to declutter some rooms and piled various mattresses, blankets, and bed parts in Metteline's old lower-floor bedroom since she had moved out for good. The stuff formed a perfect lean-to, with a mattress underneath. With a blanket draped over, and when paired with a battery-powered camping lamp, it made for an indoor campsite. I was never a treehouse kid, but this accidental assemblage drew me in hard. I loaded up Metteline's old Doonesbury books and a few Charlie Browns of my own and hid out for hours every day.

One day, Mom walked in to find me in my pit. "What do you *do* down here all the time?"

"I'm just reading," I said.

"Well, I'm only keeping these things in here for now. I'm going to take them to the dump or Goodwill at some point."

"Oh," I mumbled nonchalantly, "that's fine." It wasn't; it was devastating. I had been spending all my time in that lean-to, rereading humor scraplets because it was so reassuring.

Mom followed through on her threat some weeks later, and I acted like I didn't care. I knew it was an abnormal thing to care about, that it was, ultimately, shameful. When things were weird and shameful, I knew, we did not speak of them.

I missed the fort, because nothing would get in past those blankets. As long as I was in there, I never had to see Rick in hushed conversations with our parents and overhear things about school and the people he was hanging out with.

School in general, high school in particular, had been a bad fit for Rick. He'd never taken up with the football captains and cheerleaders. His crowd was more likely to be found under the bleachers, smoking. For fun, they set off firecrackers, incurring injured hands and accepting that as a fair price for the explosions. He was friends with the burnouts, the parking-lot shaggy guys, the kids who lived in the run-down houses where everything was a little too dark and smelled like trouble and where the parents swore and the cat was said to have magical powers. Houses with black light posters fastened to wood paneling with pushpins. Houses where someone had a snake in a fish tank. Houses where bongs were just left out in the living room because everyone either used them or didn't care who used them. Houses where everyone was supposedly into fixing cars but most of their cars didn't run and some were up on cinder blocks in the front yard. Places with guns, like the shotgun Rick had hid in his room that I found when I went snooping for *Playboys*. I never let him or anyone know that I knew the gun or *Playboys* were there. I never touched the gun.

There were many things in our family we did not discuss, but there were also many that I had trained myself not to notice. I didn't think much of it when Dad gave me a ride somewhere and I saw a small bottle of vodka under the driver's seat. I knew immediately what was going on. Obviously, he had gone to the liquor store, as all dads often do, and bought some bottles of liquor, as is normal. Those bottles had been placed in a bag, which he had put in the car, either on the passenger seat or the floor on the passenger side. Somehow, the bag had been jostled and a small bottle of vodka had fallen out. The errant vodka bottle, I reasoned, then fell to the floor and, being plastic, it bounced. The bottle must have ricocheted off the floor and then reversed direction, defying the laws of physics—much like the bullet that killed JFK—and came to rest under the driver's seat. When you're raised in a situation where you need it, denial goes beyond coping mechanism status, surpasses instinct, and becomes reality itself. I'm still terrible at picking up on clues. Every M. Night Shyamalan movie twist is a revelation to me.

My dad and I loved each other, and we spent quite a bit of time together. I had joined a youth soccer team in fourth grade, spending many happy years with my friends, my footspeed relegating me to a largely immobile position on defense. Dad was European, of course, so even though he lacked an athletic build, he was highly skilled with a ball and we'd kick one around together. He'd usually serve as a linesman at my team's Saturday morning games, and I was proud to have him there with the little flag. I was proud, too, when he would share jokes with my teammates that were just an inch on the right side of propriety. He could also toss a Frisbee surprisingly well, and we spent quite a bit of time on a weekend morning or afternoon zipping the disk across our broad suburban backyard.

Saturday mornings were about cartoons, particularly the Bugs Bunny crew. We agreed that Daffy Duck was the best, all anger and hubris. Dad said that of all the characters in Looney Tunes, he understood Wile E. Coyote the best, and he absolutely wanted him to catch, kill, and eat the Road Runner.

Sunday mornings in the fall were about NFL football games. Dad took to the game right away upon coming to America and adopted the Minnesota Vikings as his team, due to the name. We watched together as the Vikes blew several mid-'70s Super Bowls, and he tried to get me to be less upset about the losses. When the Seahawks debuted in Seattle, I was eight years old and ready to move on to the new team. He took me to some games, which were affordable at the time, but usually we sat side by side on the couch watching a team that was no less frustrating than the Vikings we had left behind. We would read the Sunday comics section cover to cover, except for *Prince Valiant* because who reads *Prince Valiant*.

I don't have a lot of memories of doing things with my dad on Saturday or Sunday nights. That's when he drank. I imagine he was home during those times—he was never much for bars—but I just don't remember.

Born in 1931, Erling Moe was living in Oslo and not quite nine years old when the Nazis marched into Norway. He was the only child in a loveless marriage that was necessitated by his imminent birth. The Nazis, who are all bad guys and should be punched at every opportunity, stayed for five years, although at the time there was no way of telling how long they'd be there or if they'd ever leave. Imagine a gun being held to your head from ages eight to thirteen.

Conrad Moe, my grandfather, was a chain-smoker who had left his large family of merry siblings (his brothers formed a beloved music and comedy act) in the country to move to Oslo. There are no extant pictures of Conrad smiling. He worked in a print shop as a typesetter. The employees of the shop, with the approval of the company's owners, would print the illegal resistance newspapers after hours, then roll the papers up tight and insert them in the handlebars of their sons' bicycles. Finally, my father and his friends would bike across Oslo secretly delivering contraband news, with the Nazis none the wiser. Heroic? Sure. Traumatic? Absolutely.

Erling grew up, married, and Metteline was born. Then the little family got on a boat and emigrated to America. When unresolved trauma and depression caught up with him, he drank to stop the terrible pain because that's what people did. The alcohol did not make it better—it made it way worse—but it did allow him to feel nothing, and soon he had trauma, depression, and addiction.

In the tiny farming and fishing village in the north of Norway where my mother grew up, people likewise carried on through the war. Their roads were teeming with Nazi troops (Hitler was convinced a Soviet invasion would come through the Soviet-Norwegian border), but mostly all they could do was patiently endure. Aase Jensen, my mom, lost her sister to diphtheria during the war, in winter. There was no morgue in town and no grave immediately available, so they had to store Elsa's body in the parlor. Windows in that room were opened to the Arctic cold to preserve the body, and other doors were sealed off. For a few days, until the grave was ready, Aase, nine at the time, was sent in to kiss her sister every night. Mom still can't really handle going to cemeteries.

In tiny Norwegian villages in 1943, talk therapy was not an option. It is unknowable if my depression comes from the inherited traumas my parents suffered, from a genetic predisposition (mental illness dots both sides of the family tree), both, or random occurrence. But it seems certain to me that the notion of putting up with things and moving forward was a family trait, and one perpetuated by the society in which my parents grew up.

So with all that somewhere on my wee shoulders, home I come from that aforementioned day with Mr. Gish at Sacajawea, home to the home that doesn't talk about mind problems, that numbs them up with pot or booze or Carol Burnett. And I tell my mom, who has been through all she has, that I'm going crazy. I fully expected to be told that it was all a phase I would grow out of, which would be the most frustrating answer but would at least give me a light at the end of this tunnel. Instead, Mom simply listened to whatever verbal coleslaw I could produce and, in the end, admitted that she wasn't sure what to do next but that she could set up a time to talk with a child psychologist. It's like a lifelong Catholic saying, "Let's go down to the mosque and talk to the imam, see what's happening there." She bucked all her programming and decided to get me professional help.

The therapist was in Tacoma, ten miles south. He was a young guy, bearded, a stock photo of "Therapist, 1981." One of the first things he explained in our first session was that it also had to be our last. The opening in his schedule was there because he was leaving his practice and moving to Boston. He would be happy to talk to me today anyway, he said, because we had come all this way, but if we wanted to leave instead, he would totally understand. "Might as well do it, I guess," I muttered with eighth-grade surliness.

It was an hour with someone who didn't know me. It was an hour with someone whom I would never see again, which suddenly held great appeal. I found my words, spoke rapidly and with passion, expressing a lot of things for the first time. It was great. He may have given me some advice on breathing or keeping a journal, but I recall it was pretty tough for him to get a word in edgewise.

Afterward, Mom asked me how it went. I told her I loved it. She asked whether I wanted to see a different therapist, and I said no, I got it all worked out, I was fine now. I wasn't. But I wanted to think that I was, and I felt self-indulgent for talking to a therapist at all. I've met a lot of people over the years who think that if they go to a therapist for a certain number of times, they will then be fine and back to normal, as if talk therapy and physical therapy work the same way. And man, that would be terrific. There's a kind of naïve optimism to that thinking that I can't help but admire.

So Mr. Tacoma was therapist number two, our relationship concluding, as it had with therapist number one, after a single session.

Not long after that one-session depression cure, I was hanging out—not playing, hanging out, because we were cool teens—with my friend Kris. I waited for a calm moment in casual conversation and revealed my obsessive thoughts about *The Groovie Goolies*. I played it off as if it were a curious blip, the "no big deal" I so desperately wished it was. "So, yeah, I just keep thinking of the Mummies & the Puppies over and over all the time. Just can't shake it," I said with a kind of chuckle.

"Huh. Weird," said Kris, in a tone of the mildest surprise, the way you might respond to hearing some minor celebrity trivia. I instantly felt lighter as this hundred-pound weight was lifted from my shoulders. "Huh. Weird." Because he nailed it. Obsessively thinking about a fake cartoon band's set list *is* weird. But there are much weirder things in the world. "Huh. Weird" recognized the anomaly but also indicated that it was a speed bump and not a brick wall. That was it for OCD.

According to *THWoD*:
Comedy Is a Helpful Tool

People with minds that have been disordered from depression often find solace in comedy. That's both strange and logical at the same time. Comedy, much of the time, is built on disorder. The Coneheads on the old *Saturday Night Live* are aliens with tall pointy heads attempting to blend in among the regular people of the suburbs. The Knights Who Say Ni from *Monty Python and the Holy Grail* hold great power over King Arthur himself because they wield the tremendous weapon of saying "Ni!," which everyone fears even though it's just a silly word. The joke so often comes from how at odds the premise is with reality.

Plenty of us have felt like Coneheads. We know we are alien to the society in which we're attempting to pass, and we struggle to understand the customs and behavior that come easily to everyone else. Likewise, like King Arthur, we have much to fear while traveling through the world, but we suspect that many of those threats, much like the Knights' "Ni!," are empty and ridiculous. We see ourselves in those Coneheads (or in their neighbors trying to piece the strangeness together), and we see ourselves in Arthur. When we make that identification, we feel less alone, and we also get some laughs that make the dissonance of the characters (and ourselves) less jarring.

It's not especially revelatory that people who eventually become comedians enjoyed comedy as children. Still, during our first season of *The Hilarious World of Depression*, I was stunned by just how often *The Carol Burnett Show* came up in conversation, almost as if it were a symptom of depression as much as it was a treatment.

I suggested to Burnett-head and comedian Paul F. Tompkins that the show's cast all seemed like friends. "Oh, John, that's a huge part of it," he said. "They seemed to have a real affection for each other. Especially for me, as a kid coming from a family where there was a lot of discord. My mother and father did not like each other. They slept in separate bedrooms. They stayed married even though their marriage was effectively over. And so to see things like *The Carol Burnett Show* or *Match Game*, the original *Match Game*, where it just seemed like these cool fun people that all were having a great time together—that to me was this window into this world of adulthood that I yearned to join. And I think I wanted to be a grown-up because I wanted to be able to be in charge of myself. I wanted to be able to maybe change my situation. To look at these people through this window and think, 'Oh my God, they seem so great, and why can't I be like that? I'm funny. Why can't I be in a world where other people think I'm funny and I'm not an annoyance?'"

Margaret Cho recalled that there weren't a lot of restrictions on what she watched. "Even Richard Pryor's movies, which I think back now and I think that's actually kind of incredible. Me and my brother, we were probably younger than ten years old watching this stuff. We didn't really even know what was going on or what the jokes are about, but it was something that brought us together."

Long before Gary Gulman was a comedian, he was a kid in Massachusetts living through his parents' divorce and latching on to the darkest mainstream comedian of the '80s. "The first guy I really noticed using that style and acknowledging that aspect of his life was Richard Lewis. So probably around nine or ten, I first saw Richard Lewis, and I immediately connected with him and his neuroses and his fears and insecurities. I must have felt the same way. So I identified with him right away, and I just adored his honesty."

Of course, not everything you consume is good for you. Writer and comedian Guy Branum grew up in rural California, trying to figure out both his place in the world and his latent homosexuality. "I watched Eddie Murphy's *Delirious* [cable special] when I was not yet ten years old in the living room of my parents' house, with my entire family crowded around, very excited for this piece of sophisticated culture that was coming to us from the outside world," he says.

"I just thought that he was the funniest and the most in control. The mix of confidence and wit and savvy. It's one of the things that most deeply made me want to do what I professionally do today. And the way that the tropes from that special echoed out in Margaret Cho's specials and so many people afterwards. Like the trope of the standup wearing a leather suit, which I understand harkens back to Richard Pryor before Murphy, but I only knew it from Eddie Murphy."

That special, with Eddie Murphy's swagger and wit, formed something foundational. "I had fallen in love with so many standup comics in that period of time. George Carlin, Rita Rudner, Paula Poundstone. But to me, the center of power was always

Eddie Murphy's *Delirious*. So in 2013, I was in New York writing on a TV show, and I was like, hey, it's on YouTube. Why don't I just watch it. And what I didn't realize is the first five minutes of that special are just him talking about how gross gay guys are."

"Gross" is an understatement. It's more a homophobic rant than standup, full of slurs and a bit about how kissing can transmit the AIDS virus.

"It was shocking because all I remembered was the good things. All I remembered is that it made me love standup and it made me love the power and confidence and certainty of standup. And then I had to watch it and realized it had sown into my brain constructions of what gay men were that had helped keep me in the closet until I was twenty-three. That made me hate myself. And it's certainly not just Eddie Murphy. It was the world that was doing that. But to have it so sharply included in this thing that I loved and was a thing that was liberating from the world that I lived in, it was a stark realization. It was a stark realization that it had done something so good and so bad at the same time."

Long before Whitney Cummings was a successful comedian and actor, she was a kid in Washington, DC, growing up in a home with addiction and borderline personality disorder. She and her father used comedy to both connect with each other and avoid family problems.

"His coping mechanism was to make everything a joke," says Whitney. "After a big fight, he would make a bunch of jokes and pretend it was all a big performance. My dad looked exactly like Dan Aykroyd, and he would even sign autographs as Dan Aykroyd when I was a kid. I mean, I now realize this is an incredibly traumatic thing to do to a kid. We thought it was so funny— like, I thought he was Dan Aykroyd until I was like thirteen.

He would act out things from movies like *Three Amigos*, and we would act out movies together. And I think it was consensual, like 'Let's pretend that never happened.' And I was so on board with the denial. We would be doing Blues Brothers songs and watching *Three's Company* and doing pratfalls, and I think I really got it from him."

Aimee Mann also had a dad who employed laughs to quash more difficult conversations that probably should have been happening, given that her mom left when Aimee was three years old.

"My father was a guy who was always pretty cheerful, but he didn't want to know," she says. "I remember times where I was sad and my father would do that joking parent thing of like, 'I think I see a smile!' And you're like, 'I'm three years old and my mother left me. Like, you probably don't. Don't bring that here.'"

Comedian Solomon Georgio came to the United States as a refugee from Ethiopia when he was three years old, and his family relied on comedy early on for entertainment and education. "We all loved comedy because that's one of the few things that we comprehended when we didn't speak the language," he says. "Surprisingly, standup comedy, too, which, even though we didn't know what was going on, you kind of see a rhythm and you know people are being entertained and laughing along. So we watched a lot of old television. Three Stooges, *I Love Lucy*, and, like, slapstick. We just immediately started watching and enjoying. So you can only imagine how disappointed I was when I met my first white person in real life and I was like, 'Oh, you're not like the Three Stooges. I can't slap you and poke you in the eye. You guys aren't doing any of that stuff out here. Okay.'"

Comedy is intoxicating to a young mind in distress. You see these famous people pointing out the ridiculousness of a world that you've never been able to make sense of. Comedians offer the hope, the chance, however slim, that it's not you that's broken but the world. And they dress up in cool clothes! And hang out with various late-night hosts named Jimmy! And they make people laugh, and those people then love them. I can't say for certain that depression leads people to a career in comedy, but it seems like the path is smoothly paved and well lit.

IMAGINED SNAPSHOTS OF
KEY MOMENTS

Let's pretend, Dear Reader, that ubiquitous photography was a thing a long time ago like it is today. Let's further pretend that we have real tangible prints from back then. And let's say the first one we're looking at is me, a few pounds lighter and with a tremendous amount more hair, embracing another young man in the Federal Way High School cafeteria. It's the mid-'80s, so I am likely wearing a shirt with superfluous fasteners.

I was a junior in high school and a few years into my effort to not betray how crazy and desperate I felt all the time. I was pretty good at acting, and the theater department gave me some recognition and a chance to hide out from reality. I'd also been listening to the handful of punk cassettes my friends and I acquired on trips to Seattle, twenty miles to the north: the Dickies, Feederz, Black Flag, the Damned, the louder and angrier the better. It was the closest thing to what my head sounded like that I could access. Oh, I was way too timid and anxious to see actual punk shows, or even hang out with the hardcore punks in the city, so it was usually just me with normal clothes and a normal haircut in my room with a Walkman. Basically, I loved listening to Henry Rollins sing "My War" with Black Flag, but I was also pretty sure he was going to get in big trouble.

The events of junior high and my ongoing storminess were enough for me to know I had mental issues. Bouts of rage, unexplained fear, the inability to read a book sufficiently to fake my way through English class. It was equally possible, I thought, that I'd end up in college or working at McDonald's forever or dead of a drug overdose. I was getting in heated arguments constantly with whoever was around over anything: politics, sports, music, the school itself. I was a pill. Incongruously, in this photo we can only imagine, I am hugging a guy.

Derek was an intermittent member of the small group of friends I clung to in high school. He was the Billy Preston to our Beatles. Probably simulating my family arrangement, I was drawn to being one of four in a group of friends: Kris, Sean, Jon with no *h*, and me. Sean was good-looking, even-tempered, and capable of drawing girls to him, and thus he became our leader. Kris, the philosopher, studied Zen Buddhism; his hippie parents were kind and welcoming and had Kris when they were young, so we all felt like they understood us better, and we hung out at his house. He had a great record collection, and it turned out marijuana and "Kashmir" by Led Zeppelin went really well together. Who knew? What a shock! Jon was the rebel, the edgy one; he used to live in the big city of Seattle, and you never knew what kind of audacious words or actions were in store when he was around. I'm not sure what role I played. Maybe I told a few more jokes than the others? Depression has solidly imprinted that era as a time when I was worthless, so I honestly don't know why anyone hung out with me.

Derek transferred in from another school junior year and was all gangly limbs, loud voice, easy laugh, and lack of guile.

The rest of us were prone to brooding, complaining about the popular kids, and spouting off leftist ideologies we didn't really understand. Derek quickly met and really liked Sean. I saw this as a threat to my own friendship with Sean and my own standing within this group. I dealt with this by being a dick to Derek, mocking him, insulting him, excluding him. I was fairly quick-witted, and Derek made for an easy target. Unsurprisingly, Derek did not appreciate this and finally told me off, calling me on all my shitty behavior, for which I had no retort. The other guys took his side, agreeing that I had been awful.

Derek's emergence and my dickishness had meant a loss in status and power for me. I had to get that power back and opted to lie to Derek, to manipulate him and blunt his justified complaints about me. School was out for the day, and I caught up with him in the cafeteria. "Hey, man. I've been a dick to you lately," I said. "I've just been really depressed, and I've been thinking about killing myself."

Instantly, Derek pulled me into an embrace, despite the appearance of such a thing among dudes at a socially backward high school. "Okay, man," he said. "Nothing else matters. I love you. You're going to get through this."

How effective my ploy turned out to be! Almost too effective. I wanted to scare him off a little, but now he believes me? And . . . loves? . . . me?

I'd been hearing about teen suicide at school, seeing brochures about it in the counseling office (where I often ended up after any one of my numerous breakdowns), and noticing a kind of social movement beginning to build around stopping it. Frankly, the whole thing had made me more interested in suicide. Was it like drugs and booze, where a thing is so incredibly great that adults try to stop you from doing it? Suicide, huh? What would that be like?

On the mile-long walk home from school, I'd think about it. Suicide would wipe away all the problems with myself, my family, school, friends, girls, and the future. And if I did it, people would say nice things about me and I'd get a big spread in the yearbook. I'd never have to face the inevitable nuclear war or live through when my brain fell apart in the next few years. The people who wronged me in high school would have to carry around that guilt for the rest of their lives, so it would be kind of like being a suicide bomber, really. I became increasingly fixated on this option. I didn't like thinking about it so much—it wasn't pleasant—but I couldn't stop. With a gun or rope or from a great height, I had the power to end all of it. I'd never had any power before.

Many years later, while I was writing this book, Derek's hug leapt to mind again. Suddenly it dawned on me that I wasn't being dramatic or manipulative in that moment at all. I really was suicidal, at least in the early stages of it. I was alone, scared, and confused. And I ended up opening up with honest words to a friend, who, as good friends do, set aside the petty stuff to forgive and demonstrate true kindness. I didn't feel as suicidal after that.

In high school, I was a frequent teary guest in the counseling office. Sandy Stonebreaker, the assigned counselor, was skilled at letting me talk and, over the years, gently guiding me toward a better life in college. I don't know if the school district would consider her a therapist, but since my work with her was therapeutic, I will add her name to the roster as therapist number three. My first-ever multisession therapist!

~

In the next photo, I'm on Interstate 80 in California eastbound between Davis and Sacramento. It's night, and I'm driving a very, very used black Pontiac Firebird. I have recently turned sixteen.

Rick is in the passenger seat. He's twenty-one, about to turn twenty-two. A slightly older guy is stretched out in the backseat, semiconscious. My eyes are wide, my hands at 10 and 2 on the steering wheel, like they taught me in Driver's Ed. The knuckles of those hands are white. No one is wearing seat belts.

Let me explain.

I turned sixteen on July 10, 1984, and took my driver's license exam that very day. I was extremely eager to get this license because I knew it would improve my life dramatically, seeing as I would now have access to:

- Dates with girls
- An ability to get out of the house
- Cool record stores up in Seattle
- A job to earn money for dates with girls and records from cool record stores

I failed the driving test. That whole wondrous world was stretched out in front of me and I couldn't get through the gate. It was like going to Disneyland but being stuck in the parking lot.

Less than a week later, I flew down to Sacramento to stay with Rick for a few days. He never did officially graduate from high school, but he had success working at airport freight companies, where he got respect, opportunities, and loads of drugs. Brains and charm can take you places.

Rick picked me up at the airport, and we drove to his second-floor apartment in a complex of three-story buildings, each with six to ten units. The complex was fairly nice. No pool, but plenty of neighbors had plants on their front steps and tiny decks, an indication that they took pride in their homes. It was already much nicer than a great deal of Federal Way. It seemed like the kind of place that a young executive on the rise would live. I was deeply impressed. Rick's was a one-bedroom apartment, so that meant sleeping on the couch. Rick owned a couch! We stayed up that night watching TV and went to bed when we felt like it.

Rick had to work the next day but left directions to the nearest grocery store. I was to walk down there and pick up some stuff for dinner, which was to be burgers. We wrote out a list: ground beef, buns, lettuce, onions (never consumed at home because our mom had an almost pathological hatred of onions), chips, pop. Rick already had ketchup. It was a mile to the store on a hot Sacramento afternoon, but it didn't bother me a bit. I was shopping for dinner. Like functional men do. I got everything on the list and made my way back to the apartment, sweaty but emboldened.

"You got ground chuck," Rick said after he got home, inspecting the haul. "I thought you were going to get ground beef."

"I'm so sorry." Panic and shame rose in my throat.

"No, it's fine," said Rick. "We'll just have better burgers. It's great." Rick knew what "ground chuck" was. There was so much I could learn from him. This was living in a golden future. You screw up and, in so doing, you improve things.

Rick had to work the next morning, too, but had the afternoon off. When we drove around Sacramento running errands, we picked up a couple of things at the hardware store and then swung by a mechanic's. Rick had a habit of driving terrible cars that he bought cheap and discarded when they finally died for good. It was his policy and philosophy. It resulted in getting stranded on the freeway a lot, but at the time it seemed to me like the height of practicality.

He parked off to the side of the garage and told me to just wait in the car, he wouldn't be long. A mechanic came out. This young guy had the same rough look as Rick's friends back home. The two of them popped the hood, and I couldn't see what they were looking at and couldn't hear them. Eventually, the hood was lowered and Rick handed the guy a ten-dollar bill. This garage thing was really a wonder. Somehow, Rick had a quick repair on his car outside the garage itself, free of the paperwork and time commitment repairs always require. A subversion of the system is dazzling for someone with a mind that doubts it can work within any system.

Back at the apartment, Rick checked his answering machine (he had an answering machine!) and was told to call Terry at work. Rick called Terry back and then told me that he needed to drive a suitcase out to Davis that night. Reuniting lost luggage with passengers was part of the service his company provided. Terry would come by to pick him up, and I was invited to ride along. It remains unclear to this day why the job required two people, let alone a little brother. But ride along? Sure!

It was getting dark as we headed out in Terry's weary-looking Firebird, me in the back. Prior to getting on the freeway, there was a stop for gas and, unexpectedly, a six-pack of Budweiser. Terry placed one in a foam cozy, covering the label, and popped the can open. Rick, lacking a cozy, placed his discreetly between himself and the car door. Then Terry offered one to the just-turned-sixteen-year-old in the back, who laughed, realized it wasn't a joke, and declined. A smoke? "Nah," I said, "trying to quit." I'd never smoked.

It was only ten minutes or so into the freeway drive that a little metal pipe emerged, taken out of the glovebox by Rick per Terry's instructions. I knew little about drugs, but even I knew what that pipe and that smell meant, and I gazed nonchalantly out the window, because although it seemed odd that they were smoking pot while driving, it must be okay because Rick seemed okay with it. I declined the kind offer of a hit.

We reached Davis. Rick was designated to deliver the suitcase and returned without incident. "How you holding up?" Terry asked him.

"Little foggy," he said. "I can drive."

"That was some powerful shit," Terry offered.

Rick turned around to me. "You wanna drive? You have a permit, right?"

Though I was pretty certain the conditions of the Washington State Driver's Licensing Bureau Learner's Permit did not allow for two stoned non-parent-or-guardian dudes to be the de facto instructors, I said yes. It was the safest choice, really: I had only narrowly failed my test, and I was sober. Sure, many years later, as an adult, the idea of bailing out two pothead idiots on a late-night suitcase delivery wouldn't sound so advisable, but that night I was flattered. Rick rode shotgun, Terry in the back.

I followed signs to I-80 eastbound and on the ramp received the suggestion of "faster" from my brother. I quickly determined that the approach needed to survive 1980s California driving was to adopt the philosophy of Mad Max movies. White-knuckled, I was keeping up with traffic at 75 to 80 mph, spotting openings in other lanes, briefly signaling, and zooming over before the competitor cars could grab them. Rick and Terry, having passed around the pipe and killed the sixer, offered no corrective notes, which I interpreted as approval. I think airline pilots must feel kind of good if the passengers are able to casually read magazines for the duration of a flight, and that's how I felt, except the magazines were marijuana.

We arrived back in Sacramento, and I executed a perfect parking job in the section designated for visitors. Terry got in the driver's seat and headed home.

A couple of days later, my parents, who had taken a brief vacation to Reno, swung through town to pick me up. Mom asked how the trip went, and Rick and I agreed it had been really great. We had been not just brothers but bros. Not just bros but friends.

When you grow up around substance use, you develop certain skills. Not ninja skills, unfortunately, but you learn to see what you want to see. Thus, I hadn't been on a harrowing night drive that could have ended in disaster. Instead, I was on an adventure with my hero who believed I was capable of great things.

A few days later, I took the driver's test again and, aside from parallel parking, got a perfect score. I've spent my life saying that my brother taught me how to drive. Rick had the greatest life I could ever imagine.

~

Our final photo is of me, on stage, in a tan suit, glasses with no lenses, and the shaggy hair popular among boys in 1986 but slicked back in a failed attempt to look businesslike. I am sweating just a bit and inwardly full of joy.

The Federal Way High School production of *To Kill a Mockingbird* was mounted in January of my senior year, held in the school's poorly heated theater—inconvenient since much of the action takes place in what is said to be a sweltering courtroom in the pre-air-conditioning American South.

I played Atticus Finch, the country lawyer who tries to save the life of a wrongfully accused black man and cool the racial tension in the town while also serving as a role model for his own children. Landing this part and being up on stage playing it was the greatest thing that had ever happened.

There was no theater department back at my junior high, but I had been cast in a small part in a production by a local semiprofessional theater company and was completely hooked on acting. When I was on stage, I had respite from my head. Acting offered everything that the real world didn't: I always knew what I would say and what others would say to me, I knew exactly how every-one felt about me/my character; there was no danger of anyone figuring out the dark secrets of what a weirdo I was.

Landing Atticus meant that I was good at something and that I had proven my worth. Only decades later would it dawn on me that normal people who never deal with depression have a sense of self-worth automatically. Just by being a person on the earth, they feel themselves worthy of respect and love and all that other cool stuff. When you're up against Clinny D, you don't have that core sense of self. So you frantically search the world for someone else to provide that sense of self for you. People might look to a romantic relationship, often one destined to be toxic, to acquire that self; kids might try to find it in sports or playing an instrument; and loads of people stay in a pattern of trying to achieve ever-loftier professional ambitions for their en-tire lives to compensate.

As for me, I tried to get it from Ms. Gorne, the drama teacher.

In the cold harsh light of thirty-plus years later, I know for a fact that I must have been awful as Atticus. There's simply no other possibility. In an almost entirely white school and mostly white town, I had never thought about what race really meant in America, especially in the South. I knew racism was bad, knew that Martin Luther King Jr. and Rosa Parks were good, that King Had a Dream, but that was mostly it.

Further, I couldn't find a way to access the gravity of that character, both who he was and the situation he was in, so in-stead I compensated by copying Gregory Peck from the movie.

In the third and final performance of the play, I managed to get myself so worked up in the courtroom scene, barking out aphorisms I had memorized but never pondered, that I sweated a little. There in the fridgelike theater, when I went to dab my brow with a handkerchief as instructed, I came away with actual sweat. "Now," I thought, "I'm really acting. I touched on something real in this moment. I am an okay person."

Ooh! Forgot to mention. I was elected a student body officer in high school, led leadership programs for other students, won the state championship in persuasive speaking, and was elected by classmates to deliver the speech at graduation. In the decades since, I've described my school in mostly disparaging terms and characterized my time there as miserable.

On Facebook, only a few years ago, I was grumbling about something or other related to Federal Way High School, and how I was scorned and shunned. Some such bullshit. Laurie, who had been my prom date senior year, finally replied, exasperated, "You were admired. You were respected. You were liked."

I would act through college, go to graduate school in pursuit of an MFA in acting, and move to Seattle to act in mostly tiny theaters and in TV commercials. Along the way, I'd have a brief professional relationship with therapist number four, a well-meaning older woman who ran a support group for adult children of alcoholics at Rutgers University, where I went for grad school. At the first meeting I attended, one guy, maybe twenty years old, dominated the conversation talking all about his dad before revealing that his dad didn't actually drink. "So he's in recovery or . . . ?" I asked.

"No," said the not-quite-adult child of not-an-alcoholic, "he just behaves in ways similar to how I think alcoholics do." So the kid had joined the group.

I asked the therapist if she was okay with this, she said she was, and I got up and left. I earned my position as an ACOA, dammit, and I'm not about to let someone unqualified into the group in which I had enlisted less than an hour ago.

As my twenties drew to a close, it began to dawn on me that perhaps I wasn't especially, umm, GREAT at acting. Good, maybe. But not sufficiently better than that. Moreover, I didn't want to move to LA or New York to try to make it big, I didn't want to work hard at my craft all the time, and I would much rather stay home in my sweatpants watching TV. So I decided to be a writer.

5

MY DOT-COM BUBBLE BURSTS

On June 17, 1990, as my twenties were opening up, I was fresh out of college and working my first day of a summer job as a counselor at Four Winds Westward Ho, a camp for mostly wealthy kids on Orcas Island in Washington. It's a camp rich in tradition, with a lot of sailboats and horses. Danielle Steel's kid was there; so was Boz Scaggs's. Kate Hudson had been a camper there a few years before. She was really normal and nice, I'd been told. The former campers working as counselors took a solemn and reverential tone in talking about the place, more like it was a monastery than a place for kids to have fun and learn to sail. I rolled my eyes a lot at this. On this first day of staff training week, a counselor approached me and introduced herself, Jill Helfrich, from Chicago and a student at the University of Montana in Missoula. She said she wanted my help in teaching a song at the staff campfire later that evening. She was cute, too, dark hair, mischievous smile, a little similar to Joyce DeWitt, so totally my type. "What's the song?"

"Goes like this," she said. "'IIIIIIII'm NOT wearing pants! I'm NOT wearing pants! I'M NOT! WEARING! PANTS!'"

"Hell yes, I'll help you teach that song," I said. Who is this cute Chicago girl who gets to this tradition- and money-rich camp and immediately decides to defy the tone of the place? I needed to know her better. She and I had been drawn to the camp, in part, for the same reason: Four Winds Westward Ho is a funny-ass name for a place, and it would be funny to work there.

We introduced the song that night with a concocted story about how we'd both attended the same summer camp in Minnesota many years ago, and there was a song we sang that was derived from a song the native tribes used to sing to celebrate coming together for a great journey. We went on and on about this, deadly serious, improvising off each other, all to build up to the actual song about not wearing pants. The swerve worked, the staff loved it, we taught it to the campers when they arrived, and it's still sung at Four Winds Westward Ho today.

Jill proceeded to be a good just-a-friend that summer (despite my best efforts, which were not subtle), a girlfriend the following summer, and a girlfriend who agreed to move to Seattle with me a while after that. We became engaged on June 17, 1994, while the world watched O. J. Simpson in his very slow Ford Bronco chase, and we got married on Orcas Island on June 17, 1995. That's a tidy five years.

Jump ahead a few years to 1998. I'm married to Jill, we're living in Seattle, I've just hit thirty, I am increasingly of the belief that as an actor I am spending all my time making someone else's dream come true: the playwright, the director, the theater company, but never my own. If I write plays, on the other hand, I can type out my own dreams for others to inhabit, allowing me to stay home and isolate myself from the world. It sounded a lot easier, and I could wear those sweatpants. Of course, now, the idea of isolation and sweatpants is a dead giveaway for depression, but at the time it seemed very sensible. I announced to anyone who would listen that I was now a writer, and since no one ever checks and there's no official state certification for that, people believed me.

As the dot-com economy dawned, the first rays of sunlight/cash hit Seattle, and there was no shortage of paying gigs. I wrote movie reviews and music reviews, and I wrote games, both board and video. After I wrote something, the client would invariably ask me to write more. "They must be desperate for writers," I thought, "or not very bright." Being good at writing was not on my mental list of options. I was doing all of this on the side, mind you, in the evenings. By day, I worked at a low-key software company called WRQ, selling software I did not understand.

I had never pursued a full-time career job doing something creative. Oh, I listened to the radio and read newspapers, and I knew people made those things, but I figured those jobs were all taken by people who were talented and smart. The people in those jobs, I figured, probably had long-standing connections that got them there or money or the ability to network and chat up the right person, and these were skills I completely lacked. Plus WRQ had free sodas. And hey: free sodas. So this was the best I could hope for. I figured I'd stay there forever and then retire and die.

I'd landed the position through my job at a temp agency, assigning so many customer service reps who loved it at WRQ that I figured I'd send myself over for a customer service job, too. Through that process, I had gotten to know Jane in WRQ's HR department, and I was pretty good at listening to her complaints about her exhausting days trying to keep up with the staffing demands of tech in '90s Seattle. She was married to Ryan, a guy I'd interviewed for temp work a long time ago. One day, Jane mentioned that Ryan worked at Amazon. Apparently he had gone in there to interview with little to recommend him but a poetry degree and was hired to be the head of HR. He was employee number twenty or so. He got the job because he was smart and nice and they needed an HR department that day. Plus it sounded cool to have a poetry guy run HR, proof that they were a different kind of company that made unusual hiring decisions, which helped them attract investors.

Ryan had told Jane, who told me, that there was an opening for an unusual editorial job there, requiring someone with a sense of humor.

Then Jane changed my life. "You shouldn't be working at WRQ," she said. "You should be doing something creative for your career." It was the first time anyone had said that to me in a professional setting. My response consisted of a bunch of vowels and *H* sounds.

Not only was it wonderful that Jane, whom I liked and respected, thought that of me, it was even better that she had given me the permission to think that about myself. I've tried to explain the significance of this to Jane many times since, but I don't think she really gets that it was a big deal. If I try to tell her again, I think she'll find it unsettling, so I mustn't.

For saddies, encouragement is revelatory. Rather than making their resolve stronger, it will implant a resolve where none had been. "Because this person believes in me," the saddie thinks, "and this person is *not* me, they may have a point."

I reported for an interview at Amazon's rented offices in downtown Seattle. Everything looked like people had moved in forty-five minutes ago: no decor to speak of, papers everywhere, harried employees bustling around. It was like some massive police investigation unit had just been opened and everyone was hot on the trail to crack the case. I interviewed with various editors and quickly realized that everyone I talked to was smarter than me. Often by a lot. So I tried to drop in words like "para-digm" and "scalability" from time to time while praying no one asked what I thought those terms meant.

After asking what my strengths were, an editor named Jean asked the age-old follow-up: "What are your greatest weak-nesses?"

"Well, you should know that I am either drunk or high *all* the time," I said, straight-faced. "So if you're okay with that, we'll get along just fine." I figured with that joke I would either cinch the job on the spot or slam the door shut. I got a call later that day asking when I could start.

∽

I learned that I was being brought in to be the senior(!) editor of Amazon's new and still-secret e-cards initiative. You know, e-cards. Animated computer thingies you send when you want to tell someone that you were too cheap and lazy to bother with a real birthday card. E-cards are electronic representations of thoughtlessness. Turns out I got the gig because I seemed funny enough in the interviews. Thanks, jokes.

A deal had recently been announced in the tech press that Excite! (exclamation point theirs), a web portal company back when those existed, was acquiring e-card site Blue Mountain Arts for $780 million. Blue Mountain's cards, full of crude watercolor illustrations and vapid sentiments, were available free to users. The idea was that when recipients went to "get" their cards by clicking on a link in an email, they would see ads on the web page where they arrived. Web banner ads were thought to be extremely effective marketing devices back in the '90s; thus the exorbitant sale price Excite! had paid. (As Americans, we were also way into Hootie & the Blowfish back then. It was a different time.) Apparently Jeff Bezos thought this business model was a great idea, so much so that he acquired an e-card company of his own. My job was to take what I could from that acquired site and build a new Amazon e-cards site—and I was expected to have it all up and running in a few months. It was like being told to build an airplane but with no blueprints and also you're a cocker spaniel. I was given an address in a different downtown Seattle office building as my new workplace.

On my first day, I arrived at a slightly decaying low-rise building at Second and Union (Amazon had been snatching up available office space all over downtown) and was given an ID badge, printed on blue construction paper and encased in a plastic holder. Nothing electronic. The guards didn't even bother to look at the badges up close. Instead, employees streamed by holding up their blue pieces of paper.

I was directed to my new cubicle in the basement. You know, the basement: where companies always put their most important talent. I had the cubicle way in the back, in the corner. There were no windows.

Soon, I met Jason and Charles, my two direct-report employees. Jason was a very sweet, soft-spoken young guy newly transferred over from customer service. He had a fondness for playing that one Alanis Morissette CD on his desk speakers over and over. Jason enjoyed drawing cartoon illustrations where all the characters looked kind of the same but he could pound them out quickly using only a mouse. He had a wall calendar of the 1998 *Lost in Space* movie with Matt LeBlanc. Charles, older and more talkative, did much more realistic, intricate, beautiful drawings, often of birds or flowers, that took days. He did them in pencil and then scanned them into a computer.

I had no idea what to do with what they were making, aside from smiling and saying, "Nice." Jason and Charles were eager to please, if baffled and, like me, confused about what I was doing there. The office space was mostly like every other office I'd been in except that it was crawling with Germans. They had been interns of the acquired e-card company. We all agreed that we were happy to meet each other. It was an exciting time to work in e-commerce on a project that was to involve plenty of e- but no actual commerce.

At the end of the first day, I met Michael, the German founder and president of the acquired company. Michael was now technically an Amazon employee, but since he was also filthy rich from the acquisition he kind of came and went. He was perpetually smiling and always, always, always wore a sweater that said "AX." I wondered constantly why this guy was always smiling and why his sweater so clearly communicated the idea of a large tool that could be used in grisly murders. Later, I pieced together that "AX" stood for Armani Exchange and the smiling was because he had suddenly become incredibly rich in an impulsive and unnecessary business deal. This chapter, I remind you, takes place in the '90s.

Michael explained that the site he had started was called Warm Hands. No, really. That was the name he picked on purpose. Warm Hands. The idea of a birthday card making you think of warm hands and how those hands got warm and what those warm hands were up to—that apparently didn't seem unsettling and/or gross to the Germans at all. This was one of our cultural differences.

WarmHands.com (which, to this day, redirects to Amazon .com; try it!) offered e-cards made up of scans of hand-drawn illustrations that the Germans found very funny but I found mostly obtuse and distressing. I can't recall the specific cards, just that the characters had big eyes and were often screaming and this was delightful to the Germans. That first day would have been quite a day already even without trying to grasp the subtleties of the German sense of humor. I mean, think of all the famous German comedians you know. Exactly.

Looking at the cards, I was distracted by the large signature of the artist who had drawn many of them. "OSAMA," it read. Their top artist was named Osama. Went by the single name Osama. This was a few years before 9/11 but many years into Osama bin Laden's terrorist career. Weren't these illustrations great? the Germans asked me.

"We might want to get rid of the word 'Osama,'" I said, adding, "We definitely want to get rid of the word 'Osama.'"

No, no, it was okay, they explained to me, because the person who had made the cards was not Osama bin Laden. It was a different Osama. German guy. Yeah, I said, I know it's not Osama bin Laden drawing German greeting cards, but still. And thus it was incumbent upon me, at the dawn of my Amazon tenure, to explain to Michael and his German interns why we couldn't keep these fucked-up Osama cards. I'm pretty sure one of the interns was named Mathias, and I like to imagine another being named Horst. There was also Maiken, a young woman from the Netherlands, who flummoxed the young Germans something awful, especially because she was smarter than all the rest of us put together. Sometimes an intern would disappear and a brand-new one would arrive fresh from Europe.

The fact that the Warm Hands cards featured opaque German humor and prominently displayed the name of a terrorist might not play big with the new bosses at Amazon, I explained. Also, I reasoned, customers might not really love being sent a card with the word "OSAMA" on it. This might be startling and make people think of bombs and dead bodies, and it might make them afraid in a kind of generalized panicky way, none of which would lead to the ostensible goal of having a happy birthday.

We didn't get much time to talk about it because we were all needed at the Seattle distribution center to fill customer orders for the Christmas rush. Back then, any Amazonian not involved in crucial day-to-day operations was expected to perform the task of picking books, CDs, and videotapes off the distribution center shelves for a good twelve hours a day. We labored alongside any human capable of drawing breath and willing to work for $7.25 an hour for a few weeks.

By this point, Metteline had been living in Norway for many years, married to Thyge, a special education teacher. They had four boys, and Metteline worked as a psychologist. Lisbet lived in Seattle with her husband, Mark, whom she had been with since they were in tenth grade. They had two kids at the time and would soon add a third. Mark was an engineer for the City of Seattle; Lisbet was beginning to teach composition at a community college. My sisters were very stable.

Rick was in town for Christmas and staying at my parents' house in Federal Way. He had been driving a delivery truck around San Diego for a while and claimed to be sober. If true, this would be a big switch from how he had spent the last ten to fifteen years. There had been several jobs and a number of moves; he lived with a girlfriend, then he lived with her platonically, then there were more roommates, then he lived with a friend and the friend's parents. Phone numbers changed and expired. I pretty much observed all this from a distance. Something that I learned after an adolescence spent trying to get my dad to stop drinking and smoking is that when you believe someone has really changed, you get burned.

Addiction is a mental disorder that messes up the logic parts of your brain and replaces them with a need to get the substance. Smokers will smoke knowing it's wrong and potentially lethal. Drug addicts will lie to everyone around them in an effort to get drugs or the money to buy drugs. They will destroy trust and wreck relationships if it means they can get the next fix. And yes, it is that person's voice and smile pulling the con and it is their own hands getting the drug and delivering it to the system, but it also isn't. It's the illness they have contracted.

But I still thought Rick was cool, and I was usually willing to buy in for another round of "he has really cleaned up" before it became obvious once again that it was either no longer true or had never been. And maybe this latest job would really stick. I figured it was a union position and involved a special kind of driver's license that required a lot of training. "He probably makes a lot of money," I thought.

The Eric Roberts tape was my first clue that reality might not match my suppositions/hopes. Rick had brought along a VHS tape of the 1995 Eric Roberts made-for-TV movie *Saved by the Light*, and when Jill and I drove down to visit one night, Rick insisted that we all watch it together, the two of us, my parents, and him. Roberts plays a Vietnam vet who bullies people and beats them up, breaking the hearts of his long-suffering parents in the process. Then he's struck by lightning, dies, and is visited by some kind of angel who shows him the error of his ways. But mere death can't kill Eric Roberts, so he returns to the world of the living, helps people, rescues a woman from an abusive husband by punching said husband, gets a horrible infection in his punching hand, briefly dies *a second time*, wakes up again, and then becomes a motivational speaker. As one does.

Rick was trying to show us that he was Eric Roberts, that he knew he hurt people and was seeking redemption. However, unless you really are Eric Roberts, nothing good can come of letting Eric Roberts explain you to your family. It was more perplexing and sad than revelatory.

Rick also mentioned, when our parents were out of the

room, that the oddest thing had happened that day. He was taking a shower, but the bathroom curtain was covered in hundreds of spiders so it was kind of difficult to get out. He told it like an amusing anecdote. Rick had always been able to sling deadpan jokes, and I laughed because that's what I chose to believe this was. But the smile afterward, the standard notification that he had been just messing with you, never arrived.

That night, we all talked about this new job I had at Amazon. I explained that, yes, it was exciting, I thought, but for right now we were all just working in a warehouse because it was the peak of the busy season so lots of temp workers were there. "Maybe Rick can come down and help," offered my mom. That confused me because that's not what people do on vacation. Rick surely had to get back to his high-paying driving job in San Diego.

"Oh, it only pays $7.25 an hour," I said dismissively.

"That's great," said Rick. "What time do you need me there? I'll need to get a ride."

"I can give you a ride," interjected Mom.

He thought I was doing the hiring myself and that I would be his boss. Oh. In an instant, he wasn't my eccentric yet still admirable hero of a big brother anymore; he was a teenager who did drugs, arrested at the stage of maturity he was in when he first started using, as is often the case with addicts. He was thirty-six years old but he was fifteen years old.

Amazon didn't need any more help, I was told, to my relief. Later, Lisbet would tell me about how Rick had been using a thing called methamphetamine.

E-cards had been given a target of March, three months away, to launch a fully functional site. This started out impossible and became more impossible with each passing day. We decided to hire freelancers for the art. Charles had been working on a contract that wasn't renewed; Jason was reassigned in the company.

Michael faded away, and most of the interns returned to Germany, hopefully having learned something but oh, come on, probably not. We kept one intern, named Alf, who was at most twenty-three but had the demeanor of a weary veteran cop who had seen it all.

Alf seemed amused by Amazon's frantic effort to make shitty electronic cards that could not possibly make money, but he kept to himself, quietly building databases or goofing off, I had no idea which. Several new employees from within Amazon came aboard on a temporary basis for things like design and software development, and we all got a new boss. My new manager, Eric, was tall, thin, angular, and French (because if the Germans can't deliver you humor, by all means call in the French), with the appearance of a snooty maître d' and the disposition of Herbert Lom's Chief Inspector Dreyfus character from the Pink Panther movies. Eric might have been twenty-eight or fifty; it was impossible to tell because when all that's ever on your face is stress and determination, age becomes a mystery. He was a tightly wound guy, eager to prove himself within the company, yet—tragically for him—saddled with a stinker of a project.

"We've got a yudge focking problem," Eric said in one of our first group meetings. I nodded as my brain translated "yudge focking" to "huge fucking." The problem involved the deadline, handed down from executives far up the chain. The problem was both yudge and focking because very little about the site had even been imagined, let alone built. It was like standing in an open field in October and being expected to open a mall in time for Christmas shopping. Over the rest of the time I worked with Eric, many problems, both small and large, were characterized as yudge and focking.

I had become friends with Ju, a fellow liberal arts grad with a deadpan sense of humor who had been placed in charge of programming the front end for our nascent site. "When he says 'yudge focking problem,'" I told her, "just mentally replace the word 'problem' with 'bowl of ice cream.' That way, you can trick yourself into thinking that he isn't looking for someone to yell at but instead talking about a large, delicious treat."

From that point forward, Ju and I would sit in meetings and have many occasions to imagine that Eric had brought out a yudge focking bowl of ice cream for all of us to enjoy. We'd nod at each other across the room. It was a good way to avoid terror even though it was, upon reflection, madness.

The e-card section was to be Amazon's fourth tab on the home page after books, music, and movies. Without the Osama e-card gallery in the cupboard and with half-explored partnerships with Hallmark and American Greetings never materializing to lift the burden of creativity off my sagging shoulders, our inventory of e-cards for this new shop was precisely zero. This meant we had to start making some. I had figured writing a greeting card would be pretty easy because, hey, they're short. As I sat at my computer in my basement cubicle for hours trying to come up with some, two things happened: I came to respect the craft of the greeting card writer, and I wrote very few greeting cards.

Over the coming weeks, I would train myself to write at least rudimentary, bad ideas even when I had no ideas. Because we could use simple animated GIFs, I had a freelance artist make a guy who pulls a birthday cake from behind his back that said "Surprise! Happy Birthday!" I used another freelancer to make a dog that said, "Let's roll around in something stinky together." I think it was a love card? I don't know. I don't think I even knew then. Does it even make sense? Hell no.

I tried to reassure myself that I would be part of a massive, widely distributed group failure instead of an individual, humiliating, getting-fired failure. There were frequent meetings, wherein every department would update the whole team on

progress, and all the team members in turn would try to portray themselves as having made some. The intrinsic problem was
that each department had to rely on all the others, and also no
one knew what the fuck they were doing and e-cards are stupid.
What each of us feared the most was being designated as "ze
bottleneck," a term Eric used for the person who was slowing
everyone else down the most. "So hoo eez ze bottleneck?!" he
would ask, perplexed and irate. Obviously, being ze bottleneck
was a yudge focking problem.

At one memorable meeting, Eric got to the question of ze
bottleneck and wondered aloud, "Is it Half?"

Confused looks all around. "Half of . . . what?" some brave
soul asked.

"Half! You know, with ze database. Half!"

"Alf?" I suggested.

"Yes! Half! We got to tell Half to get hees focking act togezer,
man."

I promised that I would pass this along to Ha—to Al—to him.
"Eet is a yudge focking problem with Half."

I never told Half that he was ze bottleneck.

Around the company, people would ask me how the Warm
Hands project was coming and then make a yucky face, either at
the name Warm Hands or maybe because they'd seen the Osama
offerings.

Or, I thought, maybe the yucky face just came from talking
to me. That was depression talking, but it wasn't all that far-
fetched. My instant elevation to "senior editor" upon being hired
engendered some degree of jealous loathing from others in the
company. Like I had been plucked off a pickup basketball court
in the park to start in the NBA. These co-workers had a point.
I was in fact spending each day acting like I knew what I was
doing, my limited acting skills in demand once more.

Which meant that I had what is known as impostor syndrome, a pattern of thinking where you believe that your success is actually a mistake and you'll soon be exposed as a fraud and hurled from your lofty position by beefy security goons. It's about as easy for a person with depression to get impostor syndrome as it is for a person falling off a boat to get wet. Most if not all successful people I've talked to about this have had some form of impostor syndrome along the way. In fact, it's the ones who have felt perfectly entitled to all their success that you have to watch out for.

Normies with the syndrome can generally get past it because they see it for what it is: a fleeting moment of doubt. For saddies, though, it can be acute and visceral and terrifying. There's simply too much of a gap between the upper-level work you're doing and your extremely low opinion of yourself for reality to hold up to any level of scrutiny. Depressed people see this gap, look for someone to blame, and immediately blame themselves because the illness tells them to.

Impostor syndrome has some root comedic value. You have achieved something only to have depression yank it away. That's kind of funny.

Even when there was ample evidence against the impostor notion, it persisted. At one point, I was asked to emcee the annual all-company meeting held at the big convention center in Seattle, and it went great. When Jeff Bezos was named *Time*'s Person of the Year, I was interviewed and photographed for the issue. However, honors like those only increased the impostor feeling because my ineptitude was being put on ever-bigger stages. I even went to an Amazon party where Bezos put a hula skirt on me, for reasons I did not and still do not understand. I was a made man, part of the gang, a beloved fixture. Reality and retrospection tell me these things happened because the company was proud of me and wanted to show me off; depression told me I was a sucker being set up. Depression steals your ability to feel happy and proud even at the moments you should be happiest and proudest.

Jill tells me that during this period I would often talk about e-cards in my sleep, starting up conversations as if in the middle of a meeting, sometimes urging her to get in touch with a certain illustrator right away. Due to the long hours we were all expected to log, Jill was among very few non-Amazon people I ever saw during my employment there, and that was because we shared a house. She was patient and supportive even as she inwardly weighed whether possible riches from stock options were worth having a husband with a nervous breakdown.

The stress, the hours, the sacrifice of my peace of mind and physical health—I knew that these were all virtuous things. That this suffering was both necessary and noble. I've never been especially patriotic or religious, but I had completely bought into the cult of labor. It's a way companies fool people into hurting themselves in order to enrich their employers.

Those of us who grew up in the '80s, perhaps more than most other generations, were raised on this notion that if you worked all the time and climbed the corporate ladder, all the material riches you could imagine could be yours. Technology was just starting to open up, so the prizes in the capitalism contest—A phone in your car! A videocassette recorder! A personal computer!—were not only culturally on display but were tools to a more advanced life than other people had. You'd get ahead and stay ahead. We watched *Lifestyles of the Rich and Famous* on television. We believed that Donald Trump was a shrewd and wealthy businessman. All this in an era when the Reagan administration tilted the federal government to benefit corporations and away from providing protection and a safety net for individuals. We fetishized our own exploitation.

Much the same spirit existed at Amazon. The power ties and hair gel had been replaced by blue oxfords and khakis, but the culture was the same. Amazon folks were expected to put in at least fifty hours a week at the time but preferably much more, and a kind of macho culture ensued, wherein employees (Amazonians, people other than me called us) would try to top each other in importance and hours worked.

"Dude, I was here until ten last night. So much to do."

"I hear you, man. I don't think I've gone home before midnight all week. My boss in khakis and a blue button-down shirt is counting on me to save the whole website."

"Right on. Tonight I'm going to be here until yesterday, and I have to kill three guys or we can never sell books again."

These conversations would go on forever, even though no one would have to stay nearly as late as they did if they would try shutting the fuck up and getting back to work. I never pointed this out, even when I got the disapproving side-eye as I snuck out at 8 p.m.

So I was a stressed-out impostor (and secretly ze bottleneck) in way over my head. But I also believed that I was, at last, on the way to being happy and that all my problems had been solved. I mean, logically that had to be the case because I had a prestigious job at a really important company. My plan was to work hard at Amazon, retire early off stocks that I was certain always went up and never went down, and then have the rest of my life to write novels or write plays or learn what it was like to fucking relax for once. It might feel like a prison (where all inmates wore khakis and most had MBAs), but I knew I would get out at some point. I just had to last five to ten years and I would have enough financial stability and disposable income to get a bigger house, have kids, and drive a better car. I'd have a future that did not involve living under a bridge in a cardboard box, contrary to what depression had been telling me since age twelve.

And it wasn't just the material concerns that would be taken care of. It was also my mental health. After battling depression my whole life and not even knowing that I had been doing so, I wasn't sure what "fine" or "happy" felt like in any broad sense, but I knew—I knew!—this new job would get me there. It would make the nebulous badness disappear. The persistent sense of something being off kilter was a mosquito buzzing in my ear, and it sometimes spiked into a deafening roar. But this new job, I was sure, would silence it.

This anticipation of problems being solved was only the latest in a very long line of incarnations of the If I Could Just mentality. If I Could Just get that one more thing, THEN I'd be happy. I wouldn't be happy in the present moment, but once the next thing was secured, happiness would be locked down. Previous incarnations of If I Could Just included:

- If I Could Just land the lead in the high school play.
- If I Could Just be accepted into a good college.
- If I Could Just land the lead in the college play.
- If I Could Just be accepted into a good grad school.
- If I Could Just get this girl to like me.
- If I Could Just move to Seattle.
- If I Could Just get hired at a steady job.
- If I Could Just get married.
- If I Could Just buy a house.

All those goals had been reached, and yet the problems never vanished in a puff of smoke. The If I Could Just approach is like trying to spot the real Santa Claus in your house, and equally realistic.

The gig at Amazon did not solve all my problems. That's the opposite of a twist ending, I know. I zigged when you expected me to zig.

The initial ridiculously ambitious deadline came and went. Eric said that this was not, in fact, a yudge focking problem. A problem, sure, but neither yudge nor focking. But while no reasonable person had ever really expected us to hit that targeted launch date, we were by now behind schedule and always would be. Between the various departments, we all tried to avoid being ze bottleneck. Alf's visa expired, and he returned to Germany. "Oh, zat's too bad," said Eric, a little saddened. "I liked Half." I can only chalk this up to relations between the French and the Germans being, by this point in history, complicated.

~

Then came the day I suddenly wanted to kill myself.

The launch date for the e-cards site had been delayed, then delayed again, and then a couple more times. But by this point the mockup of the site was starting to form, and more people were seeing the cards that I had been working on in consultation with various freelance artists. No one was telling me the cards sucked, which to a depressed person means that the cards *do* suck but everyone's either too polite or angry to actually tell you that.

Pushing the e-card site out to the public was an inevitability, and every day it didn't happen, my anxiety level climbed. But my normal nail-biting anxiety about pleasing a handful of co-workers and a perpetually about-to-snap Frenchman would soon be replaced by a need to please everyone in the whole world.

One morning, I was on the bus commuting into downtown Seattle, and I was thinking about all that I had to do that day. Smartphones and networked tablets were still years away at that point, so I couldn't *do* any of the work; I could just think about how much there was to do and stare out at a drizzly Seattle day. Thoughts of that day's workload led to thinking about the load over the next several days and weeks. Depression told me that I didn't have the talent, the ambition, or the brains to get it all done, and instead of getting more help, I would get fired. You can only blame Half so many times.

What should I do?

The answer struck me as the 61 bus pulled off the Alaskan Way Viaduct onto Seneca Street and began to turn left at First Avenue, coming to a stop outside the Seattle Art Museum. "I should kill myself," I thought. It would make everything go away. The stress would stop.

It was such a bold and weird thought that I laughed out loud. It seemed preposterous that my brain had reached such a conclusion. I wasn't going to literally kill myself over an Amazon launch? Over e-cards? I had a wife and friends and a house and a life. Wisdom took over, and I knew that this stress would one day pass and I would move on. Killing myself would be dumb, I thought, as I got off the bus and walked south on First toward the office.

Long pause. Besides, how would I even do it? Hanging was no good because it would hurt and our ceilings were way too low. Jumping off something was out because I could barely even bring myself to go off the high dive, plus I heard that survivors of jumps off the Golden Gate Bridge report regretting their decision as they plunged. The thing with the car and the hose in the garage? Nah, we only had a carport.

On my left, I saw Central Loan & Gun Exchange, a pawnshop that was armed to the teeth and usually open for business. That would probably be the answer, right? Buy one of those, drive somewhere remote, leave a note on my desk or something. Probably put the gun on the credit card; the guy at the pawnshop could help me pick one out if I told him it was for target practice or something. And it would mean not worrying about this launch anymore. And then Jill would be free to go marry someone who didn't have this secret mental weirdness. I'd be doing her a favor, really. I was ze bottleneck. I was the yudge focking problem.

People would be sad at first, but in the end they would be relieved not to have to deal with me anymore, and in time they would come to see how wise I was to kill myself. I must note that all of this was not me being strictly suicidal. I wasn't planning something. I was daydreaming. This is known as suicidal ideation, and while it's bad and a sign that you should get help right away, in my case it was a ways off from actually attempting suicide.

The ideation daydream was a long improvisational mental journey, the conclusion of which I again rejected. No, I told myself, I'm not going to kill myself. That's ridiculous. That's something in my irredeemably broken brain converting stress into despair. Probably the result of a character flaw, on account of the thing about me being weird and bad and dumb and weak. That's all it could be! I mean, it's not mental illness, I surmised, because I'm still going to my job and I'm aware of the world that I'm in and I don't think I'm Napoleon. Mental illness is for people in the booby hatch doing sad craft projects with safety scissors. I had seen *Girl, Interrupted*.

But although I had rejected the suicide option, it had taken up residence in my mind. I had normalized it. The grim off-ramp to life's freeway was built and the barricades removed.

Finally, the site launched, and it was neither a huge success nor a complete disaster. It was just a thing that most people looked at briefly and then got on with their lives. I was told to ratchet up the number of cards in the store dramatically, expand into new categories, and be ready for every major holiday with a truckload of content. I was told to hire more staff, spend more money, and "get big fast" in the Amazon tradition. And I was given my first real editorial note by Eric. "Ah don't unnerstan zese cards you make. I don't get ze jokes. Jus make some with cute bunnies or some focking puppies or whatever. Make zem cute. Okay?" I told him okay and returned to my desk to crank out more hastily conceived cards with dogs saying inscrutable things and tacitly interfere with Eric's efforts to make a name for himself at Amazon. And I tried to get ready for the next holiday.

Holidays can never be delayed no matter who is ze bottleneck, which presented a yudge focking problem for me. My brain responded by firing up its If I Could Just device once again. If I Could Just make it through this next stressful period and get enough cards finished, I would finally be happy. Then I did make it through that stressful period and emerged not happy at all. But the next one for sure! Nope. A growing problem was that each time a crisis/deadline came along, I was involuntarily presented with the thought that if I went back to Central Loan & Gun Exchange and made a purchase, this could all be over. I kept dismissing it and trying to laugh it off. It got less and less funny. It wasn't funny to anyone else because I made sure to never tell a soul.

Over the next couple of years, the stock price dropped and Amazon had several rounds of layoffs. I wondered more than ever if this whole "all problems solved If I Could Just (insert variable)" idea could conceivably have some holes in it. I gave up e-cards (the company soon did, too) to work as a senior editor in the toy store. The same nameless dread still haunted my life.

I was now stationed in a building in the Beacon Hill neighborhood of Seattle, which meant no more riding the bus that had now been more or less imprinted with suicidal ideation and no more strolls by Central Loan & Gun Exchange. I drove to work.

One morning, I had driven to work in the old purplish pickup

truck Jill and I called the Grape Ape. I was thinking about looming deadlines and co-workers who were all as stressed out and
miserable as I was. There I was in the truck, trying to keep the
specter of suicidal ideation at bay, and wondering if, when I finally got in, someone else would be sitting in my chair saying,
"Oh, they didn't tell you about the layoff? You need to go down
to HR right away, and bring your badge."

As I drove and played out these scenarios mentally, I was cut
off by someone in a very expensive sports car who had then
turned left. At least I think I was cut off. Maybe they had the
right of way and I was wrong. Might not have been expensive.
Possibly not a sports car. I don't honestly remember all that well.
What I do remember is being suddenly consumed by white-hot
rage. I honked the horn for longer than anyone ever should and
spun the Ape around to launch a hot pursuit of the offending
motorist. I accelerated rapidly, roaring up behind him. Depression shortens your fuse and then lights it.

I had already honked in a road rage fashion and figured
the driver would be even more intimidated by this ugly purple
pickup suddenly tailgating him. He would see, I surmised in my
now-blinding rage, that I was a menacing demon and was thus
capable of great violence, and he would be ashamed of his recent moving violation. I would be a hero for standing up for
justice, and all my problems would be solved and I'd be happy.
It all made sense to me. And that's because it wasn't truly me
driving the pickup any longer. Depression had seen an opening
and busted in, leaping the fence between mind and body and
taking the wheel of both my truck and me. I stood outside myself watching this all take place and wondering who that crazy
yelling guy even was, road raging in a purple pickup purchased
secondhand from a children's theater.

I am not actually capable of great violence, mind you. Or

mild violence. I am a physical coward. Oh, I can argue with anyone and am fine if those arguments get heated, but I have been in precisely one fight in my life and it was in fifth grade and it was over after one punch and I lost. But on this day I was in a truck, and as long as I stayed inside it and was fueled by inexplicably strong anger, I could feel like A Big Man.

I screamed at the top of my lungs as I drove, banging the sides of the truck's cab with my fists, hurting my knuckles, vocal cords, and sanity in the process. The luxury car drove on, very possibly not even noticing the original honk, let alone the unhinged behavior that followed it.

I was still observing the speed limit and relevant traffic laws while going flat-out bonkers with rage. My throat was sore, and the seat belt had locked in response to sudden movements. I cried rage tears, and I hadn't even known those were a thing.

Finally, I noticed the driver of the car briefly look back and noted that he was small of build and bald. This distracted me long enough to ask myself if that was, in fact, Jeff Bezos himself that I had been road raging all over. Had I stalked and bullied the founder and CEO of Amazon.com?

Later that day, I sat at my desk and waited for an email or a phone call to tell me that I could go home for the day and never return. Tried to review a toy or two. Failed at that. Hard to appreciate the nuances of an Elmo bath toy when you're having a mental breakdown after road raging Jeff Bezos.

Maybe it was too much sugar? All I'd eaten that day was a bagel. Too much caffeine? I'd had my usual one cup of coffee. This is something that people do when they don't realize they have a mental health problem: they blame every possible external factor they can think of but never bother to consider the internal ones. One thing I knew it couldn't be was depression. Because I wasn't moping. I wasn't even sad. I didn't know that depression isn't a mood. It's a set of conditions that cause a whole series of thoughts and behaviors to happen over a long period of time, often things that are wildly different from one another.

$\sim$

Once I had sweated out a few hours at my desk with no call from HR, I became a bit more confident that I would not get fired that day and that the figurative bullet had been dodged, just as the literal bullet from the downtown pawnshop had been dodged, or at least forestalled. But I knew that if this road rage had happened once, it would most likely happen again. And because I didn't know why it happened, I was powerless to prevent it.

I hung in and hung on. My mental health treatment plan was "hope for the best" and "hope this stops." My team at work was moved to new offices in the International District in Seattle, away from the top executives, and thus I was at less risk of murdering Jeff Bezos over a turn signal or some such shit.

One day, the toys editors were called into a meeting with a bunch of Amazon software developers. They were excited to show us a brand-new piece of in-house software that they called Amabot. As in Amazon Robot. If you looked at a product page, Amabot could form associations with similar pages, then conclude what copy and design should be on that page and fill it in automatically. It edited through artificial intelligence. It was very cool software, I had to admit. As far as robots rolling up to replace you go, it was impressive. The developers were happy and proud of their achievement.

"So all the things we get paid to do all day," my co-worker Diane asked, "can be done for free by Amabot?"

The software guys nodded.

"And then what will *we* do?" asked Diane.

Nobody said anything. I probably laughed a bit because it was both ominous and funny. The software guys had obviously never even entertained this question in their months of work building an invisible robot that would do my job and, by extension, take food off my table.

"You'll . . . be free to do other things?" offered a software guy meekly.

"Like look for other jobs?" asked Diane.

This time, no one answered.

Diane quit a few weeks later, writing the single word "Amabot" on her office whiteboard on her way out the door. The bits of dry-erase ink were the most atoms Amabot had yet taken up in its quest, a completely defensible quest by business standards, to kill us all.

Not long after this, I was invited to apply for a job at the local public radio station, working as a full-time writer and producer on *Rewind*, a show I had been freelancing for. No stock options, but reasonable hours and nice people and a sense that I would be informing and entertaining people instead of convincing them to buy a bunch of stuff they didn't need.

As for Amazon, I had gotten away with it. So that was good. Not so good: I had developed suicidal ideation, may have stalked and harassed the billionaire founder, and not one of my problems had been erased; instead I had grown a whole crop of new ones.

Thus began my career in public radio. That job, I concluded at the time, was a much better fit.

In fact, I thought, it would solve all my problems.

According to *THWoD*:
You Can't Solve Mental Illness by
Not Dealing with It

P eople, especially saddies (the best people), drastically overesti-
mate the value of getting stuff. They think that achieving that
next thing, acquiring that next object, or receiving that longed-
for status plateau will fix a mind that's depressed. And oh honey,
it won't. I fell for it a lot in my time at Amazon and have fallen
for it plenty of times since. I'll probably fall for it a bunch more
times in the future.

You can't achieve your way to happiness. You can't win your
way out of depression. This does not prevent smart people from
thinking that way. The people I've interviewed on the show,
for the most part, have a public profile. They've achieved a lot.
They're some degree of famous. But the people I interview often
also have this void in them that fame and achievement haven't
managed to fill.

On the first episode of *The Hilarious World of Depression*, I
talked to Peter Sagal, best known as the host of the NPR show
Wait Wait . . . Don't Tell Me. He went to Harvard, is a successful playwright (a field in which almost no one succeeds), and

has been hosting a hit radio show for decades. He is among the smarter and more successful people I know; that doesn't matter to depression. Peter's festering depression had been dormant for years, but that dormancy ended when the divorce came.

Prior to talking to Peter, I had harbored a semiconscious thought that if I had what he had, if I had his accomplishments (minus the divorce), I would be happy all the time. It's not true.

Novelist John Green, author of *The Fault in Our Stars* among many other megaselling books, has struggled with this for years. "There is this weird perpetual hope," he told me, "not just among people with mental illnesses—I don't know if it's American or if it's human or what—but there does seem to be this perpetual hope that if I just get this one thing that my life is missing, the hole inside of me will be filled."

John was once speaking to an extremely wealthy person, he recalled, who "literally said to me, 'If I could just own a plane instead of having a fractional lease situation,' and I was like, 'Stop. Stop. Hold on. You cannot seriously believe that. You can't seriously think like you're still just the one thing away. *I'm one plane away from ultimate fulfillment.*'"

At the time I was struggling at Amazon, John Green was struggling after college, hoping to get something published somewhere because If He Could Just get that, he figured, everything would be okay. It didn't work for John Green then and doesn't work for him now; it didn't work for me during those heady dot-com days and still doesn't.

"The hole will never be full," says Andy Richter, actor, talk show sidekick, and person with depression since about the age of four. "The main thing you can do is be comfortable with that knowledge."

Andy says the presence of that hole, that pit, that cavity, is extremely common among performers with depression. Depression is what made the hole in the first place, and it did so by clearing out stuff like self-esteem, a full range of emotions, and shame about wearing sweatpants in public. The problem for people with depression is that the things you try to put in those holes don't fit. You can't shove a career achievement into a self-esteem-shaped hole. Pound it with a hammer all you want, it won't go in. Same with trying to pour alcohol or drugs into the hole for a full range of emotions. It won't work.

"In fact," says Andy, "the more you try to shove things in the hole that don't belong there, the bigger the hole gets and the harder it is to ever fill."

And here's where it gets really sinister. The undue idealization with which the depressed person sees the post-achievement future is matched by a real scorn for the present. So it's not just that things will be wonderful if I achieve X, it's that whatever I've earned through hard work and talent and my endless series of small decisions to this point is insignificant.

Here in Minnesota, a lot of us transplants get to know each other because people born in Minnesota made all the friends they'll ever need in preschool. Somehow, I've had occasion to get to know Ana Marie Cox, a writer and overall smart person whom I've admired for years. And even though we're friends now, I've always had this gnawing feeling that she'll realize I'm not actually smart or cool enough to be her friend.

We did a kind of mutual interview a while back, and we noted that this running oneself down is a constant for people like us. "This is common for people with all the different things that we have," she said, "which is that if I can do it, then it must be dumb. If I can do it, it's not that hard. So everything I ever did that was like a big deal, I'd be like, oh well, I guess it's not a big deal. I thought that would be a big deal, but it's not because I could do it. So that means any idiot could do it, so on to the next thing that I think is hard. And then if I achieve it, then I guess, yeah, that turned out to be not really important either. I also come from an alcoholic family, and that's a very adult-children-of-alcoholics kind of thing, to try to fill the hole with accomplishments and achievements."

I've met a lot of people through the podcast who have what I had always wanted in terms of career achievement. Neal Brennan has Netflix specials, co-created *Chappelle's Show*, directed movies, hangs out with NBA players, and has a cool condo on Venice Beach where he lives with his nice dog, Keith.

"This is how fucking stupid my self-esteem was and probably still is in some part," says Neal. "So I did *Chappelle's Show*. And then I would tell myself that I was a good sketch writer but I couldn't write for *Saturday Night Live* because I could write single-camera sketches like for *Chappelle's Show* but I couldn't do multicam live sketches. That was my caveat. And then I went along when Chappelle hosted *SNL*, and I wrote a good multicam sketch. And then I was like, 'Oh, I can do that.'"

As a person plugged into the entertainment industry, Neal knows he's not alone in feeling this way, that a big achievement or pile of money would clean up the mind. "Everyone says money won't bring you happiness. People hear that and they go, 'Well, let's see.'

"Every single person goes, 'Oh, I may be different. Let me try.' But I've had conversations with the biggest movie stars in the world who had come to the exact same conclusion."

By the time she was ten years old, Mara Wilson had starred in five movies, including *Matilda* and *Mrs. Doubtfire*. But thanks to anxiety, OCD, PTSD, and depression, she couldn't enjoy much of anything. In middle school, "I didn't take much pride in the things that I did," she says. "And when people would congratulate me or would recognize me on the street I would be like, 'What are you recognizing me for?' It didn't feel like anything big to me."

6

BRIDGES, TROUBLES, WATERS

This chapter happens at some point in my adult life.
As to when exactly, I'm keeping that private.

Of all the lies depression tells you, and there are many, "you are doomed" is among the most believable. Nothing is good, says the illness, nothing has ever been good, and so it stands to reason that nothing will ever be good. The way you feel in your worst moments now is how you'll always feel. And later on, depending on how long you manage to survive, it will only get worse because you'll get old and sick and people around you will die and you yourself will absolutely also die and probably painfully. When you're unable to make the noise stop, a logical thought is to make everything stop.

But no. I could not do that. Suicide is bad; everyone knows that.

Then again, went my reasoning, the people who know that suicide is bad, the ones who say that, are part of the great swath of society for whom things go well. It's like when movie stars tell you to keep reaching for your dreams and never quit, because sure, *they* would say that because it worked for *them*. Those advising against suicide are the people able to handle stuff, the people who haven't been irredeemably weird their whole lives.

I knew that dying and leaving behind people who were gullible enough to care about me was a bad thing to do. I also knew more about me than anyone else did, so I knew how hollow and worthless I really was, and thus their sentimental mourning for me, if that even happened, would be misguided. It wasn't so much anguish and pain, just a cold knowledge of my uselessness. I was a dead car on the side of the road with a blown transmission and a cracked engine block; you don't repair that rust bucket, you junk it.

At this point, for the first time in my life, I had entered the "seriously considering" territory of suicide. I hadn't decided to do it, but it was in the realm of realistic options. And given that I had arrived at this new place, the only sensible thing to do was to look around. If suicide was a pair of pants (it's not a pair of pants, it's suicide), it was time to go to the fitting room and try them on. What would it feel like to write a suicide note?

Click start on the PC, click to open Microsoft Word, click on NEW DOCUMENT.

I began with an apology to Jill that quickly turned much snottier than one would expect from the format. Of course this will be an upsetting event for you, I explained, but only because you don't have the knowledge that I have. I know that I will get steadily worse, dragging everyone down with me. By getting out of your life, I went on, I am giving you the chance to find a much better husband than me, the kind of steady, stable husband you deserve. And I bet that guy will be a great dad, too. Better than I could ever hope to be.

The apology extended into ever marrying her in the first place. I had hoped that love would fix what was broken about me, and it was naïve of me to believe that. As a result, I had dragged her down into my abyss when I could have avoided it all by never hooking up with her in the first place. Then she could have married that guy from her college who she dated briefly and who opened an ice cream shop and was a big success. I said I loved her, which I did and do. That was the end.

The Aurora Bridge is a 2,945-foot-long cantilever and truss bridge that stands 167 feet above the western end of Lake Union in Seattle. The bridge opened in 1932 and connects Seattle's Queen Anne and Fremont neighborhoods. Starting with a shoe salesman who jumped to his death before the bridge was even open to traffic, there have been hundreds of deaths by suicide on the Aurora Bridge. If you're someone familiar with the suicidal urge, it is impossible to drive across the Aurora Bridge and not feel at least a little of the mood of the people who ended there. It's like a haunted battlefield.

As of this writing, fifty people have died in jumps from Aurora since 1995, with over half landing not in the water but on land, often the roads and parking lot areas around the campus of the Adobe software company. My plan, should I go through with it, was to go far out but not as far as the water. If I was to do this thing, I wouldn't want to be in the icy water of Lake Union with severe injuries even if I was about to die. I also wouldn't want to survive, have chronic injuries, and be unable to take care of myself, everyone knowing I had done this to myself willingly. Nope, just a long plunge onto hard fatal pavement, thanks.

But again! Again, again, again, I was uncertain about carrying this out. I had not decided to kill myself. I was merely trying on suicide's pants.

I parked right around the corner from the bridge, folded the note neatly in half, and left it on the dashboard right above the steering wheel. Walking toward the bridge, I realized that I would not have much time for contemplation. Either I was going to do it or not do it. If I lingered too long at the railing, that's sending a signal, that's a cry for help. Traffic would stop, cops would come, ugh. Instead I needed to appear to be simply walking across the Aurora Bridge, just like people never do. I crossed the street at the last on-ramp and was on the bridge, still close enough to the edge that a jump would mean at most a broken leg.

I spotted a point farther along the span where I knew a jump would mean certain death and where I could credibly snatch a few moments of "Oh, I'm just looking around" by standing back a bit as I looked over. It would mean that a decision would have to be made one way or the other in the span of about ten seconds. Refusing to slow down or break stride, I arrived at the designated point on the bridge and looked over. It was the moment. I could tell a few passing drivers were looking at me nervously, wondering if and how they should pull over.

Three factors immediately charged to the forefront of my thinking.

One. I had been running a mental math equation in my head for a while. News of my death would be devastating for Jill. I knew she loved me. She was a sucker, I thought, for doing so, but apparently it couldn't be helped. To this point, I had believed that the payoff for her devastation in that moment would be the better life she would have without me. It's how I imagine law school works: you go through the hard times to get to better times. On that bridge, the image of Jill receiving this news became more crystalline: phone calls trying to locate me would become increasingly frantic until there was a cop at the door. I knew she was wearing a blue sweater that morning, and I knew where she'd be standing when the cop showed up. Her pain, because I loved her, was acute in my imagining. It hurt, and it was nauseating, too. I still believed, at least intellectually, that she'd be better off without me, but how could I enable that horrible moment? How could I bring that cop to the door?

Two. It was scary as fuck, yo. Up there on that bridge? Looking down? Imagining that fall? I had walked to that bridge uncertain of what I was going to do, but to leap from that bridge meant a few seconds of falling when I would no longer have the luxury of uncertainty. To be alive without free will and with only gravity seemed undesirable. Which meant I still had desires.

Three. Jumping would mean doing something. Doing something was not really my thing. I was more inclined to not do something. I specialized in stewing.

A religious person might describe this moment—as passing motorists' eyes grew large—as God holding me back. Indeed, it did feel like hands on my shoulders and around my chest and legs, restraining me from even making a motion toward climbing over the rail. Not being a God guy myself, it felt like depression holding me back. It wasn't done with me. I turned and walked back along the bridge the way I'd come. Of course I did, dummy, because I'm writing this now.

I went back to the truck, took the note off the dash, placed it on the passenger seat, and drove back to work. Back at my desk, I deleted the document from my computer, then went to the deleted files folder and zapped it out of existence. Then I walked around the office distributing the tiny ripped-up shreds I had made of the note into as many different garbage cans and recycling bins as I could find. I didn't want anyone's concern or, good Lord, intervention. My mental state was a disaster, but it was my disaster and I was protective of it.

According to *THWoD*:
The Worst Idea Is Always Nearby

For most people, suicide seems about as predictable as a plane crash. There is no prior warning. And that's terrifying because then there is no way of knowing when this horror will happen again. For people who have known depression, even in a fairly distant past, it's never as surprising. Obviously a person could do something like that, we think, because it's a means to an end that exists in our world.

I live near the Mall of America. The largest shopping mall in the country, it has an amusement park with multiple roller coasters within it. To people around the world, the Mall of America is a symbol of a garish consumerism, a cartoonish and possibly grotesque symbol of America itself. To me, it's a nearby mall that has a lot of things, and sometimes I go there to shop for stuff that I need. The MOA, as we call it, is a fact. It isn't good or evil, it's merely nearby and reachable.

For people with depression, suicide is kind of like how the Mall of America is for me. It's a real thing. This doesn't mean everyone with depression is constantly clinging to building ledges.

Far from it; it simply means we know that it's a real place you can drive to. (Did I just compare suicide to going to the Mall of America? Well, you heard me.)

Talk show legend Dick Cavett told me about a time when he was young and institutionalized for depression. "While I was in the hospital with it," said Dick, "they said, 'We're going to take the patients for a walk.' And I thought that would be nice because I can run pretty fast and get away from the group and go over the rail of the George Washington Bridge without any trouble."

I asked him how close he came to pulling that off. "Well, we never had the walk. But that was scary. And it wasn't horrifying, it was sort of surprising. Why would I do that? And the only answer that comes back is that [it] will instantly stop this. But there's a paradox in that thought because what you mean by that is, once I jump in front of the train, I'll feel better. Because anything but this would feel better. And it's anything but this. There's no you to feel."

It's a pretty airtight argument against suicide. You want to kill yourself because you want relief from what's hurting you, but suicide doesn't offer that relief. Maybe if you believe in an afterlife, but even then you'll have to explain the hole in your head or your rather splattered appearance to God, and that's nothing to look forward to.

Sadly, the pain of mental illness can sometimes be greater than even the most fundamental logic. If this type of despair responded to reason, we wouldn't be here in the first place. This is when suicidal ideation veers hard into suicidal contemplation. Maria Bamford describes it as "that moment-to-moment feeling that all this is unbearable." Of course, a person isn't going to feel better after a suicide, but simply existing is not an option.

Maria found some solace and kinship in reading William Sty-

ron, author of *Sophie's Choice*. He wrote about his rather sudden
and extreme onset of depression in middle age in the book *Darkness Visible*. It's popular among people with depression because
it's short and because it feels good to know that there are others
feeling what you feel. Styron said, "The pain of severe depression is quite unimaginable to those who have not suffered it,
and it kills in many instances because its anguish can no longer
be borne."

Styron also provokes vigorous nods, at least from me in my
reading chair, by noting the presence of what he calls a second
self, "a wraithlike observer who, not sharing the dementia of
his double, is able to watch with dispassionate curiosity as his
companion struggles against the oncoming disaster, or decides
to embrace it."

As I write this today, there are high fences on the Aurora
Bridge, installed to create a significant obstacle to people weighing whether to make the leap. The fences are not able to absolutely prevent the jumps, but they're not designed to. They exist
to create more moments for the desperate person to see other
possibilities, glimpses of hope that could add up to getting them
to a better place. The fences, which are increasingly appearing on
high bridges everywhere, are derided by dummies and the uninformed who say, "Pff, if people want to kill themselves, they're
going to do it anyway." But that's only partially true. They might
do it anyway, but they might not. By this point they will know
that they were close but didn't do it. Then when they're getting
closer again, they can call on that experience. Sometimes all it
takes is a moment.

Comedian Mike Drucker says he can't commit suicide because all his friends will just write three paragraphs about themselves on Facebook, and "someone's going to get two hundred
Likes off my death."

Mike has come very close to suicide on several occasions. "If my parents had a gun, I would have killed myself. People should not underestimate the ability of the difficulty of suicide to dissuade someone from committing suicide. If it's inconvenient, it's like, 'I'm not going to try to do this.' For me, there's always the dull desire to not exist, but it's not an impulse to do something about it at the moment."

A few years before I talked to Mike, he had bought a variety of equipment to kill himself by asphyxiation, but he was stopped by a fear that he would inevitably screw the whole thing up. The idea of pulling off something he had never done before and getting it right on the first try was so unlikely that, in essence, he was saved by his own depression. "My own low self-esteem has kept me from suicide many times," he says.

Ana Marie Cox and I talked about how thinking about suicide—not even necessarily about doing it but just thinking of the act itself—is painful but becomes almost mundane to people with depression. "I thought everybody thought about suicide," Ana said. "I thought that was normal. I assumed everyone else, when they were going through the ways they had to deal with life, like, that's always option E. You can do this, A, B, C, D, or E, yeah? Kill yourself! Alright, no, not this time."

Ana attempted to die by suicide many years ago when she was drinking. After taking a lot of pills and slipping away for what she thought was the last time, she unexpectedly woke up. I asked if she was overjoyed to have a new chance at life and she said nope; instead, she was kind of pissed off. "I felt like my exact sort of thought was . . . fuck. Like, fine. I just remember thinking, 'Okay, fine. I'll give life another shot,' because I had this really overwhelming feeling that there must be some other plan for me."

Ana introduced me to Rhett Miller, who wrote and recorded

the theme song for *The Hilarious World of Depression*. He's become a friend even though it really bothers me how one person can be talented *and* good-looking *and* nice *and* smart. This seems unfair. But his life wasn't always beautiful. He attempted suicide as a teenager growing up in Texas. He swallowed a bunch of pills and waited to die.

"When my legs started to go numb I realized that when I died, my little sister was going to either find me or find out from someone," said Rhett. "And that tiny split second of realization, it was as if a door flew open and I knew that the thing that I had been denying when pondering meaning in life was that. That thing Sartre called Hell. Other people. And the thing that would give life meaning was the intangible connection that I had to my little sister at that moment. And then as I've tried to live what I feel is a life that's offered a lot of happiness and a lot of really deep moments of joy, those moments come from, and consequently my understanding of meaning and life comes from, this connection to other people. And so when I realized the effect that my dying was going to have on my little sister, in that moment I knew that I didn't want to die and that I couldn't die."

Rhett Miller's predicament was that he had already swallowed the damn pills.

"I started running and I ran out the back door and I ran to the railroad track two blocks away and I ran a mile down the railroad track and I hit a shopping street with a little shopping mall. I made it to the parking lot of the 7-Eleven, where I collapsed and blacked out. And there was this girl that I went to Arts Magnet with, who I would end up becoming friends with, she was exiting a Mexican restaurant across the street and she saw me collapse."

Rhett's memory of the next part is sketchy. He's been told he vomited for hours. He woke up in a hospital bed, and he had a song in his head. The song was "Blasphemous Rumours" by

Depeche Mode, which muses that God must have a sick sense of humor.

He winces now at how on the nose the unconscious song choice was, but he was and is glad to be alive.

An interjection here to say: don't do it. People care about you. I care about you, and we likely haven't even met. If you need help and live in the United States, confidential help is available at the National Suicide Prevention Lifeline: 1-800-273-8255. It's free twenty-four hours a day, seven days a week. The 8255 spells TALK on your phone.

7

IN WHICH I AM TOLD THAT YEAH, THERE'S SOMETHING WRONG

In late 2000, a human emerged from Jill's body. A boy named Charlie. Two years later there was another human, this one a girl named Kate. Though quite tiny, these babies required a ton of stuff. Cribs, beds, dressers, strollers, and so very many toys. Lots of noisy electronic toys, too, all of which were given to us by friends and family. No sane person would ever buy a noisy toy to have in their own house. Hell, I was insane and I still wasn't buying them.

Kate was born with achondroplasia, the most common form of dwarfism, which entailed a lot of medical issues and uncertainty about the future. She arrived at the same time the radio show I worked on was being canceled, and even though I managed to hold on to a job at the station, my professional and financial future became quite shaky. It was time for therapist number five, a small earnest woman working out of a small earnest office with small earnest macramé hangings on the walls. It was a relationship that might have worked out better had I been more committed to it. But I was in panicked survival mode and couldn't really open up, instead repeating the mantra "I'm strong, I'm going to be fine, I will win" over and over, which is not actually any kind of therapy at all. When Kate's health stabilized and the job crisis wound down, I cut number five loose.

The stress and sleep deprivation of parenting were tough, and so was living in a house overflowing with stuff. An innocent walk across the living room could result in tripping on some weird Elmo manifestation that then laughed, not helping matters.

So, equipped with the Grape Ape, I began regular runs to Goodwill donation boxes and, for things they would not take, the dump. The South Transfer Station is located on South Kenyon Street in the lower tendrils of the Seattle city limits. Navigating that part of town can be tricky because it's basically an estuary, the Duwamish Waterway, so you'll be looking for somewhere and run across a river or swamp with no clear idea how to get around it. Large highways are sometimes a help but just as likely to take you far out of your way, farther from the target than you had been before, and in worst cases to my hometown. Finding the dump the first few times out was difficult, and I would become increasingly angry, as had been my tendency behind the wheel lately. "FUCK!" I would scream at a stop sign, which would not respond. And at that point, contrary to the stop sign's instructions, I could not stop a chain of thoughts that whipped up in a hurry. It went like this: I was lost therefore I was lazy and hadn't planned my trip and therefore the trip would take me longer than expected and therefore I was a bad husband and father because I was neglecting my family. This series of increasingly terrible thoughts took only a few seconds.

Eventually I got the hang of it and could drive to the dump without rage attacks. On a March morning, a Saturday, I loaded up the Ape and took the smooth path to South Kenyon Street and joined an exceptionally lengthy queue of vehicles. I was listening to the radio, which held a decreasing amount of interest for me despite my being employed in the industry. Or I could listen to CDs, though music had likewise become steadily less interesting over the past several months. Finally I turned all sound off and sat there staring straight ahead.

That silent idleness served as an invitation to my frequent visitors Agitation and Negative Thinking, who happily rushed in. I was angry that there were other people in line in front of me. I hated them. I wanted to get out of the truck, open their doors, drag them out, and beat the shit out of them. Yes, yes, I thought, this is a new reaction and an alarming one. A more virulent strain of my road rage incident while working at Amazon, now with a greater threat of violence.

Looking at the vehicles in front of me, it occurred to me how much nicer most of them were than the Ape. A few beaten-down trucks here and there, sure, but also brand-new sparkling-clean Ford F-Series trucks in white. White! Who is prosperous and organized and tidy enough to own a white truck? There were Range Rovers, presumably driven by rich people who were casually consigning to oblivion pricey items a lot of people would love to own. Expeditions, Highlanders, Escalades, the kinds of multisyllabic land yachts driven by people who moved to Seattle from somewhere else and then made a lot more money than I did.

"Those fuckers," began my internal monologue. "They are in my way in every sense. Clogging up the highways so you can't even get around in Seattle anymore. Can't see around those fucking cars because they're too big. Driving the cost of living sky-high, trampling out any charming eccentricities this city once had. Fuck. Them."

That's right, to pass the time, I seethed. Even undiagnosed depressives have hobbies.

"And look at me. I'm in a truck called the Grape Ape, with dings and scrapes all over it, from 19-way-too-long-ago. It's the worst-looking thing in any given Seattle parking lot. But it's all I can afford. I'm shackled to the house because of that mortgage. Can't ever move because even though our house is worth more than it was, I'd have to buy another house in Seattle and I can't afford that. So I'm stuck in that place, or we'll move out to the suburbs, where I grew up, which would mean I'm a failure, as I already know. I'm shackled to the kids because they're kids and it's not fair to them because I'm a horrible dad. And I'm shackled to the job that I have because I'm stupid and worthless so no other employer will have me."

At the South Transfer Station, I backed into my spot and began hurling my detritus from the Ape's bed. The anger was still there. You know how when you get mad you get this warped idea that throwing something across the room will purge those feelings? And you know how that never ever works and you don't feel better?

As I hurled away, a new, bright red Chevy Silverado truck containing two rich guys pulled up. How do I know they were rich guys? Couldn't they be working class despite their polo shirts, cargo shorts, and backward baseball caps? No, I had already judged them. They were rich guys in a truck that cost ten times what mine did. I hated them before they even got out, and all the personal details I will share about them come entirely from my imagination. While Scot with one *t* climbed out of the driver's side, Bret with one *t* swung the passenger door open, dinging Ape's door in the process. Bret immediately inspected his own door for damage, ignoring mine.

"Hey," I said, "careful."

"Sorry, man," said Bret, with no remorse. Because what do other people matter to Bret? He's a date rapist. I glared some more, they didn't notice, and we all set about discarding things from our truck beds. Of course, Scot and Bret moved faster because they had each other because they had the ability to make friends, unlike me. And they were young and strong whereas I was getting old and too lazy to exercise much because I'm a bad person. They worked at an investment firm and used the nickname "Dog" for everyone. They beat their actual dogs. I could tell.

Nearing completion of our parallel jobs, Scot let slip a piece of perfectly good shelving, which fell out of his hands, off the side of the Silverado, and hit the side of the Ape, scratching the door. Scot then picked it up, mumbled, "Whoa, sorry," and threw the piece in the pit.

"Sorry?" I said. And here came the red curtain over my eyes. Anger. Temper. Rage. "You dropped something on my truck and you just say sorry? What the fuck?"

"I'm sorry," he said, in that perplexed way privileged people talk when they're confronted with the concept of taking responsibility for their actions. "You can't even tell."

Scot, a Limp Bizkit fan, was . . . right. The shelving had absolutely dented or scratched the side panel, but so had a lot of other things starting way before I owned the Ape. It was one of these marks, but I couldn't tell which one. If I had dropped something similar on the Silverado, it would have been obvious and I would have had to tell my insurance company and my rates would have gone up, but Scot and Bret would not suffer any such consequences. It sucked.

"This sucks," I said. They looked over but said nothing.

"This SUCKS!" I then hollered, unnerving Scot and Bret, who had completed their task and were getting back in the truck.

This warped semiblinding emotion began as a mix of class resentment and envy, but by the third "THIS SUCKS!" and the subsequent "THIS SUCKS!" close on its heels, it existed as rage for the sake of rage. It felt very similar to when I was sixteen years old, angrily yelling at my father, at first because of his smoking and drinking, but finally I was yelling because I was yelling and could not stop, the rage having overridden all the controls, spurred on by the futility of my actions. I imagine I looked crazed to Bret and Scot, who once played for their fraternity house's intramural lacrosse team and now smirked through mandatory sexual harassment training. I was crazed.

The Ape's bed was empty, and I tried to let the whole experience go. Another car slipped in between the departing Silverado and Ape, which was a relief and an annoyance. An annoyance because I wanted to harass the bros from one car back, and a relief because I was unable to. There were two checkout lanes, and the car between us unexpectedly stayed in line behind the Silverado, despite the other lane being open, so I pulled up there. I got weighed, paid, and left, to find the Silverado pulling out right in front of me.

"Let it go, let it go, let it go, let it go, yeah but fuck those assholes!" went my reasoning, followed by a long honk from the Ape's loud horn. Scot and Bret looked back, saw it was me, and kept going, figuring I just needed to get it out of my system. My system was just getting started. The glance back enraged me more since it was easy to fit into my narrative of Everything Wrong With Seattle And By The Way America. So I honked some more, loudly and repeatedly, as we continued down Fifth Avenue to the big intersection at South Cloverdale Street. This was where I needed to turn right, up the hill, back to my house, and so I signaled right. The Silverado signaled left.

I stopped honking, pulled up behind them, and lowered the driver's-side sun visor to obscure my face. The dump rage was now officially road rage, but it had shifted from being all yelly and screamy to something much deeper.

Had Scot and Bret actually gotten out and walked back to confront me, chances are I'd either have sped off or, if that was impossible, locked the doors and cowered inside.

But then again maybe I wouldn't have. Seething in the Ape, I daydreamed about beating the crap out of both guys. Or maybe I could be so crazed and violent that Scot and Bret, drunk by 10 a.m. during college football season, wearing athletic sandals, would run away and I would be the de facto winner. They looked back at me, apprehensive but not confrontational. They were scared. This was great.

A moment here: Boy, I spin thoughts around in my head a lot, don't I? Like, a *lot*. That's what depression does. The dance floor of your mind is never without a pounding beat, and usually the DJ is playing eight or nine songs at the same time.

The Silverado turned left. I followed and did the same.

In 1971's *Duel*, Steven Spielberg's directorial debut, a regular driver played by Dennis Weaver is relentlessly harassed and pursued by the driver of an oil tanker truck. The chase is made all the more terrifying by the fact that you never see the truck driver's face. Scot and Bret were Dennis Weaver, I was the unseen driver, and the poor Ape, who never asked to be part of this, was cast as the tanker truck. I wanted Scot and Bret to wonder what I was going to do. I wanted them to worry.

What I really wanted was to transfer what I was feeling more and more in my life over to them. All the negativity and worry, I wanted that on their heads. I wanted to be understood.

The Silverado was making frequent turns down residential streets, hoping, I think, that I would stick to the arterials and drive away. I stayed behind them, not tailgating but certainly following, absolutely looming. I wanted someone to get hurt. Me, them, it mattered less and less.

After a few minutes of this, my heart slowed down, I stopped seeing red, and I regained enough real estate in my own brain to think for a second about what happens next. Would they eventually lose me on the freeway but write down my license plate, sending the cops to my house to talk to or arrest me, leaving Jill to watch it all go down? That would be a pretty logical move on their part. I started constructing a defense in my head: "Gosh, Officer, is it illegal to drive down streets in our city? I didn't threaten them or anything. Sure, they damaged my truck at the dump, but I let it go because I don't like to start any trouble." Still, though, Jill would be thinking, "What the hell? Now we have cops at the door?"

Finally, at yet another residential intersection, I swerved the opposite direction from the Silverado and drove away. I headed home. I tried to imagine how this pattern would end. Not today, not even this year. But some time, after the fifth road rage episode, or the tenth, or the fight, or me getting shot at or genuinely shot, and not by a BB gun. And it came down to two possible outcomes: legal trouble with no one getting hurt or legal trouble with someone getting hurt. There was no scenario I could pull up where I was less angry, less miserable, less self-destructive. I was at war with the world.

The cops didn't come that day or any day after that. Encounters with other human beings continued to be problematic, as my touchiness around the kids led to plenty of smothered eruptions on my part around the house. I kept it bottled up until everyone in the house might have preferred I yell. Calls and emails from friends, invitations to participate in things, went unreturned. In this pre-Facebook world, you had to work to keep in touch with friends who moved away, and I was not up to that work. Because I made no effort, many of those people surely felt that I simply didn't like them or care about them.

It wasn't the case. I loved those people. Thing was, I didn't want them to see me like this, no fun, grouchy, a failure, a wretch. I didn't want to see myself reflected back from them as they realized what I was becoming and responded with pity or revulsion.

Of note: that's not how it really would have gone at all. My friends, being friends, wanted to see me in good times or bad, because that's what friendship is. A depressed mind is pretty adept at buying into a distorted reality.

Any door that could be closed to the world, I started pushing shut. If an encounter with another person was going well, depression told me that meant it would be a steeper drop when things fell apart, which was bound to happen. If I perceived the encounter would be bumpy or there would be conflict, all the more reason to avoid it entirely since I knew I lacked the self-esteem and confidence to resolve it amicably.

There were a few exceptions to my misanthropy, though. I loved my wife and kids. When we'd take a stroll, to get an ice cream or a burrito, maybe swing by the pet store, things were great. Yes, having young kids is stressful, but the torrents of love they provided and that I gave back to them made me feel more grounded and positive about the world. I worried, I was exhausted, but it all felt good because it was for these fantastic humans. Jill and I were always on the same wavelength of celebrating the weirdness of our little family and the weirdness endemic to families in general. When Charlie turned three, we had a Large Appliance Cardboard Box–themed party with boxes gathered from the local appliance store. (This was instead of my proposed party theme: Choking Hazards. All these things around the house that said "Not for children three or younger." I figured we'd get a bunch of marbles, small Legos, jacks, whatever we could find and then celebrate being able to play with them. Like when someone turns twenty-one and you take them to the bar.)

The extended family was another matter.

I'll back up a few years. On the day after my father retired in June of 1998, six of us went to see a live taping of *A Prairie Home Companion* in Redmond, Washington. Mom and Dad; my sister Lisbet, Mark; Jill and me. Immediately after the show was over, Dad started coughing horribly, due to side effects of what we soon learned was cancer. He went through treatment, but the cancer kept progressing steadily over the next year and a half. Dad didn't necessarily welcome cancer but made no vow to defeat it either, just accepted that his ride was here and it was time to go, which, in August of 1999, he did. All four kids had gathered at the house, Rick coming up from San Diego and Metteline having flown in from Norway with her kids for what they thought was a vacation.

Rick was sleeping some twenty hours a day in his old bedroom, either on drugs or coming off them. His chief concern during his few waking hours was the continued operation of the mail services. "Has the mail come yet? What time does the mail get here?" he would ask. In an envelope from UPS, FedEx, or the actual US Postal Service, he said, would be a check that he'd been waiting for. But we all knew the substance inside said envelope would not be paper.

At the end, we were all sleeping at the house, and Erling Moe died overnight, not wanting to make a big deal out of it. After finally waking up and hearing about his father's death, Rick's first words were "Has the mail been here?"

I knew that addiction is an illness and that Rick was being controlled not by free will but by intoxicants. If I heard about a nonrelative struggling with substance use, I would have tremendous sympathy and kindness in my heart. Not with Rick. I was furious that Rick had been swallowed up. That he had turned into my dad. Addiction had done something more sinister than merely killing my father: it controlled his actions and blunted his free will. Addiction played with my dad and brother like marionettes. There were so many memories I had of trying to connect with a father who appeared to be standing in front of me but who wasn't really there.

If you have an alcoholic parent, you build a little fortress around yourself. You don't trust people to be looking out for you, and you gather such vivid memories of being let down that you reduce or sever relationships so the risk of disappointment is eliminated. You are a rock, you are an island. If you're depressed on top of that, and you probably are, you build those walls thicker, stronger, and higher because being let down is the only feasible outcome of a relationship. You can't relax into a friendship. You can't really believe that someone will do the thing they're supposed to do. The parent is the first person you learn to rely on, and when your parent proves unreliable, that means everyone is unreliable.

We had my dad cremated, as per his wishes. Actually his wishes were that we make absolutely sure he was dead and only then cremate him. We made sure to do so, which was both grim and amusing. Then we chartered a boat to scatter his ashes in Puget Sound.

A few years after the dump freakout, Dad still dead and gradually dissipating in Puget Sound, Mom called to say Rick was coming up to visit. This always meant that she had bought him a ticket, and he would generally show up without luggage of any kind, maybe a nylon gym bag. By this point, she had sold the house in Federal Way and moved up to Seattle, where both Lisbet and I lived. Mom asked when we would like to come out to her house because, she claimed, Rick really wanted to see me, Jill, and the kids.

"Any decision I make," I thought, "must be focused on what is best for my immediate family." Rick was my brother, but he also had an unknown relationship to meth, which can make someone unpredictable and violent. Jill and I talked about this possibility of visiting with Rick, and finally I thought about what we'd do if the cast of characters was different. What if this was happening not with family but with my friend Andy?

"If Andy Jensen called," I said, "and he invited us over and he said his friend is going to be there and his friend really wants to meet us and our kids, *and* he said that his friend has had drug addiction issues for years and last we heard he was doing meth, would we go over to Andy Jensen's house? No. We wouldn't."

"We're not going to come see Rick," I told Mom on the phone. "I need to think of my kids first, and I just don't trust that he's clean. I can't take any risks."

She was stunned. I had to restate it a few times. Finally, she said, "I think he's doing much better. I don't think he's doing drugs anymore."

"I hope you're right. But I don't have that confidence, and I don't want my kids around him." Laying down the boundary felt both right and wrong. Right because it was healthy and proper and logical; wrong because I was turning my back on my family of origin. But it felt more right than wrong.

One thing I didn't bother hoping for was that my refusal to see Rick would get back to him and cause a change in behavior. I had spent a childhood, the only one I got, believing that if Dad saw how unhappy his smoking and drinking made me, he'd snap out of the substances' grasp and make a healthy decision.

With new boundaries designed to keep people out, my world was getting awful damn small. And still I looked for other things I could toss out to make that world yet smaller. There was my job, which happened to be about the coolest job imaginable. From being a junior-level public radio producer at KUOW, Seattle's NPR affiliate, I had worked my way up to delivering newscasts and then hosting shows. KUOW was often the number one station in Seattle, a city teeming with brainy, thoughtful people who love their public radio.

I was producing and hosting a weekly business and technology show; I went out and toured businesses like potato chip factories and prosthetic limb companies, and I was trusted to make the kind of show I wanted. I pitched in here and there for the arts show, which meant that people like David Sedaris would come in to be interviewed by me or the Indigo Girls would come in and perform for a broadcast audience of millions but a live audience of precisely just me. I had the greatest job anyone I knew could imagine. My boss believed in me; audiences liked me; coworkers thought highly of my work and most of them enjoyed my company. I had job security to stay there forever.

Obviously, I had to get the fuck out of that place.

Here's what the above situation looks like to someone with increasingly severe undiagnosed depression: the show I made was on the air once a week on a Tuesday night, where there were fewer listeners than if it was on during the day. That meant the station hated me and thought I was stupid. I pitched in on the arts show, but I wasn't hosting it, meaning that I was either being carefully screwed over by management or spitefully shunned by colleagues. I also didn't make as much money as I wanted and was pissy about that even though I knew the station's firm salary scale was mandated by the University of Washington, with which the station was affiliated. Oh, I could do stories for national shows in the public radio system for extra money, and I did, but still I railed against the inherent injustice of it all. Depressed people have an urge to make good things into ugly messes to better match their state of mind.

The flagship show of the station was *Weekday*, airing from 9 to 11 a.m. Monday through Friday. *Weekday* presented a mix of local and national issues, with guests to talk about those issues in the studio or on the phone and listener calls on the subjects. It was hosted by Steve Scher, a Chicagoan who was my radio hero. I wanted to be confident but not cocky, just like Steve managed to be, I wanted to trust myself, I wanted to yell at people who deserved it, and it would also be nice to be the star of the station.

That wasn't going to happen, though. There were on-air hosts further up the food chain than me who would get the job if Steve ever left, and Steve wasn't leaving. The status quo of my position would have been the dreamiest of dream jobs for me a few years before, but now it was unbearable. This was a trick my mind was playing. Of course, the career malaise was not a cause of my mounting misery, it was a symptom. The cause was depression, a condition I continued to incorrectly associate only with sadness and moping. I didn't feel like sitting in a room and frowning, I could get out of bed easily (two young kids were glad to help with that), so therefore I could not be depressed.

"I'm worried about you," Jill said one evening, having prepared her words. "You seem to be doing worse and worse, and I don't think it needs to be this way. I think you might be depressed, and I think you should go to the doctor. I want you to go to the doctor."

Obviously, this was a ridiculous idea. I was grim and grouchy, sure, and of course I didn't want to be like that anymore. And naturally I didn't like where my mood was going, but what Jill was failing to grasp, I told myself, was that the world was horrible and thus my reactions were normal and reasonable. I mean, who was crazy here? My wife who didn't see the grim reality, or me who knew everything was doomed and dying?

"Thanks. I'm just going through a stressful time. My job is hard, my commute is hard, we have two young kids. It's hard but it'll get better," I said. I smiled, hoping that would fool her.

It wasn't going to get better, and I knew that, but why drag her down with me?

There was another reason, too, one I didn't tell her. And this will make perfect sense to people who have dealt with depression and make absolutely no sense to people who never have: I didn't want to waste the doctor's time. I knew for a fact that I could not be helped, so let that appointment go to someone with solvable problems.

Reader, the whole point of a doctor is to know more than you do, assess a problem, and then help you. Seeing people and trying to help them is the entirety of their job, and thus if you are a person, you are worthy of being seen. You are worthy of help.

"I'm not going to a doctor. I mean, what if they put me on pills and I become a zombie or something? Plus, it's a copay."

Our copay at the time was ten dollars. I was not worth ten dollars.

"If you don't love yourself enough to go do this, do you at least love me and the kids?"

Oof. "Yes."

"Then do it for us."

Swedish West Seattle Primary Care Clinic is located a half mile from the house we lived in at the time. A ten-minute walk. A three-minute drive. On our insurance. My appointment was first thing in the morning. I dragged myself to the reception desk and checked in. "And what is the problem?" the receptionist asked.

"What?"

"The problem you're having. The reason you're seeing a doctor today."

My God, did she expect me to say it out loud in front of a lobby full of people, all of whom were sitting far enough away that they couldn't possibly hear me, but still? "Uh, mental health . . . issues?" I finally muttered, rolling my eyes to indicate that this was obviously someone else's overreaction and I just needed someone to tell me I was fine.

She was nonplussed and typed it in. A nurse checked my vitals and ran me through some physical exam steps. Finally, Dr. Michael Kovar entered the exam room with a smile and handshake that I sheepishly returned, still embarrassed to hassle him with my complete lack of actual problems. He asked me about energy levels (low and dropping), sleep patterns (erratic at best), social habits (none?), and whether I ever felt hopeless (Ha ha! YUP!).

"Well, you're depressed," he said. "Major depressive disorder is the medical name. You're depressed. You have depression."

"Come on," I replied incredulously, "how can you tell I'm depressed just by asking me a few questions?"

"Oh, no, I knew it the second I saw you. The questions and stuff were to make sure. And to be polite."

Good one, Kovar. He said I could try a bunch of things to address it and he'd work with me on that. There isn't any one single thing that works for everyone, he said, but there are a lot of things we can try. Right off the top, it's a good idea to get out and exercise on a regular basis. You don't need to train for a marathon, but set a schedule for running and biking. Eating healthy is always a good idea, too.

"And," he said, "I'd like to start you on some medication. We'll try the lowest dose of Zoloft just to see how it goes."

"Is there any way we could do this without pills?" I asked. "I don't want to be all altered. I want to still be myself."

"This kind of medication doesn't make you into anyone else. If it works the way it does for a lot of people, you'll feel *more* like yourself. Kind of cleans the windshield. As for not being altered, how's the status quo working out for you?"

This Kovar character had a good answer for everything. Almost as if he had been in a thousand conversations like this one and had years and years of medical training. He said looking into talk therapy would also be a good idea, that it helped a lot of people in my situation. But in the meantime, he wanted me to feel better much sooner, and thus the Zoloft.

"So, okay, fine, things have been rougher lately," I admitted. "Since my dad died, really. That was in '99. But it just feels like a bit more of something that has been going on my whole life. Are you saying that this thing I've been feeling and dealing with my whole life is depression?"

"Yes," he said without hesitation. "I mean, probably. I don't know everything you've been through, but this is a really easy diagnosis for me to make. It's pretty textbook. You're kind of boring from a diagnostic point of view."

I got in the Ape and started the drive to KUOW, trying to figure out what all this might mean and how I felt about it.

The main thing I felt was . . . great? Happy. Relieved. This thing had a name. This awful buzzing weight, this monster in the open closet, this ever-present cloud of thick smog, this was an illness, not a fundamental part of my character. I wasn't bad, I was sick.

I'd grown up in a house with substance use issues, traumas both inherited and generated, and a series of cultural beliefs that silenced any meaningful conversation or action to deal with them. I thought a strong undercurrent of pain and toxicity was part of being in a family. If I think it's normal but it has always felt fundamentally bad, it's not really normal at all. It is a problem. The problem has a name. The problem's name is depression.

I also thought this: neat! If I could live without depression, that would, I imagine, be great, even though I couldn't imagine how that would actually work. Would it be like being good-looking?

With this diagnosis of depression, I headed back out into the world, pledging to take my meds consistently and get to a therapist. In a bold twist, I did neither.

According to *THWoD*: Other People Already Know You Are Depressed

N ever let a depressed person in midepisode make your Halloween costume. Chances are he will hand you a ripped-up unitard and a red shopping bag that goes over your head and then he'll say, "There! Spider-Man! Just like in the movies!" Saddies think they're fooling everyone, but at the same time they are in such a mud pit that their ability to see straight is severely impaired. These are the people who think that no one is on to the fact that they're in rough shape.

Having your depression spotted can send a person in a number of directions. For me, it was a relief. I was being guided onto a new path that led to my mind not moaning at me all the time, and if that meant pills, well, great. I think this was because I was older when I found out and I was tired of running from the depression. But just as everyone's experience with depression is unique, so too are their reactions to diagnosis.

Chris Gethard has been a professional depressed person longer than I have. He's a comedian, actor, talk show host, and creator of a one-man Off-Broadway show about his mental health journey. His illness was first flagged for him when he was an adolescent growing up in New Jersey.

"When I was in junior high school," he says, "my brother was in high school, and he had some friends come over and they were all hanging out in our backyard. And I was just kind of sitting off in a corner by myself in a chair. One of my brother's friends who was three or four years older than me, he just walked by and quietly was like, 'Hey, man, you alright?' And I remember so distinctly him asking me that and for the first time thinking to myself, 'Oh, someone sees from the outside what's going on. I got to figure out how to put a better game face on.'"

Chris covered up his depression. That's what he was taught to do.

"I think for a lot of people who grew up working class, there's not really time to stop and say, 'Hey, Mom and Dad, I'm sad.' It's not how you operate. It just felt like what I was experiencing was a reflection of some sort of weakness. And that wasn't necessarily a thing you put out there."

Years later, when Chris finally got help and began treatment, he says his parents weren't against it but were confused, asking, "Are you getting your brain electrocuted?"

"So I remember telling my mom," says Chris, "and then my mom told my dad, and my dad asked, 'How are those pills working?' and I said, 'Good. Good.' And it just felt so awkward."

He recalls when he was finally ready to drop some jokes to break the tension. It happened at the dinner table when his mother suggested going somewhere, he doesn't remember where, and Chris said no.

"Why?" they asked.

"Because that scares me."

"Why?"

"Because I'm crazy."

That became the first joke, he says. "I'd go, 'Mom, I'm crazy. You gotta remember I'm crazy.'

"She'd go, 'You're not crazy, don't say you're crazy.'

"And I go, 'I am crazy. I'm on pills. You want me to show you the pills? What do you think the pills are for, Ma? You see the pills on my dresser? What do you think, I got heartburn? You know what the pills are for. I'm crazy!' And then she'd be laughing and then my dad would laugh and then my brother would laugh and then everybody's guard went down because of jokes."

Wil Wheaton has one of the more intriguing career paths among celebrities I've interviewed. He was a child star in the movie *Stand by Me*; he was a lead character on *Star Trek: The Next Generation*. Then he quit Hollywood and moved to Kansas to work in marketing for a tech company. It's a hard turn that doesn't make sense until you factor in depression. He couldn't take the life he was living, but instead of suicide, he chose Kansas and marketing.

"For me, living with mental illness was like living in a really large dark room with no windows or doors," he says. "And it was so unbelievably loud that I just kind of learned to exist in that loud darkness. And once my wife said, 'I really think that you should get some help for what's going on with you, because it just doesn't seem normal.' And I saw psychiatrists and I started taking medication. I saw therapists for years and that worked to a point. But I have a chemical imbalance in my brain. So seeing a psychiatrist who could prescribe medication for me, it opened up a door that I didn't know was there.

"I could suddenly see this light that I could walk toward. And I went through that door, and I didn't realize that there was this world outside of that dark cloud room until all that I had left was the ringing in my ears. And once that awful noise was taken away I became aware of how much of my life was spent just trying to exist."

Now, finally, Wil was able to start to figure out how he got in that room in the first place, so he could better avoid reentering it.

"Mental illness runs in my family. And what's weird, and one of the reasons that I think it took me so long to get help, was that both of my parents just never wanted to talk about it. They're very much from the generation that just internalized and fully believed that depression equals weakness."

For people I talked to, meds weren't a ticket to some superpower; they were a ticket to being human. Comedian and writer Jenny Jaffe remembers what happened when she got on a good prescription that worked for her. "It felt like . . . I've worn glasses since I was a little kid, and the first time I put on a pair of glasses and looked around I was like, 'Oh my God! This is the level of detail with which other people get to see the world?'"

Fellow comedian Jen Kirkman said medication "stopped me from going way under. I was under sea level and it brought me up to sea level. It didn't bring me above it, I was not happier than anyone else, I was just able to cope."

At six feet six inches, Gary Gulman is one of the taller people I've ever interviewed. His size and athletic skills landed him a scholarship to play football at Boston College, where he immediately found himself overmatched in terms of his teammates' talent for and interest in playing the sport. Despite having an older brother who had been treated for depression, Gary had never considered that he might have the condition as well. "I went home one weekend and just stayed in my room the entire weekend," says Gary, "and my oldest brother said, 'Oh, he's depressed.' I went to the trainers of the team when I got back to school that Monday for practice, and they were so understanding. One of them said that his father had suffered from this, and he was really kind and he sent me to the head of the counseling service. I met with him, and I just remember thinking, 'Wow, this is something I've needed for a long time.' I think right away. And he said, 'Why don't you just quit the football team?'"

It was a question Gary had never even considered. Depression had rotted his brain to the point where he had forgotten that he could stop doing something just because he didn't want to do it. Other people had agency over Gary but Gary did not.

There's this trick that Rick taught me when we were kids. You stand in a doorway, the narrower the better, with your arms at your sides. Then you extend them out so your two arms are pressing against the doorway, and you push just as hard as you can for a full minute. When you step out of the doorway, your arms involuntarily float up, like magic. That's what finally getting help is like. You've been pushing against this unmovable obstacle for so long that when you get out to where the normal people are, it feels like floating.

8

SEEING THE WORLD
WITH CLEAR EYES

When you've lived some thirteen thousand days largely without pills, it's hard to remember to take a pill every single morning. The burning acid-reflux feeling my Zoloft caused didn't provide much in the way of additional incentive. I would take a pill one morning, then forget the next day, take one the following day but not until afternoon, skip three days, hunker down and take one for three straight mornings, feel good about myself as a result, and then skip it again.

This isn't how you're supposed to take Zoloft, or any selective serotonin reuptake inhibitor, or any medication at all, really. In the case of Zoloft, inconsistency led to irritability, crazy dreams, nausea, and fatigue, a suite of conditions not much different and certainly no better than what was going down in my head before. When you are overwhelmed by an urge to yell at everybody nearby and then can't get off the couch after work, it becomes difficult to believe that this depression treatment protocol is going well. By extension, a saddie such as myself begins to suspect that all depression treatment is either bullshit or a lie concocted by pharmaceutical companies, which is the precise spot where depression would love to have you end up.

~

Not having studied up on how meds like these worked from a pharmacological point of view, I figured they were like ibuprofen: you're feeling bad, so you take one, and then in a few minutes you feel better, so when I really started tweaking out something fierce, I took a pill and waited. And no, that's not how it works. You need to take them even when you do feel fine, because those meds are helping you get to that baseline you couldn't reach without them.

My progress was also slowed by a suspicion that the hard work was over for the most part, that knowing the problem and solving the problem were the same thing, as if realizing your leg is broken means that you can simply nod meaningfully and go skipping away.

Dr. Kovar's diagnosis had been a revelation. But I failed to take into account the idea that properly addressing the depression would require a ton more work, work that I would be just getting started on. I knew what kind of refrigerator I was trapped in but disregarded the whole "getting out" part, which any sealed-refrigerator detainee would tell you is the important bit.

My shame over my inability to take the meds consistently, the mood swings that resulted, and the gross throat feeling when I did take them meant that after a while I stopped altogether. "I'll get back on them soon," I told myself.

The problem wasn't the meds, it was me. Antidepressants are a way of establishing or maintaining a functional mental health baseline so that you can then set out to do more of the actual work. They're like cold medicine, taking away some of the symptoms but not solving the illness that's causing them.

I had dabbled in talk therapy here and there over the years but hadn't seen much in the way of useful results. More often, I'd tell my story, omitting the parts I was uncomfortable talking about, which would be the real issues I was having. I couldn't have the therapist catching on to what a weird, bad person I am. I'd roll my eyes at anything I perceived as New Age talk, manufacture some rationalizations about how really I was fine, and then abandon the relationship by never setting up new appointments, having improved only at bullshitting my way around my mental illness more effectively. Still, despite the erratic medication intake, I was newly emboldened by the fresh diagnosis from Dr. Kovar and scheduled a few appointments. That's when depression seized on my nervousness about going and told me therapy was a waste of time. So I canceled the appointments. Depression builds a protective carapace out of your worst habits.

Now my treatment was back to only knowing I had a problem, which was not, follow me here, a treatment. A few months later, I had a follow-up appointment with Dr. Kovar so he could ask me how the Zoloft was working out. I confessed that I hadn't been taking it consistently, in part because it was hard to get used to and in part because it made my throat and gut feel gross all the time. "Okay," he said, "sounds like we should try something else." He talked about Prozac perhaps being a better option. No moral judgment, no scolding; I wasn't a weak, horrible person. "Oh," I said. "Something else. Sure."

By now it was the fall of 2006, and life started speeding up. My first book, *Conservatize Me*, was published in October of that year, and I was proud of it. *Conservatize Me* details a month I spent trying to turn myself into a political conservative. I flew to Indiana for a Toby Keith concert (having a panic attack in the hotel), met with people like William Kristol and Jonah Goldberg, toured the Reagan and Nixon libraries, and even shot some guns. The shooting range in Bellevue, Washington, had a rule that you couldn't shoot by yourself unless you were a member. If you weren't a member, you had to bring a friend. This was because otherwise people would show up, rent a gun, and kill themselves right there on the shooting range. It had become a problem. A friend, went the reasoning, would eliminate this possibility.

A day prior to the book's publication date, Jill and I had a miscarriage in a pregnancy that was several months along. It was devastating. Charlie, our oldest, had started kindergarten, and Kate, our second, was going to a ton of medical appointments, getting hospitalized occasionally for respiratory issues. So what emerged was a kind of cocktail of professional excitement and extreme personal sorrow and anxiety, all mixed together and making me scream inside my own head almost all the time. "Just get through this," I would think. "Just endure." And with love and support from each other and friends and family, Jill and I did.

For a depressed person, there's something reorienting about a crisis. It reminds you there's a world outside your head. Instead of fretting over the future or stewing over the past, you have something new to put in the brain. When it's something terrible or sad and you are still somehow persevering—waking up, making coffee, eating, going to work—it's a sign that, corny as this may sound, life goes on. For a depressed person, the notion that life will go on is always up for debate, so when it does go on, even in the face of tragedy, it feels reassuring.

There is a lot more I could say about the miscarriage, but I am choosing not to. In this way, I am setting up a boundary, which is a good and healthy thing to do.

A couple of weeks later, I got a phone call at work from Peter

Clowney, the executive producer on *Weekend America*, a news-magazine show on American Public Media, aka Minnesota Public Radio. I had been contributing to the show for a few years by this point. Peter was public radio's Wes Anderson or Jack White, the person around whom the good projects seem to form. He was new to this job on *Weekend America*, and though I'd known his name for years, I'd never met or even spoken to him.

Peter told me he loved the work I'd been doing on the show, especially a recent story about the grim fates that befell bunnies cavorting around Seattle's Woodland Park. Any new bunnies quickly disappeared. Curious why that was, I pitched a story about finding out. I liked the coupling of bunny rabbits and disappearances (thanks, depression!). The disappearances, it turned out, had the most grisly and horrific explanations possible. The bunnies were routinely either killed by coyotes or captured by hawks, who—and this is real—rip off the tops of bunny skulls and eat their brains, leaving the rest to scavengers. To hawks the brains are the most nutritious and delicious part. A volunteer trapped and collected any surviving bunnies, spayed or neutered them, and deposited them in a giant pen north of the city. This last fate, I argued, was somehow the saddest; it was mere existence without consequence or contribution. These were adorable little bunnies in a hellish netherworld.

Peter also enjoyed when I had filled in hosting the show. "So you're going to come work for us full-time," he said. "You can stay in Seattle, and you'll be senior reporter and the permanent backup host. This is going to happen."

"Wow," I said, "that is a really attractive idea. Thanks for thinking of me. I'll need to find out more about it, of course, and I need to talk to my wife and all that."

"It's not an offer. It's a fact. You're going to come work for us.

We'll pay you better than KUOW, you'll like it more, it's better for your career. Congratulations. You're hired."

Friends, there is nothing more intoxicating for a depressed person with an alcoholic parent in his past than being told you are loved and wanted. This was some Prince Charming stuff. As a funny-looking guy, I had only occasionally been in a situation where a girl made the first move on me, and every time I ended up having to stop myself from falling deeply in love with her out of sheer gratitude.

Peter had accurately predicted that I was discontented at KUOW. He hadn't known that depression had fashioned my mind such that I automatically thought that any job I was doing must be a bad job because I was the one doing it, but he was right just the same. The thing he didn't realize was that I was also very much swayed by the idea of having a regular national audience, giving me the approval and affection that I was incapable of generating for myself.

"Well, I'll think about it," I said.

"Think about it all you want, but I've already announced to the staff that it's happening. Congratulations!"

I reached out to a colleague, Robert Smith, who had gone on to work at NPR. "I really want to make the leap," I told him, "but I'd be working on a show that is still trying to establish itself. And if I stay, I have security."

"Your talent is your security," Robert said. "Your talent is what you'll fall back on. Not this station."

When you're a depressed person, thinking like that is a revelation. When I had experienced success in broadcasting, I figured it was only because the years I spent acting had inadvertently given me a good speaking delivery. When writing went well, I chalked it up to being able to slide in some jokes so that the person reading would be too amused to realize I'm a bad writer. When a huge opportunity like this one came along, well, obviously this Clowney fellow was looking to shake things up, and I was the nearest available tool to reach for. The notion that I could count on my talent as a valuable and dependable commodity was mind-blowing. I took the job. Only much later would I learn that Peter was riddled with anxiety and this Very Confident Guy routine took a lot of work. He remains one of my closest friends.

As Christmas approached, Mom told me Rick had enrolled in an experimental drug treatment program through UCLA, and whatever they did worked like a charm. He was in a steady job and had been in a relationship for several months now with a woman named Kyndra, who had two kids. They met through recovery, and the kids adored Rick. The most exciting news in all of this, she said, was that Kyndra was pregnant. Rick was going to be a father.

"Oh." I couldn't think of anything to say but managed a follow-up of "Wow."

Kyndra and Rick would be coming up to Seattle just before Christmas and would be staying at Mom's house. Given the exciting news about the baby and how straightened out Rick had become, she asked if I could please come to her house for an evening with my whole family before we took a planned trip to Jill's mom's place in Chicago for Christmas itself. I was dubious but agreed.

We arrived around 4 p.m., me, Jill, and Charlie and Kate, who had just turned six and four years old. Rick was clear-eyed and talkative at his normal half-shy level. He made eye contact and looked for all the world like someone who had indeed cleaned up his act. He couldn't wait to play with Charlie and Kate, and they were super excited to meet their uncle, especially because a new cousin was on the way. As regular visitors to my mom's house, they headed straight for the rec room, where the toys were.

Rick quickly followed them, and soon all three were wrestling and giggling. I made sure to hang around the doorway by the kitchen, so I could keep an ear and eye out for how things were going. Rick appeared sober; he was absolutely engaged, bearing the brunt of kid wallopings while making sure that the kids never got hurt. After a while, I watched them not out of concern but because it's a simple yet tremendous pleasure to see people that happy.

Talking with Rick and Kyndra as the evening went on, I wasn't able to determine where their relationship actually stood. They had been a couple, yes, but were they still? They said that the baby would live with Kyndra and her kids, and although Rick would be over there a lot, he planned to live in an apartment nearby. So they weren't a couple? But then why was she in Seattle with him? As for the pregnancy, Rick and Kyndra both smiled and said they were very happy.

Rick talked about the pregnancy and about the plans. He talked about music that he liked, his tastes having evolved from British rock to Canada's Barenaked Ladies. He did his dead-on perfect impression of my mom, which was always performed in real time, lip-syncing what she said with matching facial expressions, causing everyone in the room to crack up. Mom always played her part, too: first confused about what everyone was laughing at, then figuring it out and telling Rick to stop, while laughing along. The two of them had been running this bit for decades. Rick talked about how much he loved my book and how proud he was of me, and he talked about specific parts of the book in a way that demonstrated he had read the whole thing. Rick knew that I had refused to see him when I felt he might have been high, and it was clear to me that this whole evening was, if not an audition to get in my good graces, at least a demonstration for my benefit.

Maybe I was getting my brother back. Still, this was the person who caused Mom and Dad such anguish, continually getting money from them for what he lied and said were car repairs. Unlike me, they never gave up on him. Years before, he had tried to get money from Lisbet and me, too, by saying that his car needed repairs that very night. And why call us? "Well, since Mom and Dad are out of town, you're in charge," he told Lisbet.

"In charge of what?" she asked. He never got our money.

Addiction is an illness, but free will must be part of it, right? If I'm addicted or depressed and I kill someone, I'm still responsible and I'm still going to jail. And that free will portion of Rick and Dad was the part that made me so confused and, subsequently, angry. I was angry because I couldn't do anything.

And although it may have been selfish, I was mad at Rick for not staying my hero. I didn't like the idea that I was the one with a family before he ever had one, that I had the good job and a car worth more than three hundred dollars.

Kyndra soon flew back to San Diego, but Rick hung around for a few more days. He insisted on going skiing with Lisbet and her family, and Lisbet reported that everything went great. She said Rick had been calling his friends from high school, at least the ones who hadn't burned out or disappeared. He didn't have time to get together with these friends but made sure to have long talks with them. It all sounded like one of the steps in a twelve-step program to me, so I figured, well, good.

Shortly before he left town, I invited Rick to meet up with me in the Ballard neighborhood of Seattle, not far from Mom's new house. She dropped him off. I got coffee, he got herbal tea.

"I'm really glad you're doing better," I said, launching into my rehearsed speech. "And I was nervous about that. I was nervous that you were going to lie and say that you had cleaned up but you were still using. So I think you're clean."

"Okay?" Rick said.

"I've heard from Mom over the years, several times, that you had cleaned up and were in a good living situation and had a steady job. And that you just needed a little money to get your car fixed so you could get to work reliably. And I think that money never went to a car."

Rick smiled, grimly, but said nothing.

"There was a time when Dad was still alive and they went to Mexico for a vacation. And you called Lisbet to ask for money because you were still a couple of days from your paycheck. But you needed it wired to you right away, like that night."

Rick listened, not betraying whether he remembered that or not.

"And it's what you said to her that really upset me. You told her that with Mom out of town, she, Lisbet, was in charge. In charge. It was that phrase that got me. Because that's what our family was to you: a money source. And you didn't see Lisbet as your sister, you saw her as the assistant manager at a bank. And it was all so fucked up. You trying to sneak by Mom, you trying to fool Lisbet, her reaching out to me to help figure out what to do. It's fucked up. And, Rick, I've had problems of my own in life. It turns out I've had a depressive disorder since Sacajawea Junior High, probably. So that and Dad's drinking and Metteline leaving the country and your drugs and trying to live up to Lisbet, it's really messed me up."

Rick listened.

"But now I've been diagnosed, and I'm trying to do some healthy things, at least for me and Jill and the kids. I'm trying to kind of rebuild, you know? And I want to believe I can get better. And I'm really happy that you seem to be doing so well. I know you've had a really hard time, but I want to believe that we can repair things. It will take a while, but I'm up for trying. And I hope you are, too. To become brothers and friends again."

"Yeah. Sure," he replied. "I'm really sorry."

"Thank you. I'm sorry, too. I shut you out. I should have found ways to help you."

We kind of sat there awhile.

"The thing that hurts me the most," said Rick, "was that I wasn't there for you. I left town and went to California, and I couldn't help you. I left you here alone. I should have been there for you."

It had never occurred to me that he would see me as partly his responsibility. He had been carrying this guilt around for decades, he said, that he couldn't help me navigate through life using the things he learned and the mistakes he made.

"It's okay. I was really proud of you for going to California. I thought it was really glamorous," I said. "And I get it, leaving like that, going far away. It made sense to me then, and it makes even more sense to me now."

Then we talked about whatever we could think of, having not had many "shoot the breeze" conversations in the last twenty years. We talked about six-year-old Charlie's obsession with history and four-year-old Kate's surprising interest in heavy metal music, as well as her breezy determination in addressing the challenges presented by her dwarfism.

"Speaking of kids," I finally said, "I'm going to be an uncle again. Congratulations! Are you excited?"

"Yeah," he said, looking down at his tea. "I don't know. I'm kind of scared. I never thought I'd be anyone's dad."

"It's scary. I get it. I was totally scared. But honestly, it doesn't stay scary. They hand you the baby and something kind of happens in your brain. You realize that no, you don't know what you're doing, because how could you, but then you realize that it's okay because you'll make it up as you go along. And the baby is lying there like, hey, I'm on board, let's just wing it. And then you wing it."

"I feel like I'm going to let him or her down," he said.

"Nah. Just love the baby and do whatever you can and it'll be fine."

Rick smiled. A little. He didn't seem excited. As a teenager, he once told me that he'd never have kids because it was too cruel to bring someone into the shitty world we were living in. Seemed like he still believed that. "But it's going to be okay," I thought. "He'll come around. He'll get the hang of it."

~

I started at *Weekend America* in January of 2007. Soon a lot of cool things were happening at work all at once: more money, less time aggravatingly stuck in traffic, dramatically shorter commute, and no prescribed hours. Also: isolation. The building where I'd rented a small office was large, but it was full of tiny rooms, so it felt like a really chill prison where the inmates set their own lock-down times. I found that I didn't miss being around other people all that much and even preferred being alone. Solitude was a relief. On days the building was kind of hot, there was no need to wear pants and I could work in my boxers, a practice frowned upon in most of the contemporary American workplace. And honestly, without gossiping with co-workers, you can really get a lot of work done.

But if depression could be cured by things going well, we'd have a lot more Nirvana and Elliott Smith records.

With all the good things that had happened professionally, I was still trying to get the hang of those pills, still meaning to get to a therapist, and still hoping things were going to get better.

They did not.

According to *THWoD*:
Pills May or May Not Help,
but Let's Not Get All Spooky
About Them

The general public doesn't understand depression meds, and when people don't understand something, they fear it. And when they fear it, they mock it and/or attack it. So let's try to get some understanding up in here to calm things down. Honestly, the way you people who don't need them talk about meds, you sound crazy, and come on, that's our job, not yours.

Medications aren't one thing. You don't get a bottle that just says "meds" or "antidepressants" on it. There is a seemingly endless variety of prescription drugs available for those who suffer from depression, including Zoloft, Prozac, Fluoxetine, Cyndaquil, Celexa, and Paxil. Admittedly, one of those is actually a Pokémon and not an antidepressant.

In reality, antidepressant medication is pretty much a chemistry experiment, and a ton of things can influence the efficacy of medication. What works for one person might not work at all for someone else. The wrong dosage, too high or too low, can make you a total wreck. Taking the meds inconsistently can be as bad as not taking them at all, or sometimes worse. In my case,

I've been on some that worked like a charm for years, and then suddenly—plop—they were a total disaster.

Maria Bamford, who made me laugh so hard when I was interviewing her that I could not continue, has been diagnosed with bipolar 2 ("the sexy kind," she says, because it's what Catherine Zeta-Jones has). She's in a good, healthy, productive place now, but ten or so years ago, this was not the case. She had a breakdown and went to inpatient care.

"I went to the hospital, like I'm just going to get in here for seventy-two hours, just get my meds under control," she said. "My friend says I'm talking too fast, so I'm just going to do something about it and not bother anybody."

She got what she was looking for. Kind of.

She wanted to "get on a new medication, try this new mood stabilizer thing, whatever, but still make my shows in Chicago next week. I was just there for three days, and the hilarious part was that the psychiatrist, despite YouTubing me during the session, gave me a mood stabilizer whose primary side effects are cognitive, making it impossible to think or talk. So by the time we were in Chicago I was not able to think or talk."

Jenny Jaffe has been on some form of meds since she was a kid. The first time, she thought, "'This is the baseline people function with?' Like my brain is just processing things as they're coming in and not necessarily looking at everything as another reason to have a panic attack. And I'm letting go of thoughts more easily and I'm not necessarily wanting to kill myself right now. It doesn't change who you are; it just levels your personal playing field a little bit."

Even though Jenny's meds did a pretty good job, she was still swayed by the societal misconception that they were creating a fake self. "I think I had the thing that a lot of people—especially who start taking meds when they're young—have, which is

'Could I be more creative or funnier if I stopped taking meds?' So I went cold turkey a couple of times, and instead of becoming creative or funny, I just became too depressed to function."

Jen Kirkman wasn't taking antidepressants when I talked to her. She was getting by without them but was in close consultation with her doctor to monitor her condition and ready to go back on medication if necessary. She recalls her first experience with meds being remarkable. It was at Christmas, a time she generally hated.

"And I just remember one day not minding the Christmas music. And it was so extreme. It felt like I was dancing in the street like Scrooge. All I did was just not mind it. All I did was feel not bothered by every single thing. I was not happier than anyone else. I was just able to cope."

I talked with Andy Richter for the first season of the show. Andy's somebody I had admired for years before ever getting to know him. While he was always funny, he also seemed smart and honest and like the kind of sensible midwestern friend you want to have around. He's been taking antidepressants for years. "People have a natural aversion to the notion of being on psychotherapeutic drugs," he says. "They will say when I talk about it, 'Well, do you think you're going to have to be on them forever?' Which, I just kind of feel like you wouldn't say that if I was talking about Lipitor or insulin or, you know, freaking baby aspirin."

Like me and like a lot of other people, Andy has had the experience of a medication working well for a long time and then, suddenly, not. "It came back. The hopelessness," he said. "It doesn't matter how nice the day is. It doesn't matter how much I love my wife. It doesn't matter what kind of fun thing I'm doing at my well-paying job. It doesn't matter that my beautiful children fulfill me. And even in the misery of it, even in the real kind of emotional misery of it, I'm still going like, 'Damn it. Let's just get these pills working again.'"

The way I see it, introducing meds into a depressed person's daily routine is like how it would be if someone introduced you to a toothbrush for the first time. "Here's this thing that you have to use every day," they say. "Sometimes you'll need to go down to the drugstore and replenish." You can reject it and walk around with stinky breath and rotting teeth, or you can just do it because it produces a good result and it's really not that hard or inconvenient.

9

IN WHICH EVERYTHING CHANGES

From the window of my tiny office in West Seattle I could see a giant pile of dirt. Despite Seattle's abundant rain, the dirt pile never washed away, never lost its mound form. I'm still in the dark as to whether anyone was showing up to maintain the dirt pile—bulldozing the sides to make it more tidy, adding more dirt to the top somehow—but I certainly never saw anyone, and I spent most workdays staring at it.

Many times, while looking out at the dirt pile, I would spot a bald eagle out for a glide. There were a few eagle nests in the high trees along the West Seattle waterfront, including one relatively close to my office. Bald eagles really are beautiful animals, enormous and graceful. Unfortunately, my bald eagle neighbor was often denied his chance to inspire, because these mean crows would fuck with him relentlessly. I'd see him soar over the dirt pile and then here would come three or four crows swarming around, pecking at him, making their nasty caw sounds, and forcing the majestic though suddenly cumbersome eagle to alter course or try to get the hell out of there.

This was the ongoing entertainment from my little office window: the dirt pile, the eagle, and the crows. I loved the whole thing and found it calming. Most days.

April 4 was gray and cold, not raining but threatening to do so, as was often the case in Seattle. I had been taping a segment at a restaurant in the early afternoon. I'd asked some local chefs to come up with inventive Easter recipes for Marshmallow Peeps and interviewed them about how to make Peep Fondue and Peep-Crusted Foie Gras Torchon. It went well. I got back to the office around three thirty, and before long Jill called for a check-in. It was a Wednesday, so we brainstormed fun stuff to do when the weekend came around. Then we hung up.

Ten minutes later, the phone rang again, and I saw it was Jill. She must have forgotten to tell me something. Her tone was different, though.

"Your brother Rick shot himself."

The moment I heard those words I left my body. I was watching myself sitting in a chair, on the phone with Jill, having heard those words. Watching a knife run down my torso, my viscera spilling onto my desk. I didn't feel it; just knew that it was a thing one would feel. Rick shot himself. It made no sense for a tenth of a second, and then it made all the sense in the world. He had never been mentally ill; he had always been mentally ill. I didn't stop it. I didn't know. I didn't stop it. I didn't know. And I spoke, flatly, as I watched myself speak.

"Oh. Is he dead?"

"I'm not sure," she said. "I haven't heard that he is. You need to go up to your mom's house. Lisbet is meeting you there, and then the three of you are flying to San Diego."

"Where did he do it?" I asked.

"It was at a gun range. Like a target range."

"No, I mean where on his body?"

"He shot himself in the head."

"Oh. Okay. Bye."

I ended the call, and then somehow I was on the Aurora Bridge heading north toward Mom's house. The radio never came on.

Around Eightieth and Fifteenth Avenue, a few blocks from the house, the numbness shattered because it was pierced by horror. Gun range. I knew Rick had read my book. He read about the idea of going to a gun range and shooting yourself. And then a few months later he went to a gun range and shot himself in the head. And you generally don't survive shooting yourself in the head at close range. I killed my brother.

Lisbet was already at the house. "This is my fault," I said, not by way of confession, not in the hopes of being told this wasn't the case, but simply as a fact. "I wrote about people shooting themselves at gun ranges. That gave him the idea. He read the book. This is my fault. I did this."

"No," said Mom. "You didn't do this. He did this."

She might as well have said dogs could talk. This wasn't true. We were again participating in the family tradition of denying the horrible truth. I had killed Rick. Now I would always be a guy who killed his brother. What do we know of Cain other than what he did to Abel?

Somehow tickets had been purchased, and we were to leave in a little over two hours. I was in Ballard, the northwest part of the city, and my house in the southwest part was on the way to the airport, south of Seattle.

I wanted to be alone. In a pinch, in a crisis, in the event of my big brother shooting himself, all I wanted was to separate from anyone and everyone. And yeah, that's shameful, and I felt shame, but the desire to detach was so strong that I was willing to eat the shame.

"I'll meet you there," I said. "I'm going to stop at home, grab

some clothes, check in with Jill, and I'll meet you at the airport."
I left Lisbet to take care of our mother, who had just lost her
oldest son.

At home, I grabbed some clothes and stuffed them into a
bag. I had an urgent need to bring a book, even though I couldn't
imagine enjoying quiet reading time.

"I need cash," I thought. "Always need cash when you travel."
And I was hungry. What if I couldn't find anything to eat? They
don't serve food on planes anymore, and I wasn't going to have
time to eat at the airport, and even if I did have time, I mustn't
eat because Jesus my brother shot himself. I killed my brother.
I pulled over to stop at the Trader Joe's in Burien, right near
the airport, where I could get cash and food. But what do you
get at Trader Joe's that can travel well? What's a good portable
TJ's food to pack for your brother's suicide? Energy bars? But
which ones? Blueberry sounds kind of weird, and so does fudge.
I killed my brother. Peanut butter would work. Protein. Why am
I thinking so much about energy bar flavors? (Reader, it was because these were the only thoughts I could comprehend.) Time
was getting tight, but I made it to the MasterPark lot across from
the airport on Pacific Highway South.

I was the only passenger on the shuttle. The driver was young,
energetic, and—oh no—chatty. "Alright, we are on our way!" he
said, pulling onto South 170th, heading west to the airport.

"Where you headed, my man?" the driver asked.

"San Diego," I said flatly.

"Ah, sunny San Diego! Lot nicer than here! Business or pleasure?"

It was a perfectly reasonable question 999 times out of 1,000,
but here I was, number 1,000. And that's funny. Rick—and I
didn't know whether to think of him in the past or present tense
at this particular point—loved messing with people, especially

if he could do it so the people wouldn't know they were being messed with. So I messed with this guy, dodging around the question: "Oh, it's not really either one."

"Cool, cool," said the driver, and I could tell from his tone that as he was reading the road, he had lost the ability to read the room.

We drove a bit farther in silence. "So what's down in San Diego?" he finally asked.

And that is a bit too nosy, you must admit.

Calm as can be, I told him, "I'm flying down because my brother shot himself in the head this afternoon and I'm hoping to see him before he dies."

"Ohhsorry, umsorry."

He did not speak again on that trip. I'm pretty sure he never spoke to another passenger again. The only thing that remains a mystery is whether he kept his job or whether he got back to the lot, threw the keys on his boss's desk, and walked away. I was more terrified than I had ever been, but, come on, it was pretty funny. Rick would have thought so. Dad would have loved it.

Rick would have egged the guy on. One of his favorite things to do when he saw someone smoking was to go up and say, "Excuse me, I notice you're smoking. It looks pretty cool, and I was thinking of becoming a smoker myself. What brand of tobacco cigarette would you recommend for someone like me just starting out?"

Most of the time, the person would then urge Rick not to start in the first place. Then Rick would act confused and ask why *they* were smoking if it was so bad. The game was to see how long he could extend the conversation. Occasionally someone would suggest Marlboro Lights.

I met up with Mom and Lisbet at the airport. And it's here in the story that more parts begin to go missing. The news, sure, that was seared into my memory, not just saved on the hard drive but the first thing you see on the brain's desktop. There's a short-cut icon to that one. The conversation with Mom and Lisbet is mostly there but partially obscured by thoughts of my book and Rick at the gun range.

A flight, however, is passive. You sit in your seat and buckle up and wait to be somewhere else. I know I didn't read. I was sitting with Mom and Lisbet, and we must have spoken. Lisbet told me recently that she doesn't remember anything from that flight either, aside from our mother trying to get her to eat a cookie. I don't even remember the cookies.

Nor do I understand how, when we got to San Diego, Kyndra's mom and stepdad were somehow waiting for us. I don't know who contacted them, how they found us, how we found them. I have no memory of what their names are, and I could not tell you what they looked like.

I remember that they were very kind. I remember that they knew Rick and said they liked him very much. I recall that they were sad about what happened to him but were clearly setting that aside in order to be helpful to us. I remember that they made everything easier.

They took us to Scripps Mercy Hospital. Google Maps is telling me it's in the Hillcrest neighborhood. This doesn't mean anything to me, and in truth I had to look up the name of the hospital. We must have parked whatever car we were in and gone inside the building and to the intensive care unit, where Rick was. And that's when the memory starts to pick back up again. A small group of people were waiting, huddled together, and we somehow knew (Did we ask? Did they ask?) that they were there for Rick. One of them told us that they were Rick's friends and co-workers from the sobriety hotline where he had been volunteering for a couple of years. A mix of men and women, they all had the weathered but healthy look of addicts dedicated to recovery, and although I don't remember any particular, individual identifying features, I remember the kindness. They were huggers, which our family has never been, making for some well-intentioned and weirdly humorous awkwardness when they wrapped up Mom, Lisbet, and me anyway. People in recovery are the best huggers, and I think it's because they practice a lot. Kyndra was at the hospital. I don't think we spoke.

We walked through two large heavy wooden doors, the kind of hospital doors that are made to be locked and impenetrable for what I'm sure are important and frightening reasons. The room was bustling with activity.

Somehow—I can't remember—we were shown to a little area to the right of a desk and told to wait there and the doctor would come see us. In front of the desk, past the high-traffic area, was a section of the ICU separated by floor-to-ceiling windows and glass doors, and that's where the patients were. They were mostly concealed from view by large yellow curtains. I was able to see part of a very obese man in the bed closest to us but not much of anyone else. I looked for Rick but had no luck locating him.

None of us was crying. I hadn't cried at all and didn't see any sign that my mom or sister had either. We were going where we were told. We spoke when necessary or when we were spoken to.

A doctor came up and introduced himself. I don't recall his name, but I do recall that he was around forty years old, prematurely balding, a bit shorter than average, and kind. The doctor preempted the most pressing question by telling us that Rick was still technically alive but that brain function had stopped. If he were to stay alive in this condition, it would be in an irreversible vegetative state.

"Brain-dead," I muttered.

"Yes," said the doctor.

The bullet had entered his head from the right side, Rick was right-handed, and it was a penetrating wound, which is to say that it lodged itself in his head and didn't come out the other side. They had to work hard to try to clear out the clotting that occurs in situations like that, he said, and then I remember talk about a blood transfusion. "I can take you back to see him," the doctor said, "but I need to warn you that he won't look like himself."

Rick and I had the same parents. We came from the same place and were raised in the same house. We were both, evidently, depressed. Sure, we were different, but that was only because of some choices we had made about life path and some different cards we were dealt at random. But at root? Same. So even though his suicide was a surprise, it made perfect sense. He was six years ahead and he arrived at the place I had begun worrying would be my own destination. He had shot himself in the head. Not his heart, not his stomach. He hated what his brain was doing so much that he took up a gun and shot that brain to destroy it.

The doctor showed us to the first bed, the one that had been right in front of us. The obese man was Rick, bloated from emergency blood transfusions. My brother had never been obese. He had been absurdly fit and tan the year he worked as a roofer, and he'd held a facsimile of that appearance ever since. He had always been one of those people who just stay in good shape without exercising. He didn't enjoy the taste of junk food, he said, so he never ate it. Preferred vegetables. Didn't like the taste of beer, and neither marijuana nor methamphetamine has any calories.

So, no. This was not him. This was not my brother. Rick was many things, but one of them was always "presentable."

His body was covered in a hospital gown, and a hospital-yellow blanket was stretched over him. That detail struck me as absurd. Sure, they probably needed to control his body temperature or something, but a blanket? Like he had opted to take a nap?

Then there was the head. Or rather, there was the large sphere at the top of the shoulders wrapped in yellowish bandages. The bandages allowed a small space around Rick's closed left eye to be exposed to the world it would never again see. There were tubes everywhere.

For all the work that had been done on his head, Rick's body, though sickeningly bloated, was mostly untouched. The hospital gown had short sleeves, and his arms were at his sides. I touched his left hand, and it was warm. I didn't hold it because I didn't want to knock anything loose, although honestly how could I make things worse? I have a memory of standing by this body that was now only a body and not a person and feeling the warmth of his hand, seeing the skin that was and always had been bronzed brown. The warm skin on the hand that used to wrestle with me in the rec room, having epic battles, laughing, over who got the last pair of tube socks.

Now, we've all seen this scene in movies, right? The family member, possibly estranged, is hospitalized and at death's door (medical staff who all look like they went to drama school instead of med school bustle about), and the lead character gets the Big Scene. They poignantly say just the right thing to single-handedly encapsulate the hero's journey while also repairing the damaged relationship with the comatose patient. Then either the patient wakes up, summoned to consciousness and presumed health by the proximate eloquence, or he dies but it's okay because the scene went well.

Real life works a little differently. All that exists is trauma, screaming, fear, panic, and nothingness. It is the worst possible time for extemporaneous speaking. No words came out. My palm rested on this warm bloated hand, the one that belonged to a person who no longer existed. What was Rick without that brain that spun out jokes, lies, manipulations, love, confusion, late-in-life stories that demonstrated blurred lines between fantasy and reality, and ultimately despair? Whatever he had been or now was, it wasn't this slab of tissue.

Brothers, according to the cultural wisdom received from Hallmark cards, are always there for each other. We were rarely there for each other. That was the guilt he carried and apologized for at Christmas. And I had turned my back on him—fatally—and not welcomed him back in my life no questions asked. Sure, I had started down that road in the coffee shop a few months before, but that was the first single step on a journey that wasn't going to happen. We weren't brothers who could tell each other anything. I mean, if it was anything about The Who or Cheech & Chong, sure, but not anything substantial. We couldn't tell each other what was going on in our lives or what was going wrong in our lives. Couldn't reach out from our distant ditches.

Love was in my mind in that moment with "Rick," but depression didn't let me bring it to the forefront, not even then, not even given those circumstances. Instead, depression threw love into a salad of regret, anger, confusion, and horror. Then it reminded me that I killed my brother with my stupid book.

So I said nothing and left the room. We were shown to a waiting room just off the main lobby area of the ICU and told we could stay there and the doctor would give us more information as it became available.

At that point, it's curtain up on a long-avoided open family discussion, right? It would be a really good premise for a play. I like to think I'd be played by Ethan Hawke, but realistically it would probably be Paul Giamatti.

Part of the thing with depression is that your mind wanders.

No, we just sat there. Even if we'd wanted to finally confront all the issues our family always had, we lacked the knowledge of how to do that. So we offered each other water bottles and looked out the window. Lisbet called Mark, briefly, with an update. I stepped out of the waiting room and called Jill.

"His brain is gone," I told her. "So he's still technically alive, and I got to see him. But we don't know what happens from here."

"So he won't recover."

"The brain can't restart. It can never restart. If he lives, he's hooked up to machines forever," I said. I filled her in on as much as I knew, that he had indeed shot himself at a gun range. He was taken by ambulance to this hospital. Something Mercy, I couldn't remember the name.

"How are you doing?" she asked.

"I'm fine, I guess." I knew she meant this in the deepest, most sincere way, not like a greeting. Still, I had no idea how I was doing. In these circumstances, my brother mostly dead, me having caused it, my sister and mother in the other room, I absolutely lacked the ability to spot myself amid my circumstances.

"I mean, of course I'm not fine," I continued. "But I'm here. I . . . I'm here and I'm trying to figure out what to do next."

"Can you go outside and get a breath of fresh air?" Jill asked.

"I don't think so. We had to get buzzed through all these doors to get here. I think I need to stay here. The doctor's coming back in. I'll call you later."

The doctor from earlier was walking into the waiting room. "He's gone," the doctor said. "He has died. It happened just now. I'm very sorry."

"Thank you so much for taking care of him," I said.

Lisbet and I drew into Mom and hugged, poorly. For me, it was a performance of what people do in a situation like this, or rather what I supposed they did. Mom said she was certain that

Rick waited for the three of us to arrive before letting go. Well, I thought, no. If he was really concerned about us he wouldn't have done this in the first place. And you can't do something like "wait" when you have no brain activity. Rick was an atheist, last I had heard, so certainly his belief was that dead is dead, and thus he lacked the ability to take attendance from the spirit realm. I didn't say any of that. I just said, "Okay."

Conversations were had with doctors and nurses, and while I was an active participant in these talks, I don't remember what was said. At all. Total blank. Not sure I even knew back then, because all I could think of was Rick's bloated corpse.

My mind stayed stuck on the bandages, the yellowness, the hospital gown, but mostly how this object looked nothing like Rick. The storm that had been raging in his head for as long as I could remember had at last ended. He wasn't at peace, because there was no him to be at peace, but it had all at last stopped, leaving only this wreckage behind.

I called Jill again to say he was gone.

We got to a hotel, somehow. I think Kyndra and her family must have taken us there. The Holiday Inn Express & Suites is near the hospital and right off the freeway, perfect for the traveling business professional or guys who just had their brother put a bullet in his brain and then die. We rented two rooms, one for only me and one for Mom and Lisbet, because Mom wanted Lisbet to stay with her.

It was time to call Metteline, and I volunteered. I'm not sure I had spoken to Metteline on the phone since she moved to Norway some thirty-six years before, so she knew something was wrong.

"I'm in San Diego with Mom and Lisbet. Rick shot himself in the head," I stated. "He's dead." There was more shouting on her end of the line than I expected, an audible yell of grief and horror.

Here is a list of some of the thoughts I had while briefly on the phone with my sister, presented in convenient yet darkly ironic bullet points:

- What was Metteline's relationship with Rick?
- Did they have one?
- Were they close?
- Were any of us close?
- Is she more startled or sad?
- This is the first time I have clearly stated that Rick had shot himself and died.
- How many more times will I have to say it?
- Given that he was six years older than me, will I kill myself six years from now, in 2013?
- Is this a weird dream?
- Everyone talks about "making arrangements" after someone dies. What does that mean?
- Why can't I feel anything? Is it depression or trauma, or am I just an asshole?
- Should I cry? I tried to learn to cry on cue for a play once but couldn't.
- I think I'll get off the phone now.

And with that I passed the phone off to Mom.

Is it an emotion to want to leave somewhere? On this most horrifying of nights, when one would need to give and receive comfort more than ever, I desperately wanted to be without it. I wanted to be alone because I knew that I, at least, would be there and stay there. Not like some people who shoot themselves in the head at a gun range. Besides, I had work to do. I had to finish that radio story.

What? Yes.

The radio story about cooking with Marshmallow Peeps? That's right.

How would you even work on that in San Diego? I packed my work laptop.

What?! When?! When I left the office immediately after getting the call from Jill.

When you were in shock? Yes. I grabbed the laptop in case I wouldn't be coming back.

Are you crazy?! I think this was established some time ago.

But . . . I mean . . . ? Say it.

WHY? Because I didn't want people to get mad at me.

Yes, my brother had shot himself that afternoon, but I was still only a few months into my new job. People would be judging me based on the quality of my stories, I believed, and the best way to make sure that this story was as good as it could be was to finish putting it together myself. If I handed it off or it never ran at all, then I would be judged poorly down the line and my boss and new co-workers would think badly of me and then I'd get fired and no one would ever hire me again and Jill would leave me and I would become homeless and then die of an overdose or gunshot. Besides, working on the story even under these circumstances would show my colleagues that my priorities were in the right place: not with my family but with making a fluff story for a low-rated newsmagazine program.

A chef talking about the right way to roast a Peep will not block out 100 percent of one's thoughts of one's dead brother's suicide or said brother's bloated yellow corpse, but it's good for about 30 percent, and beggars can't be choosers. I worked until the Pro Tools software started to blur and I found there were large chunks of the story I couldn't remember because I had fallen asleep sitting up, headphones on. The sleep surprised me because I had assumed, given the events of the day, that I just wouldn't sleep again. It was clear to me that I wouldn't be able to finish the story.

I emailed my editor explaining what had happened that day and providing instructions on which server to go to in order to find the draft version of the story I'd been working on. I apologized for not completing it in a manner ready for air.

I slept.

10

TRYING TO MOVE ON WITHOUT A
CLEAR IDEA HOW

Can you be a shocked by a sunrise when you're thirty-eight years old? Around six thirty in the morning on April 5, I woke to the sunrise's weird garish light tentacles stretching across the assortment of SUVs in the hotel parking lot and poking me hard in the head. Never had a sunrise felt like a Lovecraft monster before.

The weight of what happened the day before was an instant cinder block to the chest. And no, memories of that day felt nothing like a dream. I didn't have to pinch myself; I didn't have to run through things in my head. No, I was quite aware that I was waking up to a brand-new reality. There would be, henceforth, two lives: the one I lived before Rick fired that bullet and the one after.

A few hours of sleep, maybe three, had provided the insight that my culpability extended far beyond merely writing about the rules of a gun range and, implicitly, how to skirt them in order to kill yourself with a borrowed handgun. If it was only that, I could dismiss it. No, it was all those phone calls never returned.

It was the pained and forced smile at family gatherings when Rick tried to connect with me but I couldn't let go of my suspicion enough to let a connection happen. It was at coffee the previous Christmas where I set out to rebuild—or perhaps merely build—our relationship but on my exclusive terms and with a timeline that blindly assumed we'd have years to come together with love, sobriety, and honesty. Rick's immediate danger and his urgent timeline were things I simply failed to register. Ordinarily I had humanity and compassion, I thought, and I could have and should have picked up on how desperate he was.

Dear Reader, this was not and is not self-pity. I knew the truth, and that weighty truth had now been placed on my shoulders to carry around forever. You know at the end of *Inglourious Basterds* when Lt. Aldo Raine (Brad Pitt) carves a swastika into the forehead of Lt. Col. Hans Landa (Christoph Waltz) so that everywhere he goes for the rest of his life people will know who he really is and what he did? That.

And still the sun kept coming up, the stupid idiot.

I took my meds. I've taken them daily since. Lisbet had procured muffins and coffee when I got to her and Mom's room around seven. We had a day to plan. Lisbet was going back to the airport to fly out. When she had gotten word that Rick shot himself, she had yelled out loud, "Rick shot himself," and all three kids had heard it. They began, understandably, to fall to pieces while Mark did what he could and she rushed off to San Diego. Her kids were older than mine and needed her.

I'd received the call at work, so Charlie and Kate were still in the dark about what had happened. Jill wasn't working at the time, so she could manage our household while I took care of things in the ironically sunnier place. It fell to Jill to explain to a six-year-old and a four-year-old that they would never see their uncle again, their uncle whom they had only recently met.

Somehow, we got a rental car and drove to Scripps Mercy Hospital, where, at the business office, they handed me a large padded manila envelope. It held his wallet and keys. Simple metal ring for a keychain, two keys: car and apartment. Practically nothing in his wallet. That was all he had on him. I don't remember much about the person who handed it over. I just remember she was kind. I also don't know how we qualified ourselves to receive Rick's possessions.

Mom got a call. From . . . someone? Did she have a phone by that point? Rick's car was going to be towed from the street in front of the gun range if it wasn't moved by 5 p.m. It was currently 4 p.m. We had the key in the envelope for a car that was probably worth two hundred dollars, in keeping with Rick's tradition of buying a piece-of-shit car for next to nothing, driving it until it collapsed, then dumping it for scrap. I didn't even know what this car looked like, and two hundred bucks may be overly generous.

"Let them," I told Mom. "Let them just take the car."

Mom was as task-driven as I was, since taking care of small errands was more attractive than, you know, trying to comprehend your son's suicide. The need to do stuff teamed up with her anxiety, and she wanted to go get the car. "I don't want to get letters from the police department or collection agencies," she said.

So we went to collect the car. Mom dropped me off and headed back to the hotel.

If I was writing fiction about depression and suicide, and if I had to write about a bleak and depressing gun range, and if the name I chose for the fictitious business was Discount Gun Mart, any worthwhile editor would say I was laying it on a little thick. Still, the fucking place was and is called Discount Gun Mart. Discount Gun Mart is about the size and shape of a strip mall. It has to be huge, I guess, because of the indoor shooting range.

I walked in. There's a sameness to the people you find inside a place like this. The people you see are men. They almost always have beards. Everyone looks like they smoke, and everyone is very serious. Some of them look like violent Santa Clauses.

Discount Gun Mart was the last place Rick decided to go to. As he prepared to end everything, he somehow thought of saving money. He didn't choose Luxury Gun Mart or Comfortable Gun Mart; he chose the one that advertised cheapness even before it even mentioned guns. "Fuck this place," I thought.

"Are you the guy in charge?" I asked the bearded man behind the counter.

"Yes sir!" he cheerfully replied.

"I'm John Moe. I'm Rick Moe's brother. He shot himself here yesterday, and now he's dead. I have some questions."

He asked if we could talk off to the side and told another bearded man to take care of anyone else who needed help. I'd imagine if you run a shooting range you probably always feel like you're about to be blamed for something, on account of you being tacitly guilty of a lot of things, and the guy got nervous. That wasn't my mission here, though. I just wanted to know more and asked what he could tell me about yesterday.

"I wasn't here when it happened," he said. "The two guys who were here, one of them, it's his day off today. And the other guy was supposed to be in, but he, ah . . . he couldn't. He was the one who found . . . uh, your brother."

"Was Rick a member here?" I asked.

The guy said he was. Rick had come into Discount Gun Mart in February and signed up for membership, paid a fee. "Just signed up and left. Actually, he'd never come back until yesterday."

"Do you get a lot of situations like this?" I asked.

"We've had it happen before," the guy said. "But it's been many years since it happened."

He hesitated and looked away, like there was something he didn't want to say. Then he said it.

"Here's the thing, though. When he came in yesterday, he bought a box of ammunition. And then, ah, after it happened, when they went out there, the box was still there and it was still sealed. He didn't use any ammunition we sold him."

I knew that there were no bullets found later in Rick's pockets, and the only bullets at the scene were in the box. Therefore, he must have been carrying around a single bullet in his pocket before it happened. He had been carrying a one-way ticket voucher, waiting for the day to redeem it. How long had he been carrying it around? The answer died with Rick.

The guy asked if I wanted to go out and look at the gun range. "No, thank you," I said, to his great relief.

I found the car on the side of the road with a few minutes to spare before it was tow-eligible. Dark gray, dinged-up, two-door-piece-of-shit car. It was clean on the inside. Not vacuumed but free of clutter, free of any residue of the person who had been driving it. He had prepped it for the next owner. Turning the key met with some chugging and grinding reluctance, but it started. The radio was off. He had driven to Discount Gun Mart in silence, or he had taken a moment to silence the radio. I turned it on and it was set to 89.5, KPBS, San Diego's NPR affiliate station. That's the station that aired my show.

I hit scan and ended up on a station playing Johnny Cash's "The Man in Black." Fine. The Man in Black. That got me most of the way back to the hotel. A friend of Rick's said he could sell the car for us and was possibly looking to buy a car himself. He got dropped off at the hotel, and I gave him the keys. Just take it, I said. Sell it or keep it, whatever. We scratched out a receipt, and off he drove.

There were a few other stops in those few days we were in San Diego. We had his address, and his apartment key was found in his pocket. We contacted his roommate, who said we could stop by whenever we wanted to see if there was anything we wanted to save. He had volunteered to box up the rest, donate whatever he could to Goodwill. Rick only bought burner phones with prepaid minutes. He only had the phone numbers for the landlines at his various residences, none of which he stayed at for very long. His phones and residences were like his cars: cheap and disposable.

The building and unit weren't dirty or run-down, just featureless. The living room contained an oldish couch and a small TV. There was a kitchenette. Rick's bed was a mattress on the floor in a small bedroom. There was a boom box and some CDs strewn around. Some books. My book was right next to the bed. Some clothes in the closet, maybe a suitcase's worth. Rick had lived in so many places and been close to out of money for so long that he didn't own much. There wasn't anything sentimental as far as I could tell, no photo albums, nothing on the walls, no memorabilia of childhood. No expressions of hobbies or interests or passions. We knew he kept a journal, so when I saw a spiral-bound notebook near the bed, I knew what it was, and Mom took it for her own immediately, placing it in a box we had brought. It looked like the room of a teenager. Maybe the room of a college student who wasn't doing well in school. At a stretch, the room of someone in their very early twenties. Rick was forty-four years old when he died.

I'm pretty sure the journal was the only thing we put in the box. Mom might have even left the box behind and just kept the journal in her bag. She asked if I wanted to take anything else, maybe Rick's copy of my book. No. No, I don't want to take Rick's copy of my book.

~

"It happens a lot at gun ranges. It happens a lot in places like this, too. It's happened here before."

Mom and I are sitting across a desk from, I guess, a mortician? A funeral director? We've moved on to the conversational topic of Rick's cremation after a protracted discussion of where to park outside that would be both convenient and safe.

"Wait, people come into funeral homes and shoot themselves?"

"They think they're being polite," she explained. "They figure that they'll save everyone else the chore of having to drive them over here after they've died. That's how gone their thinking is. They think that people will appreciate their thoughtfulness."

I know the mortician was on the older side. And yes, she was kind. But it was a different sort of kindness, a more earnest and practical one. In my memory, she's played by Kathy Bates. In her line of work, she needs to be kind all day long to people having the worst days of their lives, and using that kindness she needs to get a lot of business taken care of. So it wasn't an empathetic kindness where she truly opened her heart and felt what her clients were feeling. It couldn't be that. She'd drop dead (conveniently right there at the funeral home) after one day on the job. Instead it was kindness in the form of warm and wise leadership. Like a funeral-home Gandalf. I would keep this approach in mind years later when I created a podcast that involved talking to people about depression.

"So where is Rick's body right now?" I asked. I didn't know whether to refer to "it" or "him."

"Right back there. The delivery happened this morning."

Well played in regard to eschewing pronouns, professionally kind lady.

We made arrangements for the cremation and the transportation of the ashes to Seattle, because that's what Mom wanted. And what Rick would have wanted would be whatever Mom wanted. The two of them have driven me crazy over the years, and I'm certain I drove them even crazier, but they were always completely comfortable with each other.

And then we flew home.

According to *THWoD*:
Some Pain Doesn't Go Away,
It Evolves

P eople who think you can get over the death of someone close are, I suspect, people who have never experienced the death of someone close. If they had, they'd know it's not that simple.

Former child actor turned grown-up writer Mara Wilson lost her mother to breast cancer right after filming the movie *Matilda*. It exacerbated her already crowded roster of mental problems including anxiety, OCD, and depression. "I've heard of that analogy of a ball in a box," she said. "There's a ball bouncing around a box, and there's a button on it, and the ball is going to press that button. And at first the ball is in a very small box, and then the box gets bigger and bigger and bigger, so there's more space for it to jump around. But it's going to hit that button sometimes. I can't think of her and not be sad. It's something you carry with you all of the time."

For me, Rick's death is a bit like the hole after a tooth is pulled, or even the stubble after a tremendously short haircut (except with overwhelming grief and remorse, naturally). I keep feeling where the thing used to be because part of me always wonders if it's really gone.

I got ready for my interview with Scott Thompson in a different way than I did for any other interview I'd done in seventeen-plus years in the business. For one, he was more or less a god in the world of comedy, being one-fifth of the sketch comedy group Kids in the Hall. When I talk to people I admire a lot professionally, I have to switch off sections of my brain and avoid asking questions like "You're great!," which isn't technically a question.

Scott had lost his younger brother Dean to mental illness and suicide. Scott admired him as much as I did Rick.

"We were only a year apart. . . . They call that Irish twins," he said. "We literally lived together for eighteen years. I had never had my own room. And my brother and I were absolutely completely different. He was masculine, he was athletic, he was handsome; he was a lady-killer. Everything he did turned to gold. He could play hockey. You could say, 'Oh, this kid's never played lacrosse.' A week later he'd be the best guy on the team. So he was everything that a boy was supposed to be. He was the easiest to get along with. He was like a golden boy. And then at around eighteen he changed."

Scott participated in a teen program where students lived in the Philippines for ten months. "My parents had been writing me letters, telling me that things had been happening [with Dean], and I didn't understand that and I didn't buy it. I was like, 'This is crazy. I'm the crazy one. He's the athlete.' I thought he was just showing off.

"I just remember very clearly coming in the door [after returning home] and all my brothers were there and I was like, 'Where's Dean?'

"And they go, 'Oh, he'll come down.'

"He'd been in his bedroom, and he came downstairs. I remember seeing him at the end of the hall, and I just remember looking at his eyes and going, 'Where is he?' It was honestly like he was possessed. And it was just not him."

Dean Thompson was dealing with schizophrenia. Soon the world as the rest of us know it began to ebb away from him. Dean told Scott that he wanted to rewrite Shakespeare's *Julius Caesar* to include tanks. He became virulently antigay—Scott is gay—and announced that he was Jesus Christ.

"I was not a good brother," said Scott. "I was not. I did not have empathy for him."

Dean was struck by a car and was in a coma for an extended period. "When he came out, my family was so naïve we thought that maybe the car accident killed the craziness, like we really were that stupid."

Dean was involuntarily committed to a psychiatric hospital, where doctors medicated him so the voices in his head stopped— but his body fell apart. It was Dean's horror and shame at that development that Scott believes ultimately led to the suicide. I didn't ask how Dean killed himself. It doesn't matter.

Scott had a difficult time getting through our interview. He was replaying all his memories with Dean, realizing what clues he had missed, wishing he had another chance to help his brother. It was a difficult episode for me to make for the same reasons. What if I had treated Rick with more kindness? What if I had taken a few minutes to return a phone call or two? What if I had picked up on clues about his mental health, clues that in retrospect were not difficult to read?

Those are the questions that always come up after a suicide, of course. The person left behind inevitably asks them and will ask them, to some extent, for the rest of their life. Meanwhile, that person's friends will inevitably say that there was no way you could have known, you can't beat yourself up, you did the best you could with the knowledge that you had at that time.

Both sides have a point. What stings is that the argument will never ever be resolved.

After speaking with Scott, I was pretty wrung out, so, as I often do, I sat in the studio chair for a while. Kryssy Pease, the producer of the podcast, frequently urges me to go home after interviews that feel particularly resonant. "I can tell you're still kind of in the interview," she says, "processing what the guest said."

We travel together to conduct interviews a few times a year, usually to Los Angeles and New York. Because we're trying to bank as many in-person interviews as we can while we're there, this usually means multiple interviews on any given day, and generally after the day's conversations are over, I go back to the hotel and sleep for an absurd number of hours.

Talking about depression is great and healthy, but that doesn't mean it's not exhausting.

11

I CHOOSE NOISE OVER SILENCE

The kids hugged me a lot when I returned from San Diego. They were sad that they had lost this relative, this quasi-dad, whom they had met only briefly but whom they loved. But mostly Charlie and Kate were concerned about me. It was more important to them how I was doing than how they were doing, a pretty impressive feat of empathy given their ages. "I'm going to be okay," I said, answering their concern reflexively but feeling better for having said for the first time that I would be okay. Didn't really believe it but liked saying it. "But this is about all of us. I'm very sad, but you don't have to be less sad because of how sad I am. You should be as sad as you need to be." Then they hugged me some more.

Jill hadn't told the kids that Rick had shot himself in the head. We agreed that she would tell them that Rick had a brain illness, which was the truth. They wanted to know if I was going to get sick in the same way or if they could get sick in the same way. She told them that we were going to be very careful and if we started to have problems with our brains, we were going to get to the doctor right away.

That first night I was back, we watched cartoons and movies cuddled up on the couch under a blanket, and then I put each of the kids to bed with books and quiet conversations. I waited for them to fall asleep before leaving their rooms.

I knew now that suicide was off the table for me forever. It wasn't so much of a pledge or a decision, more of a realization that I simply could not ever kill myself. I was just starting to get a picture of how much damage it caused.

I would have to walk the earth like this, no bullet in my pocket, no secret ticket out of here. Which is Hell. All of the depression, the grief, the guilt, the regret, the disorientation would be mine forever and I would be awake for it, strapped into the chair like Malcolm McDowell in *A Clockwork Orange*, a guy squeezing drops into my eyes as I'm forced to watch every second of footage. The secret shame I had always lived with, the one I dared never speak of, the one that I was eventually told was an illness called depression, would be my forever burden. I've never cottoned to the idea of a big invisible space monster called God dealing out events in a wise and prudent way, but it still made a kind of poetic sense that having killed my brother, I would be cursed to trudge through life carrying the burden of my actions with me. Rick got the death penalty, and I got life without parole.

It was nice to snuggle with the kids.

Charlie had a birthday party to go to the next day, and I volunteered to take him. Jill and I ran a quick inventory of which parents were likely to be there and whether any of them would know the events of our past several days. I didn't want anyone to brush my arm and ask, "How *are* you?" with doe eyes. Seattle parents are very sensitive people, often maddeningly so.

It's not that I was scared of breaking down and blubbering in front of anyone. Quite the opposite. I didn't want to have to calmly say, "Well, my brother killed himself, so I'm not especially great," because that would be mean. Beyond that, I didn't want to have to contextualize Rick's death and make it all okay for someone else.

I didn't want to say, "Well, we didn't know he was struggling so much. It's sad, but you have to move on. At least he's not suffering anymore. It's tough right now, but I'm sure we'll get through it, especially with the help of you, Parent I Barely Know All Up in My Fucking Business."

Even "I heard what happened, I'm so sorry" was a conversation I wasn't really up for because it still required a response, still necessitated acknowledging the gesture and engaging with another person. And fuck that. Depression already saps my willingness to connect to other humans, an act that would give life more richness and meaning, but to do so in crisis? Forget it.

"No, I don't think there will be anyone there you need to worry about," said Jill. "Are you sure you want to take him?"

"Yeah. Gets me moving around. And kids have to get to birthday parties."

A few months after all this, a trained therapist advised me that my emotional reserves would be almost nonexistent for the foreseeable future, so I shouldn't really go looking for them. Depression already had me at a disadvantage on emotional reserves. You spend all day loathing yourself, burning energy you would ordinarily keep as a backup in case of problems or hassles. Then grief wants to use up even more. Together, they're a total gas guzzler, leading people in my situation to sleep a lot or be empty husks moving blankly through tasks such as providing transportation to birthday parties.

I didn't know all that stuff when I arrived at the party in the southeast part of West Seattle. All I saw was a bunch of people, maybe ten or fifteen, crammed into a very small living room and the birthday boy's dad reclined across an entire couch. No one could sit down on that couch because it was completely taken up by him. "Oh, hell no," I thought. "Get up! It's your kid's party and you have to be *on* right now. You've got to be running things, either as leader of the party, second in command to your wife, or my God at least welcoming the guests from an upright position, giving them a chance to sit." This was all a mental monologue. On the outside I was just a guy standing still, talking to no one and looking at the couch.

Six is a tricky age for birthday parties. Do you need to stay there with the kids and other parents and help supervise? Or do you leave and come back at the end of the party, the time listed on the invitation? Usually the stick-around signal for an afternoon party in Seattle at the time was beer availability, but I didn't see any. Was that supine Dad's job? Should I help? There were other parents milling about, not sitting due to lack of couch space. No one knew what to do. I turned and walked out the door. I never picked up Charlie from that party, and he's still there today, dreaming of one day getting access to that couch. No, I picked him up. The parents got divorced not long afterward. I wonder if the dad was depressed. I wonder if he knew he was depressed.

It fell to me to write Rick's obituary for the newspaper, my next published work after the book that killed him. Here's the first part of what I came up with after a week of procrastination, resentment, and forgetfulness:

MOE, RICHARD JUEL Born August 24, 1962, in Tacoma, and passed away on April 4, 2007, in San Diego, surrounded by his loved ones. He grew up in the Seattle area and lived most of his adult life in California, for the past 22 years in San Diego. He was a loving family member and a caring friend. Rick had a passionate interest in nature with a deep love for the outdoors and all living creatures. Rick had found sobriety after a long battle with the disease of drug addiction and with mental illness, both of which contributed to his suicide.

My draft included his addiction, his mental illness, and his suicide. I was a reporter, and I felt the need to tell a story about both what his life was like and why his death happened. Otherwise he's just a person who stopped existing for no reason. I wasn't confident that my version would make it through my mother's editing process, and it did not. Instead, the version in *The San Diego Union-Tribune* and *The Seattle Times* was more oblique and full of subtext I didn't want:

MOE, RICHARD JUEL Born August 24, 1962, in Tacoma, and passed away on April 4, 2007, in San Diego, surrounded by his loved ones. He grew up in the Seattle area and lived most of his adult life in California, for the past 22 years in San Diego. He was a loving family member and a caring friend. Rick had a passionate interest in nature with a deep love for the outdoors and all living creatures.

After this edit, the obit is of someone still fairly young who died without explanation. No car crash, no cancer, no information at all. And when that's the case, readers will likely figure it was suicide because they will detect that there is something the family is too ashamed to say. Sometimes an obituary might throw in coded language like "he died suddenly at home" or "she passed away unexpectedly" to let readers know that yes, of course, it was suicide—one of the top causes of death in America—but we are too embarrassed to say.

To me, that omission always has some bad side effects. One

is to give camouflage to the disease itself, because if no one ever talks about it, then everyone is much less likely to detect it. To discuss addiction or depression or other mental illnesses is to provide information about them, including their pathologies and symptoms.

Hiding the truth in an obituary is a tacit admission of guilt, as if to say: "Our son and brother died by suicide, and he is so bad to have done that, and we are so bad to have allowed it, that we cannot even bear to tell you our collective guilty truth." Even in my guilt about having led Rick to suicide, this still rubbed me the wrong way. I have long known that addiction, depression, psychosis, and schizophrenia are all illnesses, not choices. People don't enthusiastically sign up for schizophrenia, and no one is ever proud to be an addict. That's not to say free will doesn't exist or people with problems have zero responsibility for their actions—I believe it does and they do—but don't blame people with hundred-pound shoes for not running fast or for wanting to drop out of the race altogether. Help them get those awful shoes off.

I wanted to name the reasons he died. It's like if there's a serial killer named Kevin running around and Kevin kills your brother, you want to make it known to everyone that "Hey! Kevin is at it again! He killed my brother! Kevin did! It's horrible, but let's at least use this information to let everyone know that Kevin is out there killing people so STAY AWAY FROM KEVIN!" Instead, everyone acts like it's an embarrassment to be killed by Kevin. In fact, Kevin is the one who should be embarrassed that he keeps killing people. Shame on Kevin!

The disagreement over the obituary (on which I caved right away) was my first glimmer of "Hey, maybe I didn't kill Rick. Maybe it was Rick who did that." I was still pretty sure that I had at least contributed to his death, but I could now recognize this perspective as an extrapolation and not a central truth. It was the same thing everyone had been telling me, but I hadn't listened. The thought didn't take up residence in my brain, just rolled by in a convertible, briefly waved, and sped on down the road, but I had seen it.

Metteline flew in from Norway. Jill's mom, Susie, came in from Chicago to watch our kids, and soon a delegation of us traveled from Seattle to San Diego, this time under nonemergency circumstances. It was Mom, Metteline, Lisbet and Mark, and Jill and me. Mom had arranged for all of us to stay at the same hotel we had stayed in the last time. It was a known quantity for her, and even though it meant living inside the recent trauma, I went along with it. At least Jill was with me this time, and we had a different room.

We were there for the first of two services to be conducted for Rick, this one for his San Diego friends and community. Without a service to organize, our family was left with time on our hands in San Diego, which was considerably sunnier and warmer than Seattle or Norway in April. So out we all went out to . . . enjoy . . . our time . . . in San Diego?

Breakfast was at the hotel, but lunch and dinner were at the kind of spacious restaurants where one takes one's parents to have well-prepared food devoid of exoticism or menu translation, generally ones found along the waterfront. Lobsters got eaten. We were more reticent when it came to the reason we were all in San Diego, offering brief thoughts about how it was such a shame that we had no idea Rick was going through any of this. Mental illnesses, we told ourselves and each other, were very hard to detect. Mom would periodically bring up the UCLA experimental treatment program Rick had credited with his sobriety. I would ponder aloud why a university based in Los Angeles was getting volunteers from San Diego. Maybe they simply didn't have enough drug addicts in Los Angeles? I still wasn't sure there ever was a UCLA study. I still couldn't believe Rick.

After meals, we would go for walks along the waterfront, including one down to La Jolla Cove. There's a small beach there that is a favorite hangout of sea lions, who lounge and flop about lazily as tourists watch them from a pier or a walkway along the shore. You aren't allowed to walk among them during the six-month "pupping season," but otherwise this is where humans and sea lions can hang out and form friendships and then go surfing or play volleyball or something. When we were there, the area was thick with protesters who wanted much more severe restrictions imposed so that the sea lions never had to deal with people at all. So we were able to enjoy seeing sea lions up close, but the occasion was inextricably tied to feeling bad about it.

The balance between doing something recreational and feeling awful was kind of the theme of the whole San Diego trip. It was good to hang out with my sisters. The last time we had spent any extended time together was when Dad died. Jill and Mark, the spouses present, were both highly skilled at providing company and support while standing about a half step back from the larger unspoken topics.

I tried to stay engaged with everything being talked about. If I retreated from the moment to return to my mind, I heard, "WHAT THE FUCK ARE WE DOING ENJOYING A GOD-DAMN LOBSTER? HE REACHED OUT FOR YEARS AND I SWATTED HIM AWAY! INSTEAD I WROTE A BOOK IN-STRUCTING HIM HOW TO DIE! AND NOW WHAT ARE WE GOING TO DO?! GO GET ICE CREAM?!"

We did. We went and got ice cream and strolled through the park, as if this were a destination wedding.

The little pills Dr. Kovar had given me weren't doing all that much. They were a garden hose against a forest fire. All the symptoms were back and more powerful than ever. I wanted to retreat but forced myself not to. I was boiling with anger, at Rick, at myself, at the friendly veneer we all insisted on maintaining, but I kept it locked up as best I could. I wanted to sleep all the time but strolled through parks instead, eating a fucking mint chip cone.

The VFW hall where the service was held was spare but not unfriendly. It was a place where large men laugh and hug and drink and have heart attacks. The service had attracted around eighty people, most of whom looked like they had gone through a lot more living than their calendar ages might have indicated. A fair number of smokers outside, more than a few coffee drinkers inside. It was a sobriety crowd, and man, were they huggers. One by one, strangers would approach me, identify their connection to Rick, and pull me into their bearlike torsos. "I'm sorry," they said. "I loved him so much. He was a great man."

I had met some of the mourners during that hazy night at the hospital. I couldn't remember most of their names. For Rick's friends, the loss was immediate. The guy next to them in the truck was gone forever. The guy working the other phone was gone. The soft-spoken, slyly hilarious guy with the perpetually slightly haunted look was never going to be there again. I mourned for them. And I was jealous. They had spent years of casual time with Rick.

After Rick died, I'd asked a lot of questions of anyone I could find and tried not to sound like a pushy reporter in doing so. Rick had apparently been to a doctor who had recommended he get a lot more aggressive about treating his mental health problems and consider going to an inpatient facility to treat a brain that had been through a lot. Instead of getting help, though, Rick felt ashamed, as if he had let everyone down by being mentally ill. As if he had chosen it.

Many people got up to talk about Rick at the service. His sense of humor kept coming up, the jokes he told and pranks he pulled that you wouldn't even put together for another few days, only to find him smirking when your brain finally caught up to his. None of the sobriety friends seemed particularly shocked by his death. Suicide was nothing new to them. Rick was a beloved army buddy who had fallen in combat during war.

The guy he was supposed to drive with on the day he died was most shaken. Rick had called in sick, and it had struck his co-worker as troubling. He had been trying to reach Rick that whole day to check in, leaving messages, calling people they both knew to find out if they had heard from Rick, all the while doing the two-person runs and deliveries on his own. It wasn't until much later in the day, near the end of the shift, that he learned what had happened. He offered a story about the two of them driving together one day and Rick spotting an injured bird along the freeway and insisting on pulling over. Rick wrapped the bird, might have been a crow, snugly in an old T-shirt and gave this guy directions, which Rick knew by heart, to the wild animal rescue place. "He did that kind of stuff a lot," the guy said, earning some laughs and nods from the rest of the assembly. This, apparently, was classic Rick. Saving addicts, saving birds. We all thought about the lifesaving he did, and then our minds returned to why we were in this room.

Other speakers talked about the labor Rick put in to try to fix himself. Gambling had become a problem for him after he was off drugs, we were told. He needed to get that high somewhere. Apparently Rick had done pretty well at the casinos, so it wasn't the financial losses that worried him, just the dependency on the rush he got. To address it, Rick banned himself from all the casinos, which is a thing you can do. You go there, get your picture taken, and sign something that says you're not allowed to gamble there and will be kicked out if you show up.

Being the noisy one in the family, the professional talker, it fell to me to represent the family of origin at the mic. I spoke extemporaneously and told stories about the roughhouse pranks we had played on each other. I told about the M-80 firecracker that he lobbed onto the deck when I was out there reading in the sunshine. I mentioned the revenge I got by hiding in his car at 6 a.m. when he came out to drive to his roofing job, then grabbing him around his chest, necessitating his silently walking around the backyard for ten minutes to shake that one off. They were good stories, and I know how to talk in front of a group.

It felt like being on the radio or doing standup. Like giving a wedding toast. If I'd spoken from the heart, it would have just been screaming and maybe throwing some chairs.

I wasn't telling the truth about how I felt; I was merely slipping into a skill I had, one that let me talk and work the room and make the audience happy. As if this were a gig and not my brother's memorial. I slunk back to my seat furious at myself for acting like everything was alright. It wasn't even close to alright.

My storehouse of anger, however, was not entirely self-directed. I was also furious at Rick. Everyone he left behind would have to carry this horror and confusion forever. Not just me and my sisters and our mother but also his daughter, who was still two months from being born. She's going to learn that her father died by his own hand before ever meeting her. She's going to need to live with that forever. She's going to need to cope with that and find certainty in the truth that it wasn't her fault. I was angry on behalf of Kyndra, who was left to manage that issue for their daughter. Months later, Mom would tell me that I had to let go of my anger. I told her no, I wasn't going to let go because I wasn't done with it yet. I was still using it.

In Seattle, we held Rick's memorial at Lisbet's church, University Congregational United Church of Christ. Jill and I loved our pastor at our own United Church of Christ in West Seattle, a blunt-talking transplanted East Coaster named Diane. Diane was more about being good to people than trying to save our souls. I told her at one point that I didn't think I should even be going to church because I was pretty sure I didn't believe in any kind of Christian God. She shrugged and said that wasn't a deal breaker.

I invited Diane to accompany the family on the boat to scatter Rick's ashes on Puget Sound. It gave Jill and me a little strength to have someone we knew along, someone who could be direct in a way Norwegian Americans could never hope to achieve. It was Mom's idea to scatter the ashes in the Sound, just as we had done with Dad. She even set up the same deal with the same boat and crew we had sailed with not quite eight years before. Another dead male member of the family, let's dump him in the water, and now we have a pattern. At this point and forevermore, I saw Puget Sound as a family burial plot and could easily visualize being dumped in there myself one day. I did not wish for this fate, just viewed it as a grim inevitability.

On the ship's manifest would be the crew, Mom, Lisbet, Mark, Metteline, Pastor Diane, Jill, and me. No kids. We got to the marina, and Metteline opened the hatchback of the car to retrieve the box of ashes. "Is there anything worse than the word 'cremains'?" I asked Lisbet quietly. "It's this weird pun right at the worst time."

Lisbet nodded. "Plus it sounds a little like Craisins."

Rick would give us permission to make these jokes. He'd encourage it. I mean, if he hadn't been a pile of cremains. As it was, he didn't say much about it one way or the other.

For reasons I've never been able to deduce, Mom asked Metteline, "Is the box heavy?"

And with a setup like that Metteline had no choice. "Well," she offered, "he ain't heavy . . ." And let it hang there. We all felt just as devastated as before, just as devastated as we would feel for the rest of our lives, but we had to laugh as she finished up, a little sheepishly, with "he's my brother."

A lot of things got said that day. I would imagine, anyway. The only thing I remember verbatim was Diane saying, "We shouldn't be here." She then elaborated on the larger point that there's a unique pain that comes with the loss of someone who died before they were really supposed to, and who died by their own hand. We needed to recognize that it feels wrong because it is wrong. It's not the way the world should work. It's unjust and dissonant. It helped to hear it out loud. *We shouldn't be here*.

I don't remember anything else that was said. Oh! Wait! Yes, I do! It was a bit windy that day on the water, so during the scattering of ashes, a bit of ash blew up from the water and onto Metteline's jacket. "Rick! Get off me!" she said. Way to go, Metteline. You were two for two that day.

The first thing I noticed at the public service was that several of my co-workers from KUOW were there, even though I had left the station months before and none of them knew Rick. Most of my friends and nearly everyone I worked with did not even know I had a brother, because I never spoke of him. The rest of the guest list was mostly family friends from a long time ago, people who had known Rick before he moved to California, back when he was a charming kid. Annette, who lived down the street from us, was there along with her son Dean, my best friend for years who shot me with a BB gun, and Gene, her husband. Punkin and Buffy, their OCD-inducing dogs, were not available, having both died long ago. The O'Briens, Dagmar and Bob, were there. Rick's old girlfriend Audrey, who was in Lisbet's class in school and who my mom always wished Rick could have stuck with, was there. Rick and Audrey moved to Sacramento together, but she returned to Seattle when Rick went off the rails.

There was a milling-about opportunity before we went in and sat down. One by one, guests made the rounds to Mom, Metteline, Lisbet, and me. One by one, they said how sorry they were and one by one I resisted the urge to suddenly look confused and say, "Sorry? Oh my God, did you kill him?! And all this time we thought it was suicide! Wow! There's been a big mixup! But I'm glad you're sorry. I think we *all* learned a lesson today." Rick would have approved. But I refrained. Instead, I smiled and thanked them for their kindness.

Then a steady parade of parents' friends from long ago shared sweet memories they had of Rick. They recalled the camping trips and the day trips to Mount Rainier or to the Washington coast. They remembered how clever he was, the funny but always harmless pranks he would play, his creativity, his energy. The stories were always set in an era when Rick was full of possibility, when he was seen as an impish handful and not a kid unable to contain or focus his energy. These mourners, these well-intentioned friends of the family, had understandably not been part of Rick's life, so all they recalled was the boy they'd once known.

Still, I thought at the time, that wasn't who Rick was. That was not the Rick who did the thing that brought us all here today. Their version of Rick was the opening chapter or two of a very bleak biography. A history of the Beatles that ends in Hamburg. There's more to the story, family friends. And as all these stories of Rick piled up, I became increasingly frustrated and felt the anger duct open. They were leaving out the parts where Rick fills his body with drugs and where he fills his head with a bullet. They didn't have stories about the Rick who had a shotgun in his bedroom.

After a while, I stopped nodding and saying thank you. "Well, he had a lot of problems," I said. "And for a really long time. He started doing drugs when he was working his first jobs at the airport. He was fifteen or sixteen years old. And addiction runs in our family." Then the person I was talking to would have a sudden need to go talk to someone else.

"Thanks," I'd offer. "I had no idea his mental problems were driving him to this. He must have been suffering for a long time. Rick and I hadn't been very close for the last twenty years or so. He was kind of in and out of homelessness, and he was a drug addict, of course. I will live in regret and guilt forever." Then the conversation would draw to a quick conclusion. Next.

"That's a great story. At the time he killed himself, you know, when he shot himself, I had been mostly out of touch with him. He appeared to have cleaned himself up, but I still wasn't sure whether to believe it. Because, as you say, he was charismatic, and an addict with charisma is dangerous because they will use anyone and tell whatever lies they need to tell to get the substance they need. It's an illness." And off they went.

Audrey, at least, wasn't like everyone else. She was there when Rick started to slide. She had known addicts and seen people get lost. Audrey was shocked when Rick died but, like the sobriety community of San Diego, not at all surprised.

After a little while, I became cynical about the event in general. The only thing anyone had said that made any sense was on the boat earlier in the day when Diane said that we shouldn't be here. This service shouldn't be happening. Rick should have been alive when these friends of my parents died. He should have gone to their services. That's how it's supposed to work. Maybe I should go to his service, but I should be decades older. My kids should go to his service, but not until they were like fifty years old.

Society should have been evolved enough to notice problems he had with hyperactivity when he was a kid. Schools should have noticed his learning disabilities and addressed them, rather than concluding that he was a bad kid and a dumb kid. He shouldn't have accepted that assessment. He shouldn't have thrown away his school career as a result. Those guys at the airport shouldn't have offered drugs to a kid. He shouldn't have accepted the drugs. I should have had more sympathy. I should have called him back. America should run a mental health care system that isn't shameful. America should offer people with mental illnesses like addiction, depression, and psychosis a chance to get help and stay alive.

And yet here we were.

And here was this thing, mental illness, that can be helped simply by talking about it. If Rick had been able to overcome the discrimination against mental illness in our society and in his own mind and talk to more people about what was going on, he could have gotten help, and then we wouldn't be here. That's not all there is to mental illness or suicide, I realize that, but if more people were able to freely speak about mental health, there is no doubt more of them would get help and improve and not die at the Discount Gun Mart.

But what do we as a society choose to do instead? We freely elect to NOT talk about it. That is so goddamn stupid. It's like we could administer the polio vaccine by saying the words "polio vaccine" but elected to not do that. I guess to respect polio's privacy?

Fine, then. I'll be the loudmouth.

According to *THWoD*:
Good Things Happen
When You Talk

It's not like people avoid talking about depression because they're scaredy-cats or weenies or dumb chuckleheads. They have good reasons. Few among us, when we were kids, were taught by the adults in charge to talk about such things. I get that not everyone is in a position to talk about their innermost vulnerabilities on a widely heard podcast or even freely in public. And I understand that as a white heterosexual man with a college degree, I am spreading my message about openness from my castle high atop Privilege Mountain. But I do encourage listeners—and society in general—to open up to people they can trust and people who can help, because I see a clear and consistent benefit being enjoyed by people who have. My decision to become/remain a loudmouth has been pivotal. And this has been the case for a lot of people who have appeared on the show.

Peter Sagal, the host of NPR's *Wait Wait . . . Don't Tell Me!*, a comedy quiz show with infuriating punctuation, often cordially mingles with the audience after taping an episode of that show. He shared his struggles with depression on the *THWoD* podcast, and it became one of our most popular interviews. So now, some *THWoD* listeners approach Peter after *Wait Wait* to tell him the full story of their own struggles.

"The most gratifying response I got is from someone who would not be pleased with my airing familial bits of dirty underwear in public," Peter told me, "and that is my father. My father, who is eighty, comes from a particular population of Jews who do not believe in parading one's problems in front of the goyim, as my grandmother would have put it. The idea being that if you have domestic difficulties or personal problems, you do not talk about them. You do not expose them to the world.

"Time went by after the podcast came out, and my mother called first. And my mother is eighty as well. And she said something to the effect of 'I saw your blog and I just think it was wonderful.'"

Not a big deal, said Peter, because she's been praising him "since my first solid stool."

He was waiting to hear from his father, who is far more reticent. "It was months after the podcast came out, and he called me up and said, 'You know, I listened to that podcast. You came out as a depressed person.' And I said yeah.

"He said, 'You know, there's a family history of this.'

"And then we proceeded to discuss it."

So a thirty-eight-minute podcast episode was enough to pry open a vault of information that had been sealed for decades.

Like Peter, Andy Richter was gracious enough to agree to appear on the show before it launched, which meant he really didn't know what he was getting himself into. Andy appeared on Dax Shepard's podcast, *Armchair Expert*, a couple of years later and shared a story of the response he got from being a loudmouth like me.

"A guy named John Moe has a podcast called *The Hilarious World of Depression*. I did an episode of that, and I don't think I've done anything that's had as much of an effect. One morning, I went to the gym early at Warner Brothers, I'm getting coffee in the commissary, and this guy with this soft southern accent came up to me and was almost crying. He said, 'Just you talking about it made me go to therapy, which I'd felt like I should do for years. My parents were always against it, and they're still against it. But it saved my life.' I'm a fucking clown," Andy concluded, "but just being honest helped somebody."

Gary Gulman's episode of the podcast was one of the more wrenching ones we ever put out, because he was in a really dark place when we recorded it. He was coming off a stretch of professional success and recognition but had found it so difficult to simply function in the world that he had moved back in with his mother. Editing Gary's episode took forever due to all the "ums" and "uhs" he used, unable to summon up words to describe his life.

We talked to him again about a year later, and he was a different guy. He talked clearly and with verve. "I think partially my interview that I did with you, after that I started to get feedback from people who thanked me for talking about depression. And at first I thought, well, it wasn't such a difficult thing, and I appreciate you thanking me, but I don't see any real contribution. But then as I started to talk about it on stage, I would meet people after the show and they would give me this incredible feedback and thank me. So when people say 'that must've been very difficult for you,' it would have been difficult if people had told me to stop or if people had been really negative about it or were uncomfortable with it. But people were so positive and encouraging that it was very easy to talk about. And it was a revelation that I could have such an effect through my comedy. My observational comedy was popular, but the stuff about the depression seems to have reached people on a deeper level, and it's been really satisfying, gratifying, and redemptive in many ways."

Gary Gulman's standup material about depression caught on so well that he turned it into an HBO special produced by Judd Apatow. My point is that if you just talk about depression, you will get to work with Judd Apatow and do an HBO special. It sounds crazy, but I guarantee it works every time.

12

THE HELL WITH THIS,
I'M MOVING TO MINNESOTA

I took to grief and recovery like a duck takes to calculus. I knew all the right things to believe: that Rick's death wasn't my fault, that things would get better, that I wasn't him. But somehow I couldn't always believe them and would become sullen, resentful, short-tempered, and kind of a jerk. Sometimes I would feel nothing, as if I were watching a very dull movie of my own life. Jill would tell me years later that during this period, she would think, "Is this who he is from now on? Is this how it's going to stay? And if so, I'm not sure what my move is here."

Among the moves she made was one I couldn't do for myself: she found a therapist who specializes in people left behind after a suicide. The millstone of Rick's death was dragging me down to very bad places indeed, but I resisted casting that stone off because I felt like I deserved the weight. Plus, again, that ten-dollar copay. "His name is Mark Hoagland," she said, "and he isn't on our insurance, so you'll have to bring your checkbook and pay him for each session."

"I don't know, that's going to be expensive. I'm pretty crazy."

"If we need to, we'll take out a loan. We'll mortgage the house again. We'll make it happen. You need to do this."

She and I don't speak in a lot of absolutes in our marriage, with the understanding that when we do use one, it's a big deal.

Hoagland, therapist number six in my lifetime collection, was soft-spoken but direct. Yes, he said, he'd handled a lot of people in my situation, and no, there's no easy path. "It's not a matter of getting over it," he said. "You'll never get over it. Nothing will ever be the same again. You'll have your life before this happened and your life after. But you can walk through it. Feel the whole thing, know the whole thing, but keep walking."

That was fine and good and made sense. What was dissonant about this experience was that I didn't deserve help or counseling. A murderer is not generally asked how he's coping with the untimely death of his victim. And sure, survivor's guilt is a thing, and I get that, I know a lot of people feel responsible when they really aren't. But here's the thing: I really was. I practically goaded Rick into the Discount Gun Mart. I explained all this to Hoagland and said, "Isn't it a little convenient for me to say that I'm not responsible for his death? Wouldn't I selfishly be making my own future that much easier if I released myself from culpability?"

He shot right back, "Isn't it a little convenient to say you *are* responsible?"

Touché, Mark Hoagland.

He said people get this idea that they're incredibly important in everyone else's life, and it's a kind of fallacy we imagine because we're important in our own life. We're all the lead character in our own movie, having the meet-cute, defeating the supervillain, winning the championship. But in other people's movies, we're character actors. Maybe the best friend, tops, who may contribute to the hero's decision-making process but certainly doesn't have control over it. Most of the time we're not even the best friend, we're a face in a crowd. We're the gas station attendant who has two lines. Hoagland reminded me that, family or not, it's pretty hard to believe I held much sway, given that Rick and I never really talked.

I took in what he said. It felt good. But depression, now supercharged by grief, wouldn't let it go that easily. I thanked Mark Hoagland for his time, wrote him a check, went to many sessions after that and got a lot out of it, but still mumbled to myself, "Yeah, I did kill Rick, though."

Rick had died in the spring of 2007. By spring of 2008, Jill and I had made a different life. My radio show was based in St. Paul, Minnesota, and on a visit there, I started lobbying Peter Clowney to move me out of Seattle. I wanted to help the show and the company more, I told him. I wanted to get away from the traffic, the high cost of living, and the experience of seeing a graveyard every time I looked at Puget Sound. Much like my parents hitting the FUCK THIS reset button in 1960 Norway, Jill and I packed up our stuff, sold the house, and headed midwestward. Contributing to the decision was a new pregnancy, and when you're planning on having three kids, you really can't stay in Seattle. That's too many kids. That's like having cows in your house. You need to move to the Upper Midwest. Thus ended my relationship with the really fantastic therapist number six.

A little over a year after Rick died, we were in the Twin Cities, where a few of our friends lived and none of our family did, meaning few built-in supports when Margaret, our Minnesota baby, our native speaker, arrived on May 1.

Here's what happens when you move across the country just before age forty: you kind of, hmm, I don't know exactly how to put this, die. I died. The me I was in Seattle, in the greater metropolitan region of my youth and lots of adulthood, ceased to be. Sure, there's Facebook and email and, I guess, phone calls.

There are visits, and we've made a few back to Seattle over the years. But really, I killed that version of me and I danced on his grave. Gleefully swung the wrecking ball into that life.

I still went by the same name, had the same body and the same chronic mental illnesses, and rooted for the Seattle Mariners as best I could. But the context of who I was in Seattle—the home, the neighborhood, the nearby friends and family, the workplace—that was gone. The weather was different, the TV networks were all on different channels, and the precipitation had turned from liquid to crystalline. When I was ten, my parents had decided to move us all to Boston, where my dad had been offered a job, but they backed out at the last minute. I didn't find out about any of this until I was fourteen and became fascinated by the life that could have been. Would I have had the same problems? Different ones? Would I still have been me?

In Seattle, there were always plenty of reminders of the worst parts of who I was and what I'd been through. As saddies, we tend to look for those totems and readily find them. A mention of Federal Way on the news brings up memories of all that terrified anger and all those crying jags. A drive through Ballard to see my mom includes a glance at the coffee shop where I spoke to Rick for the last time.

Now that was all gone.

When a depressed person is kept busy and occupied, the symptoms of depression can fade out of the picture for a while. It's not the same thing as being cured, not at all; it's just that the brain is too busy making sense of the current stimulus and making decisions around it to spend the usual time examining (and steadily eroding) itself. Soon after the monumental move and the arrival of the baby, we bought a house in St. Paul. This happened right around the time I was promoted from reporter to host of *Weekend America*. And all THAT happened right as my new home of St. Paul was hosting the Republican National Convention, the one featuring the Bambi-on-ice-style debut of Sarah Palin on the national stage. From there, it was on to the economic near-collapse of America and the presidential election soon after.

Through all this, Kate, our middle child, started kindergarten, Charlie started second grade, and Margaret was a baby. I think Jill and I may have slept at some point, but looking back I can't be certain.

It wasn't all that long, just a few months, before a lot of the stress, the preoccupation that kept my mind from crashing with depression, seemed to lift. The more dramatic and visible effects of the economic crisis passed, Barack Obama was elected, and *Weekend America* was canceled. The show was expensive and the crash dried up a lot of the corporate support.

As the show ended, Peter told me that the number of stations carrying it had been going up with me as host, and the ratings had been steadily climbing. The CEO of the company came to my office and apologized that this had to happen, hoping I would not get discouraged. The executive under him took me to lunch and vowed to create and develop a new show for me to host, urging me not to leave the company out of frustration. I wasn't going to leave, of course; I had just bought a house and welcomed a baby. But after all these people above me had made great efforts to say I was good and valuable, of course what I felt was bad and worthless. The show had been on me, and I failed and was a bad person.

These thoughts, these bleak distortions, came as a kind of dark relief. When good things fall to pieces, it validates the depressed person's mind. "See? Everything IS terrible. I was right all along!"

Now I was in a netherworld of coming up with new programming ideas and beginning the long process of trying to convert them into reality. I had almost no meetings on the calendar, plenty of time to just think. Mentally healthy people can intuitively regulate the time they spend in self-contemplation and balance it with time they spend just living. Normies such as these might do some yoga or meditation, possibly make lists of goals, read the occasional self-help book, but then they'll hang out with friends drinking Chablis at Olive Garden or seeing a Bradley Cooper movie. Look, man, I don't really know how the normies spend their time. They don't have to worry about getting trapped in their own worst thoughts or running from those thoughts for years at a time; they parry away those thoughts with languid élan. It's an instinct for the normies, like being able to show up to parties.

Saddies, on the other hand, have a tendency to seize upon any idle moment to leap into our own brains, use depression to beat ourselves up about the past, use anxiety to beat ourselves up about the future, and generally berate ourselves for sucking.

It was time to give therapy another chance.

I've been with Jill since 1991, the George H. W. Bush administration, so although I don't recall much of what dating is, I'm told looking for a therapist is kind of similar. You check someone out online, set something up, and then see if there's any chemistry. So I hit the therapist dating scene, hopeful but cautious. By this point, I wasn't anywhere near sure how to deal with my brain, my memories, my guilt, the low but constant thrum of utter despair, but at least I knew what I was up against. At the initial intake sessions with therapists, I'd give a rundown on my pathology. It was the stuff about my book's connection to Rick's suicide that always seemed to take the air out of their sails.

"Wow," the inevitably bearded therapists would say, "okay." I stumped them. I could spin a good narrative about what I'd been through because, come on, I'm a public radio guy. I understand the arc of a good anecdote. And I generally ended up giving the story something of a happy ending. Something like, "But you know, life goes on. I've been through some things, but all I can do is move forward." Flash a small smile, believable and still a bit grim, and that was that.

There were no sparks, no second date/appointment arranged with any of the therapists I saw. "I'll call you," I would say on my way out the door, and subsequently throw away the business card I'd just been given. We'll call these people therapists seven through ten. I couldn't remember them if they were standing in front of me. Not getting any help there. Maybe change up my approach? Try the support group route?

After some Googling, I ran across group meetings for survivors of suicide and picked one relatively nearby. It was a hot weeknight, so I stopped at the convenience store before the meeting and bought a huge bottle of Gatorade, huge being the only size available. Then I followed the directions north on the freeway to the suburb of White Bear Lake and to the prescribed address. It was a funeral home. Yep! This support group for survivors of suicide had been holding regular meetings for some time in a funeral home. For me, I don't know, it didn't give me that "life goes on" vibe. More of a "life stops right here at this address and in those boxes over there" vibe. But okay, let's keep an open mind.

I was the youngest by at least fifteen years at this meeting and one of very few guys. It was mostly elderly Minnesota women. Women are more likely to attempt suicide in America, but men are much more likely to succeed at it because they use guns. People summarized why they were there as a means of introduction, most of us giving brief summaries of our most horrible days. Jan, the oldest woman of the bunch, didn't really cotton to the brevity concept, so she just dove right in with her whole story. It seems Jan had been a little worried about her husband for a while; he was quieter than normal (kind of a hard distinction to make among elderly Minnesotan men), but nothing to raise any major alarms. Then one night, and this was a few months ago, she was on the phone and her husband walked by. He asked if that was her sister she was talking to, she said yes, and he said, oh, okay, tell her hello for me. Jan did, and he walked out to the garage. A moment later she heard a gunshot.

Jan hung up the phone, went to the garage, and found him there, dead, part of his head gone. She called her son, and he called the police, and then she sat in her house waiting for them both to come. The police got there first, asked Jan some questions, and then asked her to sit in the back of the police car, which, they explained, is standard procedure in situations like that.

"I don't know why they did that," Jan told the group. "I didn't shoot him. I wouldn't do something like that." Jan wasn't particularly interested in talking about her grief or sorrow; to her the important part was her confusion and disorientation, the story of an elderly woman who didn't know why these things were happening. Her husband's final words were "tell her hello for me"? And then he's dead? And then she's in a police car?

We commonly associate certain feelings with losing someone to suicide: pain, guilt, grief, anger, sadness. Confusion isn't mentioned nearly as often as it should be. "How could this person be dead, through their own deliberate action, when I never knew that was a possibility?" Because if you never see something that huge coming, that means you live in a world where anyone you know might do the same thing, and then you're adding fear— terror, really—to the confusion. You were going about your day, and then boom, this happens, so maybe you've had the universe figured wrong the whole time.

Back home that night, I was rattled by how ordinary, how

mundane, Jan's story was. It took place in a world, the real world, the noncinematic world, where death doesn't clearly foreshadow, doesn't dress in a costume, and doesn't have a swell of ominous music. Where you don't get foreshadowing. The banality of it was what was terrifying. Death walks by asking about your sister. I had finished off that whole bottle of Gatorade but had failed to take into account that Gatorade is packed with sugar, so when I tried to go to sleep that night, it was difficult. I stayed up until four, mostly staring at the ceiling and thinking about Jan and her husband. It was the last funeral-home support group meeting I would attend.

I looked for another group that was closer to my house, that fit my schedule, and that wasn't at a funeral home. The only one fitting those criteria met at the St. Paul Police Eastern District Station in St. Paul. Attending that one meant passing security checkpoints and guns, guns, guns everywhere. Apparently it was impossible for area facilitators to hold meetings of this nature in places that did not reek of death and violence. Would a coffee shop's back room be so hard to book?

This was a group with more age and gender diversity. It was also enormous. Suicide is an endlessly renewable resource, and rates in the US are climbing, so there are new loads of confused people left behind every day. Once again, everyone went around the room introducing themselves, but this time everyone gave their whole story, abandoning the notion of summarizing. It's probably from working in radio for so long that my producer's brain switches on in situations like that. "If this is a ninety-minute meeting and there are twelve people here, everyone should get seven and a half minutes. Round that down to seven to allow some general housekeeping time. But even better would be three minutes each so we'd have time to actually discuss."

I was about number six and tried to show everyone how it

was done by busting it all out in a tight four minutes before tossing to my neighbor, who proceeded to go on for another ten to twelve. The stories varied: children lost to suicide, fathers, mothers, boyfriends. A few people had lost someone ten years before; others had lost someone the previous month. Some had found the body; others received terrible phone calls. For whatever reason, maybe the Minnesota communication style, no one focused on their emotions all that much. Little to no time was given to how it felt for this to happen or strategies in moving forward. Still, emotion gets through whatever you use to tamp it down, and there were tears and even a few laughs. But above all what came across was, again, confusion over how we came to be in this situation.

The support group experiment hadn't alleviated any guilt or grief or anything else regarding Rick's death, because it had been all anecdote. There was no discussion, no searching, that could lead to real commonality or camaraderie. And it sure didn't help my depression at all. The only real takeaway for me was "You're cursed and lots of other people are also cursed."

I've never been to journalism school. David Candow, a former CBC executive who spent many years traveling around as a consultant to public radio organizations, gave me my only real training. David died in 2014, and I miss him terribly. Among the things he taught me was that the best interviewer in the world was a three-year-old child, because three-year-old kids ask "Why?"

If they don't understand the answer to that question, they'll follow up with "But why?" and continue along those lines until you tell them a truth they can understand or until your spirit breaks. That three-year-old doesn't care whether they are perceived as knowledgeable or educated. It's unimportant that they come across as an expert. They ask in order to learn and understand, and they demand clarity. In my radio work I've found that a simple "Why?" is often the best question you can ask, along with the even shorter "Oh?"

My problem with group support meetings was that there was neither time nor format to ask people follow-up questions. What was the first thing that made you feel better after this suicide happened? Was the person who died close to his or her family? What role did drugs or alcohol play in any of this? What's the best advice someone gave you? What's the best advice you gave yourself?

It didn't seem like so much to ask, to gather with people who had a similarly profound trauma and then help each other, but it continued to elude my grasp. I quit the support group. Meds became the beginning and end of my mental health efforts, pills that weren't making me better but at least stopped me from getting worse. They were the DayQuil of mental illness. All I had to do was wait for the whole deep-seated mental illness and horrible traumatic grief to work itself out OR keep taking the pills until I eventually died of something else. SEE? PROBLEM SOLVED!

Matthew Baldwin, a friend from Seattle, led a project in the summer of 2009 called Infinite Summer. It was an online book club for people who all agreed to finally get around to reading David Foster Wallace's *Infinite Jest*, the 1,079-page bestselling abstract expressionist novel. Matthew was getting essays from various writers about their experiences reading the book.

We were coming up on the one-year anniversary of Wallace's own suicide, and Matthew asked if I'd like to write about how, in light of Rick's suicide, I wouldn't be reading the novel.

Here's part of what I wrote:

I picture every Wallace book I see on a shelf as being soaked in tears. David Foster Wallace and Rick Moe, born just six months apart, were completely different people. I know that, but I have a pretty hard time drawing distinctions sometimes. They both had brains that didn't work in the same way as most other brains. I admired them both in ways that transcended any other admiration I had felt. With Rick, it was, again, the golden glow that older brothers have, on their bikes and skateboards, with their strength and jokes and cars. With Wallace, it was reading some of those *Harper's* essays and experiencing Shea Stadium Beatlemania and a kind of loving fear all at once. Oh, so that's a writer, I thought, sweating, screaming on the inside. As someone who wanted to be a writer, it was incredibly inspiring and absolutely soul crushing. Being a writer in a world that features Wallace would be like playing basketball in a world that has Michael Jordan, only none of us even know how to play basketball and we're all injured toddlers with broken lacrosse equipment.

The exposure I felt when this was up online was a bit nervous-making, but it felt good to finally state some personal truths. Then the comments started racking up, and people were linking to the piece through social media. It went as viral as a suicide piece could go; readers responded with gratitude and their own stories.

I didn't expect this. The piece was merely an accounting of my experiences. And yet people who knew neither me nor Rick related to it, and it seemed to help them.

"Hmm," I thought, "let's make a note of that."

According to *THWoD*:
Therapy Is Neither Good nor Bad,
It's an Adventure

Look, it's an uncertain and chaotic world, and therefore something like talk therapy isn't going to be a fail-safe solution every time. And just as you won't fall in love on every date, you won't necessarily connect with the first therapist you see despite everyone's best intentions.

In season three of our show, we made an episode called "Adventures in Therapy" where we gathered stories from listeners about their great and not-so-great experiences seeking help. We wanted to portray how wonderful good therapy could be, and we wanted to hear about bad therapy situations people had moved on from. We were deluged with responses. Here are some favorites.

> After seeing a couple therapists on and off through student
> health, I finally got sent to a private practice so someone could
> see me for more than six weeks. When I called to make my
> first appointment at the first therapist on my list, the last thing
> she said to me after setting up the appointment was "Oh, on

Thursdays I bring my golden retriever to the office. Is that a problem for you? Let me know and I'll keep her home."

I spent every Thursday for the next eight months sitting on the floor with Skyler as we worked through my general anxiety depression and family issues. And then when my class schedule changed for my last semester, Skyler's schedule changed, too. She started coming on Tuesdays to see me. Skyler wasn't a trained therapy dog, just a goofy golden with a pure heart, very soft fur, and a very amazing therapist as an owner. Seven years later I still haven't found another therapist team as amazing as Missy and Skyler.

—Kat, Atlanta

I went to a therapist after my sister passed away and I was already dealing with depression and I was dealing with grief on top of that. And I really wanted to just go to a therapist to find some coping strategies. I went to a therapist through my employee assistance program and it was this random guy in an office building that smelled like Goodwill. And there was a boom box playing '70s music in this little closet that I guess was supposed to be a reception area. I walked in and there was nothing on his walls except an Elvis clock with just his pelvis going back and forth with the second hand. It was so loud and distracting and when I asked the guy for coping strategies, just ways to kind of get through my workday, he freaked out and he said, "Coping strategies?! I don't think you understand how much you've lost! I don't think you understand how profound this is! I mean every holiday, every Christmas, every Thanksgiving, every Easter, you're going to be thinking about your sister on her birthday! I mean, this is terrible! This is going to affect the rest of your life even on Flag Day!"

Like, he brought up Flag Day, which at the time I didn't even realize was a real holiday. So I left crying, but now every Flag Day I laugh because it's just one more day to grieve on a day I didn't even know existed. So thank you, therapist, for that.

Erika, Boulder, Colorado

[My therapist] had a rocky relationship with her annoying husband, she hated meal prepping, she was in the process of losing a ton of weight. And when I tried to share my frustrations with struggling to lose weight she immediately recommended a doctor to me that would prescribe me weight loss meds instead of actually dealing with any of my emotions. At one point I remember sitting on the couch pouring my heart out about my weight issues and dealing with my own self-worth, when she interrupted me to say, "Oh my gosh I know what you mean. I can't even look at my wedding pictures because of how fat I was. Like seriously how did I have friends back then?" She then proceeded to come sit on the couch next to me and show me all of her Facebook photos of her wedding day, where she continued to berate and belittle herself based on her weight and what she looked like. For over five minutes.

—Crissy, Plano, Texas

When I was in college my cousin and best friend of twenty years was killed in a car accident. I had already been depressed for at least four years and this really kicked me while I was down. I wondered if I wanted to even keep living and felt worthless and insignificant. On the recommendation of a friend, I went to see a therapist on campus and we set up a weekly session. The first meeting went okay but the second just seemed to rehash the first. At the third meeting, I walked into my therapist's office and she gave me a puzzled look and said, "I'm sorry, who are you?"

I said, "Well, I'm Travis, your three o'clock appointment."

She then said, "And what are you here for?"

And I paused for a second and said, "Well, among other things, I've been feeling pretty insignificant." And at that point I felt it was best to just turn around and walk back out. That was several years ago now and I can laugh about it, but at the time knowing that I had been forgotten by the person who was supposed to help me gain some sense of self-worth, that was pretty brutal.

—Travis, Oklahoma City

I stopped seeing my last therapist for a few reasons but one of the main ones is that I never quite felt a human connection because she always kept a really stoic face and tight body posture. I just started with a new therapist and I'm really hopeful about her. On my first visit, she greeted me at her door, and as I followed her into her office I noticed her dress was accidentally tucked up into her underwear. I let her know and we both started laughing. The authenticity and humor from that initial interaction led to a really quick sense of trust and connection, and that lasted throughout the whole session. I'm looking forward to my future visits with her.

Laurel, Seattle

13

THINGS THAT MAKE ME STRONGER

Nothing works for everyone. But for most people with depression, there's something out there that will make a positive difference. It might mean a long and laborious trial-and-error period, and it might also involve a serendipitous discovery in unlikely places. Here are some things outside meds and therapy that work for me.

Dogs

Get a dog! Get two dogs!

Much like having children, it can sometimes feel like you made a horrible mistake bringing dogs into your life, what with the noise and the poo and the expense and the sleep you'll lose and never ever get back. But unlike a child, a dog will almost never crash your car, spill truth about you in a memoir, or go to an expensive liberal arts college. (And if those things do happen, you've got a very clever dog indeed and can exploit it for money.) It's conclusive: dogs are better than children. I would apologize here to my own children, but I'm confident they can construct the same argument in the matter of dogs v. parents. Besides, they never read my books, so who cares.

In our Seattle days Jill and I owned a beagle named Lucky. But after Kate came along, Lucky simply couldn't handle life. Terrified that a new baby would mean no more food for her, she began making every effort, safe or reckless, to acquire it, leaping to countertops, falling off countertops, wedging herself behind the fridge, and anything else she could think of. At one point, she was so determined to get inside a plastic lid–covered container she thought contained food (it did not) that she ended up dislodging her lower jaw, requiring an emergency trip to the vet with a slack-jawed, crazed beagle who somehow regretted nothing. We chose to side with our human children and found Lucky a new home, with a woman who lived alone and loved beagles.

So we had seen how the dog thing could go bad and needed only the mental image of a beagle with a slack, swinging jaw to remind us. In 2009, we had lived in St. Paul for a year, and Charlie, now eight, and Kate, now five, had begun an earnest lobbying process. They acquired library books about dogs, and they would find sections about their preferred breeds and leave the books open to those pages around the house. When we mentioned it was a nice day and they should go outside, they would note how fun it would be to play fetch with a dog if we had one, which they could not help but notice we did not.

The crushing blow came when, at their request, we watched the movie *Hotel for Dogs*, a family movie about a hotel for dogs. Don Cheadle, who also starred in the not similar *Hotel Rwanda*, plays the social worker who ends up running a dog hotel while somehow never being overpowered by what must be a debilitating stench of urine. The kids' tears and lamentations at the end of that movie caused Jill and me to cave.

I cautioned Charlie and Kate that dogs are not toys. "They need a lot of care. Feeding, walks, cleaning up. And it's emotional, too. And one day they die."

"That's not true," said Charlie, scowling at my ignorance. "That's not how dogs work."

"Yeah, of course it is," I replied.

"Dogs don't die the same day you get them," he said. "Usually, at least."

"I said 'one day they die.'"

"Oh!" said Charlie, "I thought you said 'in one day, they die.' Yeah, we know they die, Dad. Everything dies."

"Baby, that's a fact," I said, winging a Bruce Springsteen reference over his head.

Dave was a small, nervous mixed breed who, though only a couple of years old, had been through a few owners already. All the wires were connected wrong inside Dave's brain, and as a result he did a lot of things backward: when I would come home from work, Dave, instead of rushing to greet me and deliver affection, would bark ferociously as if I were a persistent robber who broke in every day at five thirty. Dave did not enjoy the company of other dogs, had no use for toys, and would turn his nose up at treats. On occasion, he would get a used corncob, fall in love with it, and growl at anyone who came near. Playfully tossed tennis balls bounced off his head and he did not blink.

But in calm moments, Dave would cuddle, and every night he would sleep on Charlie's bed. Through the social pitfalls and challenges of Charlie's childhood, Dave was a reliable friend, asking nothing in return, just wanting to be there. Dave found the person in the family who needed him the most, as dogs usually do, and did his job. He also pooped on the floor quite a lot, which was not his job. Mixed performance reviews.

Many years later, when my radio/stage show, *Wits*, was canceled and I was hitting a nasty wall of depression, we decided to get another dog, maybe this time a dog that did, you know, dog things. Played. Ran. We loved Dave, but as he got older he was more like a screwed-up cat than a dog. Plus, getting a dog is a better response to a midlife crisis than buying a sports car or having an affair, and somewhat cheaper.

Into our life came Sally, a five-month-old black Lab–pointer mix from the Humane Society. She loved Dave right away and tried to engage him in play almost constantly. Dave never saw the point of it or intellectually grasped exactly how play works. Nevertheless, Sally persisted, forming a dynamic not unlike Sponge-Bob SquarePants and his neighbor Squidward. We often took the dogs to Crosby Farm Park down by the Mississippi River, where they could go off leash and run through the brush and where Sally could swim while Dave stared at her not knowing how or why someone would do that. Sally's favorite game to play at the park was to jump right over Dave. This was Dave's least favorite game, and he would bark and growl. That made Sally love it more because she had at last gotten him to engage in some way.

In June of 2017, on a walk through the park, Sally heard something in the brush and dove in to investigate. Obscured by the thick shrubs and trees, we heard the sound of an altercation and, oddly, the gobble of a turkey. At that sound, Dave rushed in to save Sally. A moment passed and Sally came bounding out, happy as could be. Dave did not. We called him once, which was all it ever took, and he did not return.

We went into the brush after him and called him some more; nothing. Went to the exact spot where he had gone; nothing there. Spent the next hour searching but no luck. It's not unusual for dogs to disappear, but they're usually found unharmed.

Over the next several months we tried family searches, cooking stinky meat near the spot he went missing, forty friends plus strangers from Twitter in a concentrated search, employing a volunteer dog search organization who provided us a dedicated case worker who was tireless in her efforts, food and water stations in front of trail cameras we set up, and two separate pet psychics. Months went by. Dogs would be spotted here and there, some of them in shelters; we would investigate, but it was never Dave.

I had lost dogs to cars when I was a kid, I had lost them to disease, and it's a horrible, horrible experience. For my family, this was worse. We started to lose hope, but logically speaking we could not regard Dave as dead, since we really didn't know. At the same time, we couldn't reasonably expect him to be alive, especially when a Minnesota winter came through. He was Schrödinger's dog, neither/both alive/dead.

A few months after Dave vanished, I took Charlie, then a high school junior, to look at colleges, putting us together in the car with nothing to do but talk. Along the way Charlie ended his months-long stoicism and broke down in tears. "He was my friend when I had no friends," he said. "He always liked me no matter what."

It wouldn't be until the following summer, over a year after Dave's disappearance, that we all came to accept that something must have got him out there. Many, many tears were shed and will continue to be. The stress of not knowing was terrible; the knowledge that we'll never know is almost as hard. Maybe a coyote hurt him or killed him. Maybe the rather large hawks or eagles that lived nearby played a part. I simply can't believe a turkey killed Dave, because that is too weird even for Dave. I theorize that because things were so backward for Dave, some instinct kicked the wrong way and a bad situation got worse.

When I was in that car with Charlie, when he was finally letting the pain out, I scrambled to think of words of comfort.

"All Dave wanted," I told Charlie, "was to get into your heart and get you into his. He wanted to put love in your heart and let you have that feeling, that knowledge, that warm wonderful certainty of a connection. And he gave you that, right?"

He had, Charlie agreed.

"And it's still there. And it hurts like crazy right now, but it's love and it's good. A dog comes to a person or a family as an ambassador of love. And we put up with all the barking and the floor poo because of that love. Once that love is established, the rest of that dog's life is a party to celebrate the mission being accomplished. And as Prince tell us, parties aren't meant to last."

Yeah, that was a stretch, but Prince is the primary prophet of Minnesota, so worth a shot. I continued.

"We never get enough time with anyone we love, especially dogs, because of biology. I wish we had more time with Dave, but I know that love is still there and always will be."

"That helps," said Charlie. "Thanks, Dad."

After Dave disappeared, Sally was out of sorts. Not sad, really, but nervous. Every night at around nine, she would find me and more or less demand to be held and petted. It was a ritual that came to be known as Reassurance o'Clock. After a few months, we decided to get another dog for Sally. Sally was our dog, and we'd get Sally a dog of her own.

At the Humane Society we met Brenda, a blond mutt of no recognizable breed, rescued from Alabama. In the little visitation room, Brenda timidly went from family member to family member, demonstrating hesitant affection and allowing herself to be petted. "What a nice mellow dog," Jill said, a bit surprised. We adopted her but unanimously agreed that "Brenda" sounded more like a junior high science teacher than a dog, and we renamed her Maisy.

Whereas Brenda had been polite and timid, Maisy, after we

brought her home, was bonkers—tons of energy, always wanting to play-wrestle with Sally, who was completely down for that
kind of roughhousing, and enjoying toys with a feral, growling,
presumably Alabaman intensity. No dog could be less like Dave
than Maisy, except in one crucial area.

Maisy fell in love with Charlie. Not to sleep on his bed and
provide gentle comfort but to play, play, play. While everyone in
the family had grown weary of Maisy's favorite game, Puppy
Wants to Bite You but Doesn't Understand When to Stop, Charlie loved it. He thought her default demeanor—a kind of genial
toothy nihilism—was hilarious. Dave's thing had been to be a
kind of anti-dog, while Maisy's shtick was to be the doggiest dog
of all dogs. Maisy would hop up on Charlie's bed, mouth agape,
teeth bared, while he was at his desk working on homework, and
she wouldn't quit giving noisy clues until he agreed to engage in
the kind of mock combat that is, at heart, both a dog playing and
a dog for real biting you. Maisy taught Charlie to keep loving dogs.

Dogs don't worry about the past or future. No depression,
no anxiety. Right there, that gives dogs role model status. While
we mustn't emulate a dog's "present only" approach to life (our
careers, families, and homes would fall apart), we can still see it
as heroic.

I don't believe it's possible or even advisable for a human to
love another human as demonstrably as nearly any dog loves
almost all humans. I mean, you can't go knocking people down
like that and licking them all over while whimpering; it's im-
polite. But it is useful for a human to see such regular demon-
strations of what love looks like. For depressed folks, it is also a
reminder that it is indeed possible to feel things, and feel them
profoundly. Even Dave, when barking his head off at me, would
always be wagging his tail, so I knew what he meant even if he
never knew what he meant.

Dogs are also highly effective at ratcheting down humans' sense of self-importance. "You and me," say dogs, "are both mammals. We eat, we poop; we run around; we like to sleep in soft places; we enjoy toys although we define them differently." Spend any time with a dog and you realize that you have quite a bit in common on a basic survival level. I read somewhere that dogs don't really give much thought to the idea of species distinction and that the reason they think people are so great is because they see us as exceptionally clever dogs.

"Check out *these* dogs," dogs think. "They walk on two legs and can reach things. They can open the fridge and take out meat and cheese, and even though they don't eat it all right away—still don't get that, doesn't add up, not sure I'm even impressed, just baffled—the point is they can do it. I want to hang out with these *amazing large hairless dogs*."

Depressed people who can comfortably house and take care of a dog should really consider adopting one. Or maybe two. One dog is an ongoing abstract monologue, but two is a bizarre farce.

Bands

Everyone in the world should join a band. If you cannot find a band to join, the government should assign you one. If you don't wish to join a band, you should join a band anyway. Don't listen to yourself, listen to me, because it's good and right. This way, everyone is in a band and we're all much better off.

But John, you say, I have no musical ability or talent. It doesn't matter. Neither do I, and I've been in bands for decades. There are no excuses. I've thought this through. It can work.

I've idolized rock stars ever since I was first made aware of them. When I was five, Metteline explained the Beatles and taught me their names and archetypes—Paul/cute, George/quiet, Ringo/funny, John/deep. "The Beatles are my favorite band," I announced, and carried that knowledge around for months. It made me feel in touch with a greater world beyond our house. My favorite song of theirs was "Uncle Albert/Admiral Halsey," which was, unbeknownst to me, from Paul's second solo album.

It was a brief honeymoon of fandom before Metteline noticed my persistent use of the present tense.

"You know they broke up, right?" she asked. I was crushed. How could they do such a thing? I had never heard any of their music.

In fourth grade, I felt ready to open my heart again to new bands. *Rumours* by Fleetwood Mac was the hottest album on the charts, and I received the vinyl LP for my birthday. The album is a masterpiece, of course, but what really got me hooked was that it was the only album I owned that did not feature cartoon animals on the front. It was mature. *Rumours* was recorded when the band members were going through a series of hookups and breakups, and they channeled all that into some brilliant songs that are, by turns, wistful, bitter, angry, perplexed, hopeful, and despairing. I understood none of this. But I could tell something was going on with all those voices. Still one of my favorite albums. And Stevie Nicks ignited certain tinglings.

Over time, my fascination with musicians grew. Some bands seemed friendly: Bee Gees, Men at Work, Van Halen. Others seemed neutral but a bit troubling: Queen, the Who, Led Zeppelin, the Police. And some scared the hell out of me: KISS (who struck me as bossy), AC/DC (seem to enjoy Satan), and, oddly, Elton John. His weird nasal tonality and outrageous costumes made me feel like he existed outside the codes of society. Plus he plays piano?! Elton was overdue to get in trouble somehow, to get yelled at.

But one thing all bands and artists had in common was that they played concerts. They all got up on stage, strutted around, and showed off, and not only did no one tell them to simmer down, people loved it. People paid good money just to be in the room to watch them show off and then screamed with approval about it. Rock stars, I observed, received unconditional love and approval, even Peter Criss when he goes home from the concert, still in his cat makeup, and talks to his family, who are also in cat makeup. And their cat, who wears human makeup. So much love in that family, I surmised.

Of course I wanted to be a rock star! Of course I did. But there was a problem: no musical talent. A fifth-grade foray into learning the French horn resulted in so much stress about my lack of progress that I developed searing stomach pains that were diagnosed as the beginning of an ulcer.

When I first moved to Seattle, I lived for a time in a duplex near Green Lake with Sean, my old good-looking pal from high school, and Joe, who I knew from grad school in New Jersey. Some friends were putting together a series of backyard theater performances under the name Beer Theater (you get the idea), and the three of us decided to play some songs, using Joe's guitar, some pots and pans, harmonicas, and our car keys as instruments. We named ourselves Free Range Chickens, after an item Sean and I spotted at the grocery store.

Free Range Chickens' first gig consisted of "Willin'" by Little Feat and "I Know You Rider" by the Grateful Dead, plus a fair number of jokes and gags. It was well received, and I came off the stage exhilarated. I had sung and the audience hadn't hated it. This led to invitations to play at various other variety / cabaret performances around town and a silent thrill that maybe I was in a band now? I was a . . . band guy?

My days were being spent in the offices of a downtown law

firm that had gone out of business, where I was part of a small crew sorting and mostly discarding decades' worth of files. Randy, the only remaining full-time employee of the firm, was sporadic in his attendance and slack in his supervision. We got along and he played the bass, so I invited him to a practice. Scott, a close friend from college, played drums, and I roped him in as well, making us a five-piece.

And I felt like I was in a dream. With one guy from each of the four phases of my life—childhood, college, grad school, and real world—a rock band had been formed. It's hard for me to know if we were any good, since depression brain tells you you're lousy all the time, plus we reflexively called ourselves bad because if you do that, you preempt other people who might say it. It's musical vaccination. This isn't to say we were not bad, mind you—I suspect we were—but you can't count on a view you see through a cognitive-distortion prism.

Jill's friend Ethel had taught her sewing when she was a kid, and Jill had a knack for big showy Halloween costumes. She asked if she could make us all chicken outfits for whenever the next show was. Feathery yellow hoods, she proposed, along with bib/poncho things likewise decked out in feathers. "Something easy," Jill said, "that you can slip on and off." To my surprise, everyone supported the idea.

A week before Christmas in 1994, I got a call from the people who ran the place where we sometimes rented rehearsal space. A band had canceled for a December 26 show at the Lake Union Pub, the dive-iest punk bar in town. Our pay would be beer. The Lake Union Pub wasn't known for actual violence, just for loud angry obscure music and fans who danced by slamming into each other. "So we have to decide," I said at the next practice, "if we want the gig, and if so, if we wear the suits."

By then, the whole band was fiercely loyal to the suits and

the "just kidding" vibe they projected. Joe, our oldest member, spoke up. "So what is the absolute worst-case scenario here?" he asked. "That we get chased down the alley in our feathery chicken suits by angry punk rockers. And what a great story that would be if we survive!"

The show was sparsely attended because of Christmas and the refusal of anyone we knew to show up at that bar. We played a spirited set, in costume, for an all-male smattering of leather-clad punkers who stared in disbelief for the first three songs and then proceeded to cheer us on more and more lustily. It was at this show that another side of me emerged. I raced around the room, I rolled around the floor, I was a David Lee Roth/chicken hybrid. I didn't understand what was happening to me, but I didn't worry about it. I introduced myself on stage that night as Little Jackie Chicken.

I was out of my head. I wasn't thinking; I was in the moment, and the moment was good. It was different than acting because instead of playing my perfectly calibrated part, I was doing what occurred to me on the spot. It was a vacation from my head. All I had to do was sing to punk rockers while dressed as a chicken. A bargain!

"Hey, man," said a smiling, tattooed, green-haired attendee afterward, "usually I'm sore from slamming at these shows, but now I'm sore from laughing."

The band stayed together another six years, bassists coming and going, our onetime sound guy, Steve, showing up for a rehearsal with his guitar and joining the band. We made a demo. We got better. Weird Al Yankovic accidentally saw us play once and said he enjoyed it. We may have actually been good. But the most important thing about the band was that it was a hobby. We didn't try to get famous or even signed to a record label. Every other creative project I had worked on in my life carried a small

seed of "maybe this will make you hit the big time," and therefore included a lot of stress and varying degrees of emotional
lows when the big time was not hit. With Free Range Chickens,
I had hit it as big as I ever really wanted to hit just by going on
stage. Speaking, I think, for the rest of the band, too, I would often say that some people have bowling leagues, some people are
in rec league softball, and I'm in a band. Same purpose.

The band dissolved after family demands increased, Sean
left town, and I stopped getting along with the new bass players. It wasn't fun, so it ended. A few years later, Jill threw me a
surprise thirty-fifth-birthday party that brought the band back
together, in costume, with a bass player I had never met, and
we played a surprise set. Possibly to Jill's dismay, this led to a
re-formation of Free Range Chickens under the name Chicken
Starship ("Starship" being the designated term for when a band
really should break up but doesn't), and we played several more
years, in costume.

When I moved to Minnesota, I assumed the band days were
over. I hit forty, so my presence in a band would be not so much
"a fun lark" as "What is that sad dad doing?" Peter Clowney, the
executive producer who had brought me to Minnesota, was in
a band that had real skill and a degree of ambition. When that
band collapsed, as all bands must and should, he asked me about
trying to make something together. No chicken suits.

Our venture eventually came to include a math professor
friend on bass, and that math professor's math professor friend
on drums. So we had an all-math-professor rhythm section and
public radio creatives on guitar and vocals, which is really the
classic pedigree for any great band. U2, Radiohead, they did the
same thing. We called ourselves Math Emergency after a brief
crisis our bassist had when another mathematician was about to
publish a math paper that threatened to scoop his math paper.

It was more dramatic than I ever thought math was capable of being.

We've played maybe five shows in the last five years. Possibly only four. There is no Little Jackie Chicken in this band, no rolling on the floor. There are rehearsals, though. Nearly every Sunday night we gather in the drummer's basement to play and rehearse songs we've written and to write and arrange new ones. And to drink beer and get away from our families for a couple of hours. As I write this, it's been a year and a half since our last gig, so the guise of "we're rehearsing for our upcoming show" has more or less collapsed.

I no longer seek a lead singer performance to take me out of my head. What I need now, as I get old and rot and die, is to fuse music making with my actual self. With Math Emergency, I employ only as much humor as I might use in regular conversation, and I write songs about identity, marriage, kids, my family, and getting old. I needed to be Little Jackie Chicken for a while, for him to show me how to cut loose, and now I'm okay being me.

So yes: GET IN A BAND!

Videos of Spooky and Possibly Fake Things

When life gets extra difficult, I watch videos about ghosts, Bigfoots, and UFOs on YouTube. It's not that I necessarily believe in the veracity of videos with highly dubious credibility. I rarely do. But I do believe that there's more to the world than what we've proven or observed. I'm a fan of the idea that there might—MIGHT!—be something hidden and wonderful out there.

My dad loved telling ghost stories from the times he went camping with his father in Sweden. In one story, they were driving on a country road at night and kept having to stop because they'd see feet crossing the road in their headlights. My grandfather would get out of the car, confused as to why there were so many people at night in the countryside, and see no one. As the story went, after this happened a few times, he finally saw several pairs of feet stopped and facing the car, at close range. He got out again and saw no people, only the remains of a bridge that had collapsed. As I type this now, I get thoughts like "They never owned a car" and "I know for a fact that when they camped they took the bus" and "What kind of headlights only show you the road at feet level," but at the time the moral of the story was always "GHOSTS ARE REAL" and, to a lesser extent, "DEAD SWEDES ARE CONCERNED ABOUT TRAFFIC SAFETY."

We tended to see ghosts on camping trips in the summer. On a camping trip to Vancouver Island, Canada, we visited an old military fort that had been converted into a park. We were free to roam around the somewhat dilapidated concrete bunkers, but the rooms themselves were locked. One bunker had a grating on the door we could look through, and we saw a faint glowing light that came and went. There was no doubt in my mind that this was a ghost. A rare daytime one.

Later on that same trip, I was walking on the side of the road with Lisbet. The road was on a hill, and a red convertible came down the hill with a smiling bald guy in the passenger seat and NO ONE in the driver's seat. The bald guy smiled and waved at us as we gawked. Who was driving the car? A ghost. That's who. (A few months ago, I suggested to Lisbet that it was probably a British car. I think she was disappointed by this explanation.)

For a depressed kid, a kid who didn't realize he was depressed, a kid who thought he was shamefully weird, the ghost world was a tremendous comfort. As awful as the "real" world could sometimes be, it wasn't the only world out there. There was at least one other world where you got to float around, mess with people (and thus have an advantage over them), and do cool magic things like go through doors. You even got to stay up late at night! And if there was a ghost world, there could be other worlds, too. The existence of ghosts pointed to the existence of more than just this life in my house with this family and these schools and a future where no one would ever marry me or hire me for a job. Also, I loved my family and I kind of dug the idea that once we all died we could either hang out on clouds in heaven or fly around bothering people as ghosts.

Bigfoot offered something similar but smellier and meatier and more immediate. For a kid in the Pacific Northwest, Bigfoot wasn't a legend or a mystery; it/he was a fact. Everyone knew that Bigfoot was native to our part of the country and had been spotted many times and talked about in Native American legend forever. So when a rumor got around in third grade that a Bigfoot had been captured alive, we all believed it without reservation and looked forward to reading about it when it eventually came out in the newspapers.

The '70s were a big time for Footkind. The Six Million Dollar Man fought one on TV, and there was a burst of documentaries produced with rickety cameras and even more rickety journalistic practices. One had a re-creation of a couple's story of Bigfoot pelting their remote wooded cabin with rocks and then ultimately appearing at their door when they opened it. I've watched this on YouTube, and the creature shows up in the fakey, fakey, fake, fakiest mask people have ever made. But it scared me more than anything else I've ever seen on a screen. Because I knew Bigfoot lived in my general vicinity, I went to bed every night for a while convinced he would emerge from the tiny suburban forest patch in the backyard, scale the side of my house, smash through my second-floor window, and beat me up. (Why would he beat you up, John? I have no idea, parenthetical questioner.)

As the years passed, I came to respect and admire Bigfoot

for the same reasons ghosts held such appeal: there is a world beyond that which we know. And I might really be comfortable in this world, in the deep woods, where Bigfoots have a whole society probably, and most likely some buildings. A brain like mine might be okay there and accepted, not to live there, just to visit sometimes. Bigfoot represented hope that there was more to the world than the life I was forced to live.

Now I approach these phenomena more anthropologically, interested in the believers more than the objects of their belief. To hear from the diehard believers is to pry open my own mind and get ever-so-gently triggered into imagining thinly disguised alternate realities and to take tiny vacations, occasionally at my desk at work, from the present and hopefully not lone reality. If there aren't any good Bigfoot or ghost videos surfacing, I'll make do with UFOs or conspiracy theories for a while.

Personally, I tend to favor the YouTube channels that play it straight or at least make an effort to do so. A very serious, somewhat worried-sounding British guy narrates videos on the Top5s channel, featuring titles like "5 Strongest Signs of Aliens & Alien Life" and "5 Creepiest Ghost Sightings Caught on Tape." On the Slapped Ham channel, a different British guy offers up selections such as "10 Creepy Church Ghost Sightings Caught on Camera" and "7 REAL Bigfoot Sightings That Will Make You a Believer." On both channels, the narrators, when faced with a more dubious piece of "proof," will go with the "some say" or "make up your own mind" feints, and I think that's adorable.

None of the footage I've seen on YouTube has made me a believer in ghosts, Bigfoot, UFOs, or anything paranormal. But I remain a big fan of daydreaming about worlds where I might not be gripped with anxious thoughts while trying to commute to work.

14

A TREATMENT I STILL
DON'T FULLY UNDERSTAND
BUT DO APPRECIATE

R ick haunts my Twitter feed.

After I received stronger-than-expected responses when I tweeted about his life and his death, I began an annual tweet-storm about Rick and about depression and mental health. I urged people to get help to treat a treatable illness. I explained that a suicide reverberates and damages the people left behind. I pointed out, stridently, that this is a common illness, and it's treatable and potentially fatal, so do something about it.

The responses were overwhelming. People thanked me for talking about it, which was nice, but they also opened up about loved ones they had lost, and they promised me, a stranger, that they were going to make appointments to try to get better. They wrote to me, months later, about how things were improving in their lives.

Coming forward about my own condition was a different story. I was afraid. If I told the world I was depressed, it seemed pretty likely that my professional opportunities would dry up fast. Who would want to work with me? Who would be able to trust me? Would other employers want to take the chance on a rapidly aging and openly crazy host? At the same time, I simply could not continue to preach that people should open up about mental illness while not doing so myself.

Being a public figure associated with the brand of my employer, I likewise worried that American Public Media, aka Minnesota Public Radio, could take heat and damage from the disclosure. I met with Jen in the HR department and explained that I would like to come forward on Twitter about my depression, to "out" myself, and asked if that would be okay with Minnesota Public Radio. "I think you should," Jen said, "and the company will stand behind you on this. And personally I hope you do, because it's something I've been dealing with for years and I agree with what you say about it."

I took to Twitter. "The truth is, I haven't done all I could do. I haven't been forthcoming. I haven't lied but I haven't told the whole truth. The truth is that I've been living with the disease of depression for many years," I wrote. The positive response came in a tidal wave, people thanking me for being open, coming out of the closet themselves, again vowing to get help. The negatives? No one has ever told me it's a mistake for me to share stuff like this.

I was invited to give speeches at mental health events around town, based on me being on the radio, kind of, but mostly based on tweets. Tweets! "Either I'm really good at talking about this stuff," I thought, "or people are absolutely starving to hear someone talk about it and no one but me is coming forward." Might have been my smoldering good looks, too. You never can tell.

So in the Twitter sense, Rick had been haunting me like a friendly ghost.

After a few years in Minnesota, my professional life could not have been going better. I had helped start an on-stage interview series called *Wits* that morphed into a music and comedy variety show on public radio stations across the country. We taped at the Fitzgerald Theater in St. Paul, home of *A Prairie Home Companion*. In the course of hosting *Wits*, I found myself in situations I'd have never dared dream of: performing sketches with Fred Willard and David Cross and Maria Bamford; being on stage for intimate musical performances by Neko Case and Brandi Carlile and Rufus Wainwright. I couldn't imagine a dreamier dream job.

Putting a show like that together, however, was a whole lot of work and meant a degree of pressure I had never experienced in a professional setting. Besides being host, I was also the head writer, overseeing freelancers and doing a lot of the writing myself, endlessly reworking scripts in hopes that what we brought on stage would be funny and engaging. Putting out twenty to twenty-five new shows a year meant that there was nowhere to test the material before it went in front of an audience, at which point I just had to hope (because there is no science to comedy) that it would get a laugh. If something fell flat, my mind told me, it was because I'm an unfunny person and a bad person and dumb and I've let down the audience and all the other people working on the show. If something wasn't working, it was because I didn't care enough or work hard enough, I told myself.

Although *Wits* toured a little, most of our shows were in St. Paul. This meant constantly trying to come up with performers our producer might be able to talk into flying to Minnesota for not much money in order to appear on a show that was struggling to find a national audience. The guests had to be famous enough to help sell a thousand tickets at the Fitz but obscure enough that they'd be willing to actually do it. A surprisingly narrow band of celebrity. Our invitation list always needed new names.

If Jill and I were trying to relax in the evening and watch a movie, I would be noting who was in it, wondering if they'd be a good guest, could they sell tickets, and would they be willing to fly out. I was constantly pulling the car over while listening to the radio, Shazam-ing the song being played, investigating how famous the musician was and whether they were on tour and already coming to Minnesota. Entertainment had turned to evaluation; distraction had turned to stress.

The depression engine was roaring. "But how can I be having constant bleak despair when I have the dream job of a lifetime?"

Which is a dumb question. Depression doesn't evaluate your career. Depression wants to kill you. "Oh, you got a raise? Oh, you got passed over for promotion? Oh, nothing happened at work? Cool, cool. Whatever. Don't care. Listen, I want to kill you," says depression. The show was a bit of a deal with Satan: get your dream job, become friends with accomplished people you love, soak up fame and adulation, and all it will cost is your happiness and peace of mind. You get all the pizza in the world but pizza will taste like lettuce. Real *Twilight Zone* stuff.

So now I'm rocking my midforties, on meds for the depression but not doing anything to improve my mental health. By this point, I've spent decades essentially stalling, attempting to find ways to put off dealing with this thing. Actual thought from this period: "If I can stop depression from overwhelming me until I die, then I sort of . . . win." The problem with putting it all off until later is that later will one day show up. The stress of the dream job was a little rock hammer that busted a hole in the dam. And that made me remember that I had killed my brother.

Ah yes, we haven't heard about that idea in a while. It had taken some heavy damage after good counseling from Mark Hoagland, but that had been years ago. How horrible was I to live this Minnesota life with a loving family and a successful career when I had given Rick the idea to get a membership at Discount Gun Mart, then go in there and fire a bullet into his head?

How could I live with myself after killing him? How could I even do radio when he had left all those messages about hearing me on the radio, the messages I never returned, the messages I barely even listened to on voicemail before deleting them?

Of course I knew, deep down, that I hadn't killed him. I understood that. But deeper down, of course I knew I *was* guilty. Depression looks for the most horrible option on the menu and selects that every time.

The thing about a traumatic fixated-upon memory is that it is exhausting to the brain. I wasn't just haunted by this memory, I was tired all the time. Ever wonder why saddies can't get out of bed? For many, that's one of the reasons: an obsessive memory simply wears them out.

As if the knowledge weren't enough, my brain offered a constantly looping visual aid: the memory of Rick's body, stretched out and yellowed, bloated beyond recognition from the transfusions, connected to endless tubes and monitors, on an ICU bed in San Diego, just as he was about to die. I saw that body more and more often; it was posted on the backs of my eyelids when I tried to go to sleep at night. And I couldn't go to sleep at night. Insomnia, which runs in the family, raged. I was lucky to get four hours some nights, so I had to stare at that body in bed for hours. Knowing I did it. Reader, I was going—and allow me to use the proper medical term here—nutso.

You can't move to Minnesota and get away from all your problems. Or Seattle. Or New York or Los Angeles or Rome or Melbourne or Mars. Your problems have maps, and they will find you. And when the problems of depression and shame and anxiety and grief and guilt started piling up again, well, friends, I felt so tired. Depression was my oldest companion; it had been with me since before Jill ever came along and was sticking close through every move. I was accepting that.

What I did not wish to accept was a lifelong attachment to that picture of Rick in his final moments. You can't spend all your time in a jump scare. It simply won't do.

Carol was therapist number eleven in my life. I finally had enough therapists to field a theoretical and highly pensive football team. My relationship with Carol was intermittent; she lived way out in the suburbs, so I used her services only when things were trending toward crisis. It was kind of like calling the fire department a lot instead of working hard to put safety measures in your home.

On one visit I was explaining to Carol the obsessive looping recurrence of the horrific image of Rick's body, how I couldn't stop thinking about this real thing I had seen. "Do I have post-traumatic stress disorder?" I asked.

"Well, are you going to work and getting things done? Are you showering and wearing clean clothes?" she asked. I was.

"Are the kids getting to school and getting fed? Are you doing your part to make sure that happens?" Yes.

"It sounds like you're functioning. So I wouldn't call it a disorder at this point. That's all the word 'disorder' really refers to. But you certainly have post-traumatic stress."

"Okay. I guess that's good to know."

"Have you heard of EMDR?" she asked.

"Sort of. I think," I said. "No. What is it?"

She explained that it was a technique to work through traumatic memories, to make the brain do something different when those particular harmful thoughts and visions return to make trouble. The patient recalls a painful or traumatic memory and focuses in on particular aspects of that memory. As that happens, the patient is asked to look in particular directions, signaled by the therapist's hand or a pointer or buzzers in the patient's hands. Through this, the patient can form new associations with that memory. For instance, a victim of a violent crime can replace the terror of that moment with a new association that they are strong and a survivor. Essentially, it's like cleaning a wound so that the body can set about healing itself without irritants and infections, except in this case the wound is mental.

~

I'd hold hand buzzers, little electronic pulsers, and she would talk to me until I was in a very calm and receptive place. This sounded like either the dumbest pile of crazy or the craziest pile of dumb I'd ever heard of. But I figured that worst case, it would make for a good story and I'd be no more miserable than I already was. Best case, I could stop carrying heavy, awful memories that were dragging me down.

To pull off that best case would mean trafficking in some psychotherapy clichés like finding your happy place or resolving mother issues. These are terms dragged out when someone wants to make fun of therapy. In popular thinking, imagining a happy place in order to help your brain is a denial of reality. This is a common way to dismiss mental illness and to dismiss possible ways to address it. This thinking often comes from the same people who believe that the best way to treat depression is to "snap out of it" or "pull yourself up by your bootstraps." These are the same people who will bemoan "political correctness" when asked to treat those different from themselves with at least a minimum of politeness. Their mockery, their eye-rolling, and their scorn are, to my way of thinking, the result of being taught the same discriminatory perspectives shared by the people who raised them.

So these jerks make jokes and roll eyes, and the average person gets a little more hesitant to go to therapy and work hard at it because they've been told that these issues—which might be causing a lot of pain and stunting development—are ridiculous. As that discriminatory mindset further infests society, people might believe that therapy itself is ridiculous and that people who seek it are ridiculous. And then people who need help don't get it.

Getting better is not ridiculous, and using whatever means you can to get there isn't ridiculous either. Imagination, like a thumb, is a tool available to humans, so we should use it. Establishing a peaceful place you can return to with imagination is genuinely beneficial. Most people who are serious about this stuff don't refer to it as a happy place because "happy" isn't really the point here. The point is to establish a sense memory of a place where you are calm and serene enough to conscientiously recalibrate your stormy mind. Maybe you get happy, maybe you don't, doesn't matter.

One of the first things I did in EMDR with Carol was establish where my peaceful place was, a location I'd been to where I felt the most calm and relaxed. This was not difficult. The tiny town of Oceanside, Oregon, is right on the Pacific Ocean. Jill and I have spent at least a dozen vacations there, and it's my favorite place in the world. My exact peaceful location is one specific spot on the beach, looking out on some huge rock formations in the water. It's warm and breezy, and in my imagination I'm holding a Tillamook Brown Cow ice cream cone and my kids are there and somehow being civil to one another.

Carol took me deeper into that place, encouraging me to notice the smells, the sounds, the sensations under my feet. Am I there alone or with other people? What am I wearing? At this point, I was pretty relaxed and, I guess, hypnotized? We established that spot on the beach as a safe place and rehearsed how to return to it in my mind, both during the impending EMDR sessions and in other parts of life.

The goal in my EMDR work was to take what I knew intellectually to be real, that Rick was responsible for his own death, and make it what I actually feel as the primary response whenever I think about how he died. The nightmare trauma image of his body was a problem, yes, but more than that it was a symptom of a larger problem: the irrational responsibility and guilt I had over his death. Carol and I established a three-word phrase to keep in mind: *Rick shot himself.* All the issues over culpability, the long rambling monologues of guilt and self-loathing, led to the factual statement that after everything else he held the gun in his hand and squeezed the trigger.

Yes, but I wrote this thing in my book about gun ranges—Rick shot himself.

There were all these phone calls, and I just turned my back—Rick shot himself.

I could have done so much more—Rick shot himself.

Rick shot himself. Establishing that was the only path to feeling something other than that I also deserved to die.

Now let's get to the hand buzzers. She used gizmos that went by the delightful name "TheraTappers." These were slightly bulbous disks, one for each hand, connected by cable to a box she held, which was used to control the intensity and frequency of the pulses. The pulses and the directed eye movements that follow them guide the memory to a safer and more manageable place, so that the patient doesn't routinely fall into horror when the thought comes up. If you're thinking the TheraTappers sound like Scientology's E-meters and thus scientifically dubious, well, brother, I was right there with you, especially because the equipment didn't look so much "state-of-the-art medical device" as "failed RadioShack home project from 1978." But again, what the hell did I have to lose besides my desperate shrieking?

So with eyes closed and TheraTappers tapping, I set about recalling the sight of Rick's body in that ICU. And as I had done with the safe place on the beach, I recalled all of it. The sounds of hushed personnel, the smell of both disinfectant and grievous bodily injury, where the desks were, the other patients in my peripheral vision. None of these sensations needed to be retrieved so much as let back in, me holding the door for the long-suppressed demons waiting in the lobby outside. With the sense memory came all the feelings of that moment. Whereas back in 2007 shock prevented me from fully experiencing the present, no such shock existed now. I was consumed by the pain of the past. It was awful. Really awful.

From there, using TheraTappers—I am not a paid endorser of TheraTappers, I just like the name a lot—we redirected my brain to connect the feelings, the sensations, the image in my mind with the phrase *Rick shot himself*. It wasn't easy, it wasn't fun, it wasn't comfortable, and it took more than one appointment. After each appointment, I could barely drive myself home because I was so exhausted. Once I got there I napped, hard, because my brain had just run a marathon. But the whole EMDR thing worked. The guilt and all the other thoughts about Rick's death, which had several years to mutate and calcify, now went to the thought that Rick shot himself, a horrible truth that both made sense and allowed me to live my life. It all worked. I still can't believe how successful it was.

That said, I wasn't exactly celebrating. The goal of my EMDR was to form a thought pattern that told me that my brother shot himself and died. Sadness and loss, while devastating, at least adhere to a world I could navigate, whereas the old association "I killed my brother" did not. Carol said that if the old thinking acted up again, I could always return for more EMDR (and TheraTappers!), but it's been several years now and the fix has held.

EMDR surely does not work for everyone, and plenty of people dismiss it as pseudo-science without enough underpinning in provable outcomes. The people who practice it aren't certified by the state and are more likely than most health care practitioners to have macramé wall hangings. It's very possible that EMDR worked for me simply because I wanted it to, because I wanted to believe in something that could get me somewhere better. And that is fine with me. I've always admired religious believers who know that there is order to the world. I could never get there. I never much went in for alternative medicine either, which as a resident of Seattle in the '90s meant my eyes were more or less locked in rolled position for a decade. So perhaps I was simply so beaten down by life, I got on board with TheraTappers in a way that I couldn't with Jesus or crystals. But it worked, and that's good enough.

Now, when I think of Rick's death, which happens daily, and get around to my possible culpability, my brain directs all those thoughts to *Rick shot himself*. It feels like the truth all the time. Not long ago, my daughter was sledding with some friends. She was part of a group that encouraged a kid to go down a particularly steep run. The kid ended up fracturing a vertebra and missed some school. My daughter came to me devastated with guilt, cursing herself for causing his injury. Instinctively, I blurted out, "Brandon chose to go down that run himself!" Which was true.

15

IN WHICH I POSIT
THAT DEPRESSION IS, PERHAPS,
HILARIOUS

In the summer of 2015, Jill and I went to Maine to celebrate our twentieth wedding anniversary in the land of uncomfortably rocky beaches and cold gusty weather. This is because we know how to party. While there, I made the decision to quit my comedy job because I simply could not imagine putting up with the stress any longer. It turns out many other people felt the same way (my employer, audiences, stations), and upon returning to St. Paul, I was told *Wits* had been canceled. That night, Jill took me to see the movie *Trainwreck*. NBA star LeBron James was in it, and he was the most skilled comedic actor in the cast. This fact, coupled with the cancellation of my comedy show, led me to wonder if I had ever known anything about comedy in the first place.

Peter Clowney, my boss, jumped ship to go work at Gimlet, the very hip emerging podcast company, although he would continue to live in St. Paul, presumably so our band could continue to practice. Peter was—and is—one of my best friends, so his departure from work was a huge bummer on that score alone.

He was also the person who hired me, then brought me to St. Paul. He served as my biggest advocate and cheerleader within the company. Over the years, I often thought, "Wow, I'd be so screwed if he ever left." Then he left.

I knew that thinking of myself as an extension of a show, making no separation between self and performance, was messed up. But when it was all over and canceled, I wasn't sad so much as annihilated, since the thing I had placed myself in had been destroyed. A parade of well-meaning colleagues came and went through my office and email in-box, offering condolences. I found myself in the unlikely position of having to soothe them by saying I'm fine, I'm fine, life goes on, everything must end, no one got hurt, I'm just glad that it existed at all, blah, blah. I think I even said "blah, blah" a couple of times.

Depressed people do this all the time. They take their fragile, underdeveloped selves and put them in what they hope will be a sturdier and more nurturing container. A shitty, ill-fitting carapace. In my case, the carapace was a show, or many shows, or a lifetime of shows, on stage and on radio. For other people, it might be unhealthy relationships, or relationships that become unhealthy. It might be religion or a sports team or a political orientation. It's all a form of giving up on yourself and putting your identity, your self, in the hands of other people.

It's dangerous for saddies to farm themselves out like that, and it never really works.

I had a few new behind-the-scenes things to do for the podcasting department at work, but without a show to make, my schedule slowed way down. Shrewdly, I filled that time by sitting at my desk and staring straight ahead and letting my mind do whatever it wanted. What my mind wanted to do was kill me. Bad strategy. Of course, the other option for saddies, besides torpor, is keeping frantically busy.

Here are two terms that I think are largely useless. One is "feeling sorry for my/yourself." People use that one to knock people who are trying, usually unsuccessfully, to deal with something. They're not feeling sorry for themselves; they're trying to deal with a situation and are often severely outmatched because their temperament, experience, and emotional makeup are not up to the task at hand. But! But! They are trying to handle it. So instead of describing folks that way, maybe try to help, or at least cut them/yourself some slack. You monster.

The other term I find less and less use for is "processing," as in trying to move forward after trauma. "I'm still processing his death," for instance. It implies a promise that can't be fulfilled. "Process" is a series of actions undertaken to accomplish an end result. Computers process data in order to achieve a product. So a person said to be processing will come out the other side sounding a chime and delivering a result. And trauma just doesn't work like that. I never processed Rick's suicide; I kept going because I had to keep going, and nothing ever was or ever will be okay. If a computer processed like that, I'd throw that computer away.

Popeye was a weird cartoon. I promise I'm going somewhere with this. You got the sailors with rage issues, the steroid/PCP qualities of spinach, and this guy Wimpy whose whole thing is that he wants hamburgers but is broke. But what does Wimpy do? He promises he'll pay you on Tuesday if you buy him a hamburger today. And I would watch that and think, "Why don't they show us what happens on Tuesday?" Because on Tuesday, Wimpy has either come up with cash (unlikely) or has to answer to some sailors who have a habit of resorting to violence as their primary means of resolving conflict. Tuesday is going to be HELL for Wimpy.

The cancellation of *Wits* was my Wimpy Tuesday, and I took

a mental thrashing. Never mind that I had wanted to quit anyway; this was the world rejecting a show that I had taken to considering as an extension of myself.

In the days and weeks that followed, I could not handle living
in the present moment, and the idea that life was just a long series of present moments horrified me. Suicide had been off the
table permanently since Rick died, and even if it hadn't been, I
knew how dumb it would look to kill myself over the loss of
a show that featured a recurring character called Murder Cat,
just as it was ridiculous to have existential dread over Amazon
e-cards. But I found the present moment unbearable.

On weekends, naps stretched out for way too long. There's a
kind of facile response that normies have when they hear about
saddies going to bed and staying there. The normies think that it's
about being bummed out or lazy. That may be a factor for some,
but a much more common reason is that, again, we're exhausted.
Having a brain spinning like that, having a brain bottoming out
like that, carrying around that psychic baggage all the time—it
wears you out. The body might be expending very little actual
energy, but the mind is running a marathon combined with an
obstacle course. Are you depressed and find yourself tired all the
time? That may be because you do a decathlon every day.

The pain over this cancellation wasn't anything like what I
felt after Rick's death. There was no horror to it, no shock to the
system. This was a kind of physical and psychic fatigue, and it
felt like the last straw, professionally speaking. I had been striving
my whole life, trying to get the next big thing that would surely
make me happy and solve all my problems. And over and over
again it all went south.

They say the most successful NFL running backs always keep
their legs running forward even if they're being tackled because
they might break free of what's dragging them down and be

able to keep going. When *Wits* ended, I felt like my legs had been pounding away for years, but now they were really sore and maybe it was time to get tackled. Attendant to all that was an accompanying shame that I was depressed at all. I had a wife who loved me, children who loved me and who were going to be good adults, a home. And I still had a job. I also had all the privileges society could provide. I was a straight white guy with a college education, so all the machinery of our civilization was arranged to protect me and help me. What the hell did I have to complain about?

The thing is, I knew better than to think depression was a result of something. It's not a reaction, it's a medical condition. But knowing it and feeling it are different things. I didn't want to die, but I wanted to take my brain out of my head for a while. Just store it in a jar for a few weeks and then put it back in after I'd rested.

I called our insurance company to see what I could do about this, describing in vivid detail what I was going through, and ended up on the phone with a triage nurse. She referred me to an inpatient treatment facility in town. On the phone, the intake person heard about my state of mind and suggested a day treatment kind of thing, and maybe sooner rather than later. Like day camp instead of sleepaway. The plan would be to take two weeks off work, sick leave, and go to the facility from 9 a.m. to 6 p.m. every weekday. They'd monitor my meds, have one-on-one and group therapy, and try to get me to relax a little. Being home in the evenings would be good, they said, to be with my family and sleep in my own bed.

I kept the phone number and the name of the person I talked to. But I didn't call back and never went in. The name and number were enough to improve me. I had an option if things went deeply south. You might not need them at a given point, but it's nice to know where in a building the fire extinguishers are kept.

My family helped during this time. Sally, the loving new puppy, helped, too. And I had stumbled on an idea. We had made dozens of *Wits* episodes over the past few years, and many comedians had appeared on the show. In talking to them or reading interviews with them as preparation, I was always struck by how many had dealt with depression. Often in their act, sometimes behind the scenes, but it would come up again and again. Part of that might have been that as a saddie myself, I was drawn to saddie comedians.

Patton Oswalt had been on the show a few times. He has this great bit about going to the grocery store on a Tuesday morning and ending up in the frozen foods aisle to buy some Lean Cuisine meals. "And as I'm looking at them, Toto's 'Africa' started playing on the ambient music," he says. "I have never felt more peacefully, effortlessly, joyously suicidal. It wasn't even despair. If I had a gun, I would have just brought it up, one smooth movement, like 'Oh, they have French crust pizza, doo doo doo doo doo' (Bang!)."

Maria Bamford has tons of material about her bipolar 2 disorder, of which depression is a big part. Richard Lewis's whole act is about bleakness and despair. And those topics are no laughing matter. Yet here they are presented by comedians, and people laugh.

What about a series of interviews about that? For podcast, of course. I knew it was way too niche to turn into a radio show. I had become friendly with Patton and Maria, as well as loads of other comics who had been on my now-dead show. I was curious: Had they gotten into comedy because they were depressed? Had the isolation of being a traveling comic, combined with the necessity of marketing one's self as a brand, made them more depressed?

Unlike most ideas I get, I stayed fixated on this one. And other people at my work were instantly on board with this "talking to comedians about depression" thing. Maybe the only reason no one ever said, "Are you crazy?!" was that built into the concept was the admission that yes, I am crazy.

Within a few months, my new boss, Steve Nelson, and I were on a plane to Los Angeles to record interviews for a pilot of something temporarily called *The Hilarious World of Depression*, though everyone agreed we should eventually change the name to something less weird and unsettling. Patton Oswalt agreed to be our pilot episode interview and asked Steve and me to meet up with him at a combination record store and barber on Sunset Boulevard to talk.

One of the first things Patton did was call into question what I thought was the premise of the show.

He doesn't believe there are more depressed comedians than there are depressed dentists; it's just that comedians talk about depression as part of their job. "More than any other profession, if a comedian is depressed, they have to very aggressively battle that state of mind in what they do. They're up on stage, and if they're depressed and very open and natural on stage, they're going to talk about that. A guy that is a bricklayer or a cabinet-maker, their depression might not find its way into their art, the way it would a comedian."

So I'm sitting there among heavy metal albums and Patton Oswalt's hair clippings as Steve tries to hold a boom mic in just the right spot and I'm wondering if my whole show has fallen apart before it even had a chance to happen. But the more I talked to Patton, the more things he said that hit awfully close to home about how depression presents itself.

"I didn't really deal with depression until I started earning a living just purely being a standup. It was this goal I'd always worked for of 'I just want to be able to pay the bills only doing standup,'" he said. "And then you get to that point and then all you see around you is—oh, you gotta take the next step. What's the next step? What's your TV show? What's your movie? I was happy on this plateau. I didn't know that by getting to this plateau, I would see this other rock face spiraling into a mountain and all my friends were scrambling up it. I thought we were all happy on this plateau."

When we got the tape home to Minnesota to construct the pilot, it was clear that the question "Why are comedians depressed?" had become less interesting. What I wanted to ask of future guests instead was a bit simpler. What the hell is depression? What does it feel like? How do you go on living? What works for you and what doesn't? How does depression bend your mind? At the heart of the work I had done in radio were people and stories I found fascinating, stuff I wanted to share with the general public in such a way that they would find the subject as fascinating as I did.

The advantage of talking to comedians is that good ones like Patton are highly skilled at talking about complex issues in a clear and compelling way that cuts through the fog of everyday life and connects to an audience's humanity. Audience members then realize that the comedian has described something they didn't know anyone else thought or felt. They realize they're not alone in having this often worrisome thought; they have company, they are okay. And that's when the laughter happens. The laughter is an exhalation of relief.

People laugh about Patton feeling suicidal listening to "Africa" near the Lean Cuisine in part because it's a dissonant juxtaposition, but really that bit is about how an intrusive suicidal ideation can show up when you least expect it, how true deep despair appears out of nowhere. That is terrifying because it feels like a killer on the loose. Audiences laugh because it echoes and relieves some of their own darkest thoughts. Those thoughts are less terrifying when a comic at the top of his industry is saying them out loud on stage. I think you would need to be a pretty big-time comedy geek to want a podcast about comedy theory as it pertains to depression, but a podcast that finally talks about this illness, and does it with jokes, that could work.

Back at the office, the idea kept on getting traction as I wondered why people were humoring me. Depression talking there. Like, was I eventually going to show up for an important meeting where everyone would point at me and laugh? What if someone was late for that meeting? Would the group wait for the tardy person, or would I see the tardy person in the hallways, running toward the meeting while pointing at me and laughing? Is public broadcasting capable of making me Punk'd?

Around Christmas of 2015, I was asked to supply my co-workers Nancy Cassutt and Kate Moos with a bunch of CD copies of the pilot so they could be sent to HealthPartners, a combination insurance company and medical provider based in the Twin Cities. Then I was invited to join them to meet with that organization.

At the meeting, I sat in a very nice office with very nice well-dressed women, and I wondered how Patton's jokes about being tied to a truck and anally raped in a post-apocalyptic hellscape had gone over and whether sponsorship money would be forthcoming. "Comedy is really something," I mused, somewhat grimly.

HealthPartners had started an outreach program called Make It OK. They wanted to get across the message that a lot of people have mental illnesses, and a whole lot of those people are your friends and neighbors. They're a clerk at the grocery store or a cop or a doctor or a lawyer. If more people understand the reality of mental illness and get disabused of the Hollywood myths about it, the stigma about getting help will diminish, and then we'll live in a healthier society. On their website, makeitok.org, you can read stories from people who have experienced mental illnesses, stories of hope about how they got better. There were tips for what to say to someone you're worried about and what not to say. Part of good health care is preventing an illness from getting severe before it gets treated, so if you're an insurance company that's what you want to do. And as a human, that's also what you want to do. Donna Zimmerman of HealthPartners explained to me that the only problem was that they couldn't seem to get much traffic to the site.

Then it was my turn to talk. I had a lot to say. Having thought about what the show could be, I compared what I wanted to do to how I used to get my kids to take their antibiotics when they had ear infections: slip the medicine into some ice cream. "Basically, the message about depression, that's the pill. But if a podcast is just a pill, no one will want to download/swallow it. What you gotta do is drop that pill in some strawberry ice cream, mush it up if you have to," I said. "The ice cream is Patton. Or Maria Bamford or whoever else we get. For a show like this, we could get a doctor from the Mayo Clinic to talk about how a selective serotonin reuptake inhibitor [SSRI, a common form of antidepressant] works or we could get Maria. But the thing is, more people will download Maria because they know it will be fun. We want to rack up those downloads in order to spread the message and because we can then make money on more sponsorships to offset the cost of production. And most of all, if we reach more people, then we REACH MORE PEOPLE."

When you've been on the air for fifteen years of public radio fundraising drives, you learn to instinctively steer the conversation toward the case for getting money. "Well, we really loved the pilot," said Donna.

"Really?" I asked. "Even the part about Patton in the post-apocalyptic hellscape?"

"It was unexpected," she said, and laughed. "But we thought the show sounded great."

They had already decided to sponsor us. Effectively, I was the car dealer in the passenger seat as the customer drove home in the new car, saying, "I think this car really fits your needs!"

Donna officially gave us the news a couple of weeks later. We were funded. We were going to make a season's worth of episodes of what stubbornly insisted on still being titled *The Hilarious World of Depression*. Millions of people all over the world deal with this illness, but I was about to do something very rare in the depression community: I was about to go pro. Yep, I was *that good* at feeling bad. Low five!

16

A POTENTIALLY HILARIOUS WORLD
OF POTENTIAL DEPRESSION

*W*its was fading slightly in the rearview mirror, feeling less like a personal failure, and the validity of *The Hilarious World* was coming into focus. One day, Jill and I were driving to the off-leash dog park, the two of us, well, four counting the dogs. Our dogs have never been fully trained, obedience never being of interest to them, so the park is a place they love.

If you give me enough years and a wise wife, I can eventually start piecing things together. And it helps if that wife pieces them together for me and simply tells me. Without the kids in the van, Jill and I could talk more freely about subjects like Rick, and I recalled the last conversation I had with him, where I thought things were about to get back on track. "And then there was the whole thing during that trip when he was calling his old friends from growing up," I said. "Remember? He tracked down the Olson brothers and Jay. Or he tried to. That was so weird. I wonder why he did that."

"Well," said Jill, with some hesitation, "he was saying goodbye."

"What do you mean?"

"You didn't know that?" she asked, very politely, as though talking to a rather dim child. "He went skiing with Lisbet's family, he called his old friends, he met up with you and apologized for never being there for you enough growing up. He had made up his mind to die, and he was saying good-bye to everyone."

Silence.

"So it wasn't a twelve-step thing?" I mumbled.

"No! God. Really, you didn't know this?"

This revelation about Rick came soon after Jill dropped another fairly obvious truth bomb on me. I had told her the story about staying with Rick in Sacramento just before I got my driver's license and how he'd reinforced his image as my hero. "And he had something going on with his car, so he stopped by a mechanic and the guy looked at his car off to the side, Rick slipped him a ten-dollar bill, and that was it. No receipt, no nothing."

"Well," she said, "I mean, he was buying drugs."

"Oh. You think?"

A long pause while she evaluated her marriage choice. "It's 1984, ten-dollar bill, some sketchy mechanic he knows, secrecy? Yes! Or selling. Probably buying," said Jill.

"Well, come to think of it, I don't recall any actual car repair happening."

Poor Jill. It was too late. I had already fathered her children.

Jay was Rick's first best friend in elementary school. He lived down the street and was the warmest and gentlest member of an eccentric blue-collar family that believed their Ouija board could transport itself around the house. Through some Facebook connections, Jay tracked me down after we got to Minnesota, and we spoke by phone. Jay hadn't really been in touch with Rick down through the years but was nonetheless screwed up by his death. "How could he do that?" Jay asked me, nonrhetorically.

"He was sick and he didn't get enough help to get better," I offered.

"But he called me when he was in Seattle at your mom's. And he had my number after that. Why didn't he call me?"

"I don't know," I said. "I think he didn't want anyone to know how bad it was. I don't know, Jay."

～

It was summer 2016, and I was in Chicago for a podcasting conference.

I was completely jonesing to get *THWoD* launched and on the air so my voice could go out to strangers and I could feel like a person again, but it was taking a long time. We were months past getting the green light but still weeks from making an episode. Steve and I had hired Kryssy Pease from the Minnesota Public Radio newsroom to produce the show. She was smart, hardworking, and creative, and she had dealt with both depression and eating disorders, so that was great news. The joke construction of "(Person X) has a history of (mental illness A, B, C, and D)! Isn't that great news?!" is one we've relied on from the beginning, taking grim pleasure in someone's chronic mental misery because it means we can use it for our actual jobs. "Paul F. Tompkins has depression *and* childhood abandonment issues? I am so delighted to hear that!"

Anyway, Chicago. My company throws a little reception in the evening and I drag myself there, feeling sheepish because it's promoting our current shows and while I used to host one, I no longer do. So I'm just some dude at a party, my personhood no longer validated by the outside forces I require. *THWoD* had not yet been publicly announced. Peter Sagal was there. Peter is a friend, although I'm not entirely certain how we became that way. It's tempting to say that when you host national public radio shows, all the other hosts welcome you into their fraternity, but I had never gone camping with Ira Glass, and brunches with Robert Siegel never seemed to materialize. If there are late-night Ping-Pong parties at Terry Gross's place, I've never been invited. Instead, Peter and I probably met by making similar jokes on Twitter. At this party, he pulled me aside.

"Hey, I heard about your show. The comedy and depression thing? I want in."

"In? What do you . . . I don't . . . How?" He has a show. He can't host my show. No fair.

"I want to be a guest. I want you to interview me," he said.

Kryssy and I already had a pretty good list going of potential guests who had publicly stated that they had dealt with depression. Peter Sagal was not on it. He runs marathons. Lots of them. He's funny and smart, with an Ivy League education, and he is the host of one of the only hit shows on public radio. True, he recently went through one of the ugliest divorces I'd ever heard of, and I know he was devastated by that. But going through something awful is not the same thing as having a chronic mental illness.

"Peter, I had no idea you were depressed," I whispered.

"That's because the only person I ever told aside from medical professionals is you, right now."

He had read my tweets about Rick over the years and was struck by my descriptions of the effects of a suicide on the people left behind. I've been saying for years that the bullet that hit Rick effectively kept ricocheting off everyone he knew and would continue to do so forever. Peter had never been near suicide, not even in the depths of the divorce. But like anyone else going through something horrible and not knowing when or how it will end, he naturally ran through some options in his mind of what to do about it. In such an inventory, suicide often shows up on the list even if you have no intention of ticking that box.

A couple of weeks later, I was back in Chicago at public radio station WBEZ with Kryssy to record what would be our first official interview for *THWoD*. "Thwod," we pronounced it around the office; my earlier attempts to refer to the show as "H-wod" were met with revulsion. During over fifteen years in radio, I always brought a few pages of notes and questions to interviews that pointed to a rough outline of where I wanted to go, but after writing up similar material for Peter, I decided not to bring them along. I had no idea where the interview would or should go, and I just wanted to ask him the questions that came to mind. I know his work, that's enough, I gambled. I still don't bring notes to *THWoD* interviews. I follow the conversation instead of leading it, and the interview ends up being about the person I'm talking to instead of about where that person fits within predetermined suppositions.

Peter described a life and a marriage that were going okay and then took a sharp dive. "Then, to paraphrase President Lincoln, the war came. It became a living nightmare."

He had been a depressed person all his life, and people like that have a warped perception of reality that tends to make mountains out of molehills. But then he ran across an actual mountain in the form of a horrible divorce that included his kids cutting off contact. This got his perspective realigned. He said he used to worry about whether he would be invited to appear on one of the only other hit shows in public radio, *This American Life*. "If you're somebody who loses sleep because you're worried [*TAL* host] Ira Glass doesn't like you personally, then you'll die when your kid starts telling you they hate you."

~

People can have excellent life circumstances and still experience depression, and people can have horrible circumstances and not be depressed at all. But I've met plenty of people already predisposed to depression who encounter some trauma that fans that spark into a bonfire. Peter Sagal, an actor and a playwright, had been able to maintain a façade for over fifty years, but the traumatic divorce made the depression impossible to ignore.

That made sense. What I wasn't clear about was why he wanted to come out of the closet now. Here. On this podcast. With me.

"Because it is really, really, really, really, really hard to go through this shit alone," he said. He was hoping to hear from other parents who had been alienated from their kids. And he was willing to bare his innermost pain as part of that reaching out and to let other people who felt the same know that they're not alone.

Kryssy and I walked out of the stately WBEZ studios and onto the incongruently garish Navy Pier a bit shaken about how weirdly well it had gone. As with all guests, we hadn't paid Peter anything, and his show didn't need any visibility from our un-launched podcast, yet he had gone, as far as we could tell, to the depths of his soul to tell us about his worst and most vulnerable times. And the reason he did it? He felt it would help himself and others.

Before the summer ended, there was a family vacation to be taken, a West Coast road trip as a follow-up to the previous summer's East Coast swing. After a few days in my peaceful place of Oceanside, the way back would take us through Grand Teton National Park, where, in an event not included in our itinerary, Jill began to die.

During a chilly camping night, she remarked that she had a stomachache, which we all chalked up to campfire hot dogs. It was a lot worse the next morning, so we rushed off to urgent care in Jackson, Wyoming, where a doctor said she just had a stomach bug and should wait it out. Should be fine by tomorrow.

One thing for sure, he said, it definitely was not appendicitis. The pain persisted into South Dakota as we all waited for the stomach bug to lift. Somewhere around Sioux Falls, our old gray minivan became an ambulance and I sped toward St. Paul. Jill wanted to get back home because if we ended up in a hospital somewhere else, there would be a much greater chance of sky-high hospital bills that might or might not be covered by insurance. Would South Dakota hospitalization mean $20,000 of debt? More? Soon she was moaning in pain.

I pulled up outside the ER doors at the hospital in St. Paul as Jill, almost unconscious from the suffering, blearily admonished me for parking in the ambulance spot. "It's okay," I said. "We are one." The triage nurse put her in a wheelchair immediately and wheeled her out of sight. Her appendix had been perforated. A few hours later, the surgeon said that the infectious goo inside the pointless yet murderous organ had been contained and she should be fine. Over the next few days, there were many sedatives, and a lot of tests, as her release was repeatedly delayed. Only after we got home did we get to see the doctor's notes. In fact, there was contamination and a diagnosis of sepsis. The notes also included a suggestion that the option for palliative care should be left open. End-of-life care. She lived.

I was forty-eight, and a stomachache at a campground had very nearly led to me being a widower with three kids, all because my wife, like all people, had an appendix, a ticking time bomb inside her body, and hers happened to detonate. Jill had told me many times over the years that she wouldn't be any more surprised to drop dead at thirty than at one hundred. I would always say she was being unnecessarily morbid, but after the appendicitis I knew she was right. Any of us could simply end at any given time. We don't come with warranties. Death is everywhere, I had been reminded.

Well. Huh. What is this all for?

In the prolonged effort to catch my breath after the appendicitis, depression hit hard. It was about how close we'd come, thanks to chance and a terrible doctor in Wyoming, to Jill losing her life, to me losing her, to the kids losing their mom. And it laid bare a hard reality about existence itself: one day we're simply not anything anymore. There is no meaning.

Now, this was in part depression talking, telling me all this "life is pointless" jazz, and although it's all logically correct, it was getting tediously predictable. Depression was my personal New York Yankees or New England Patriots, and I was tired of it winning so many championships. So how, then, to fight back? How to go on? Be a good dad and husband, sure, but other than that, what?

~

Getting back to work on the show, we had more episodes to fill out for our first season. I leaned on funny people I already knew for some of the slots, because we figured it might be off-putting for people to be invited to tell all about their chronic mental illnesses to a stranger on a show that had not yet debuted. Maria Bamford, Andy Richter, and Paul F. Tompkins had been on my previous shows, so they trusted me enough to go along with it. Dick Cavett had been speaking out about depression since the '70s, and he also agreed to participate. He even volunteered to go to a public radio station in the Hamptons for the interview. I'm often an inch from becoming a squealing fanboy, and this was one such case. If I'd taken a moment to acknowledge I was speaking to Dick Cavett(!), the interview would have fallen apart, but I managed to hold out for forty-five minutes.

A pretty good celebrity lineup meant that we could reserve a spot or two for comedians who were relatively obscure but had a story to tell. I went to Brooklyn to talk to Sam Grittner, who had dealt with depression and addiction and was coming off a suicide attempt some months earlier. We sat in his apartment, the same one where he'd taken a pile of sleeping pills, in what I soon realized was the toughest test yet of the premise that a discussion of depression could have laughs in it. Sam said that he took the pills and "just closed my eyes and just tried to be at peace, tried to make peace with myself. I fall asleep, and then six hours later I wake up. That is still the most surreal experience of my life. And my first thought was 'Fuuuuuuck! I managed to screw up my suicide attempt!'" He ended up taking the subway to the hospital in order to avoid the massive expense of a short ambulance ride.

I wish I had prepped our borrowed recording engineer a bit better. Matt was used to recording stuff about business and the NASDAQ for *Marketplace*, and here he was making sure we got good sound levels in a discussion of suicide and depression. Matt seemed a bit shell-shocked leaving Sam's apartment, and I felt the same. I went back to the hotel and slept a couple of hours. I've found that even on trips to record interviews, I have a hard time doing more than two in a day because they are emotionally and psychically exhausting.

Some buzz began to build leading up to the December 2016 launch of the show. In the aftermath of that presidential election, many people approached me to say something to the effect of "I COULD REALLY USE SOMETHING THAT MAKES ME LAUGH RIGHT ABOUT NOW AND THAT ALSO HELPS ME DEAL WITH THIS SUDDEN MASSIVE DEPRESSION I AM FEELING." They spoke in all caps.

As our December launch date approached, we had several interviews in the bank. Andy Richter had talked about playing Simon & Garfunkel's "Bridge over Troubled Water" over and over again at age five in the immediate aftermath of his parents' divorce. Maria Bamford welcomed us into her home in Los Angeles and told about her breakdowns, her involuntary commitment to a psychiatric hospital, and the fact that her pugs were married. Dick Cavett, who had been depressed as a Yale student, recalled his hospitalization.

Kryssy and I, along with Kate Moos, who served as editor and executive producer, had to figure out how to turn tape into an actual show. We eventually settled on a narration model, where we play tape but then I do voice-over through it in order to explain stuff like where the interview happened and the guest's biography. That leaves the guest free to explain the really good squishy emotional stuff. Lots of podcasts and public radio shows like to pack in loads of music to accompany the stories. When it works, you barely notice the music; it serves to emphasize the tone of the conversation and draw it into sharp relief. When it doesn't work, you get obnoxious sound that tries to manipulate the listener into feeling something that the actual material doesn't deliver. "I kind of don't want to score any of the conversations," I told the producers tentatively. "I just want the words to hold themselves up." We were all on the same page there.

We figured we needed a theme song. Kryssy and I happened both to be fans of and friends with Rhett Miller of the Old 97's. Rhett is nice, funny, makes gorgeous music, and also happens to be the survivor of a suicide attempt. I texted Kryssy one night that we should try to get someone who sounds like Rhett to do the theme song. She pointed out that Rhett sounds like Rhett. Oh yeah. Let's ask him. Five minutes later she texted to say, "He's in!"

The tasks of editing the interviews and writing scripts fell to me, and as I pounded through hours of conversations about depression, anxiety, suicide, hospitalization, divorce, and generalized despondency, it occurred to me that perhaps this might not be an ideal job for a depressed person. Also: "Hmm, I should have thought of that before becoming a professional saddie." I would edit for a while, get up and stretch, edit some more, go to the restroom, edit a bit, weep, edit, go for a walk, and so on.

On those walks, I listened to music. Probably my favorite band to blast positivity and energy is the Hold Steady. One day, I was on their album *Separation Sunday* and the track "Charlemagne in Sweatpants" rolled around.

A few minutes into the song, Craig Finn, a Minneapolis native, speculates on what kind of story he wants to tell. Boy meets girl? Murder mystery? In the end, he decides it's best told as a comeback story.

Craig's talking about some drugged-up Minneapolis teens or maybe about Jesus—that's how Craig rolls—and soon the song returns to something approximating despair, but the lines on their own struck me. Any story I was going to tell on *THWoD* would be a comeback story. Maybe the person found the right treatment and is feeling better. For Andy Richter, depression will always be there, but he can manage it. "It's a bad back that I've learned to cope with," he said. "I've gotten to a workable level. That's not to say it doesn't still affect my quality of life, because it absolutely does. But, you know, so does a bad back."

Even the guests who weren't doing well had at least come on my show to talk about it. They were opening up, knowing that this thing has a name, and inviting dialogue about what people with depression go through. That might be a long way from absolute top mental health, but it is nonetheless a comeback story.

The show felt like a comeback for me, too. I felt good about the episodes we were making, it was nice to work closely with other people, and Kryssy and I turned out to be very compatible work partners. Kate Moos has been in public radio for a long time and used to be the lead producer on *Speaking of Faith* and

On Being with Krista Tippett, so she knew a thing or two about smart and emotional interviews. I kept waiting for Kate to tell me I was doing everything wrong, but she never did.

This didn't cure my depression, of course, because that's not how it works, but it bottled up the symptoms enough to let me get some good positive work done. I had what I considered a pretty solid prediction of what would happen next: the show would go out, a handful of depressed fans of my work would find it and say nice things, HealthPartners would get a modest bump in web traffic and be pleased, and then we'd pat ourselves on the back and move on to other ventures. Hopefully I would not get fired.

We launched the show.

Late the next night, I got a text from Kryssy that we were at number two on the charts among all podcasts, or, among podcasts where no one gets murdered, number one.

Over the next few weeks and several new episodes, we slipped from number two, but not all that much. People were sticking around, subscribing, coming back for more. *The Hilarious World of Depression* was a hit. I'd never had a hit before. "How long is it," I thought, "until it all falls apart and we get canceled and I get fired and my family leaves me and I'm living in my car in the Walmart parking lot?"

17

SCOURING THE NORDIC COUNTRYSIDE FOR TRAUMA FOSSILS

Somehow, as a result of all the decisions I had made over the course of fifty or so years on the planet, I was standing in front of a hundred Minneapolis snowplow drivers, telling them how sad I've always been. Since *THWoD* took off, I've been invited to give a lot of speeches about depression, mental illness in general, and my own journey from ignorance to awareness. The speech to the plow drivers was a tough one since they tend to be taciturn Minnesota men, not prone to sharing.

I was there as part of a larger wellness campaign by the city's HR department, and the way they got the guys to show up was to put me on just before they announced who got which plow route for the coming winter, so everyone was pretty keyed up. I admitted I am less likely to know how to fix a car engine, more likely to write a poem about a car engine. Nonetheless, and as is usually the case when I speak, a few of them approached me afterward and laid their burdens down, admitting to struggles with depression that they had never been able to seek help for.

These dudes head out on the streets in subzero temperatures and deep layers of snow to clear the roads, but speaking with a professional, or anyone sometimes, was a bit too scary.

A week or so later, I ended up in the dining room of a historic private club in St. Paul, giving a mildly tailored version of the same speech to a group of doctors and surgeons. It was intimidating in a different way. Yes, I'm able to feel inadequate among both surgeons *and* snowplow drivers. Tremendous range. Getting ready to step to the lectern, I realized that all I do is talk about illness on a podcast, but these people cure illness. I was fully prepared to open the speech by saying, "There's been a terrible mistake."

The representative from the hospital sponsoring the event introduced me. She got out her notes to read from the standard bio everyone uses, but she prefaced her remarks with a six-word dependent clause: "Prior to finding his true calling." I was grateful that there was more bio to list after that because I was breathless. Had I found my true calling? Hard to dispute.

At the same time, I was meeting a lot of *THWoD* fans out in public. Walking through the produce section, right by the oranges, at the downtown St. Paul Lunds & Byerlys grocery store, I was approached by a guy in his sixties who politely introduced himself and shook my hand. He kept shaking it as he explained, "I've liked everything you've done, but this podcast is very special to me. I've had a hard time talking about my depression for many years, but to hear other people talk about their issues, that's made me feel like I'm not alone and I can do something about this. So, thank you. I really think you're making a difference for a lot of people." I thanked him and tried to make small talk about the big topic. And at some point I realized he had stopped shaking my hand but had not actually let go. So I was pretty much just holding hands with a dude by the oranges, talking about chronic mental illnesses. Though I had been in the public eye for several years by this point, this was new.

Consciously or not, we had made a show that addressed big gaps in the collective discourse about mental illness. We talked openly, shared stories, and made jokes. Unlike the grim funeral-home support group, we included some well-earned laughs about depression, and unlike the support group at the police station, we could ask specific questions and edit what we got. And with all that solved and gratitude from listeners pouring in, I was no longer depressed and never would be again.

Kidding. A bit more serene at work, maybe. The sense that everyone hated me was less overwhelming. When my boss's boss came to a meeting and got choked up from reading some of the listener emails, that seemed like a pretty good sign. Depression can't be cured by positive life circumstances because depression is not a reaction to circumstances. Regular emotions, the kinds that normies generate effortlessly, might show up in response to life, but deeply embedded chronic mental illnesses that have held on for decades? Nuh-uh. You could have a million people hold your hand by the oranges and those won't budge. The feelings, I mean. The oranges would definitely budge with a million people in the store.

A month after our second season ended, I agreed to write a book, this one you're reading, about events in my life that traced a biography of my depression.

Season three of the show was coming up soon, which meant twenty episodes and twenty straight weeks of a production cycle. In the calm before that storm and in the spirit of piecing my mind together enough to write about it, my family took a vacation to Norway. As long as you're not hung up on having spice in your food, it's a great place to vacation. It was two weeks of seeing relatives and fjords and wondering what forces carved them both out like that.

We visited Sortland, the small town where my mom grew up, north of the Arctic Circle. It's not much bigger now than in the 1930s and '40s, and some of my extended family still lives there, dying at advanced ages and steadily replacing themselves with new babies.

We saw the barn where my grandfather hid his radio from the Nazis. Radios were contraband, and he risked everything to keep his, an act of defiance that has always made me proud to work in radio. The barn is now the home of three sheep: Frank and "the Ladies."

We sat on my cousin Else-Berit's deck one night. It didn't seem like night since in that part of the world the sun comes up in late May and stays up until well into July. People mow the lawn at midnight, children's bedtimes are forgotten, it's all a kind of cheerful vitamin D–drenched euphoria. On the deck were Else-Berit, her husband, Per, Jill, Metteline, and me.

Just before this trip, I had interviewed the celebrity chef Andrew Zimmern, who had experienced a good bit of trauma in his childhood that translated pretty quickly into a downward spiral of addiction. "Trauma that is not transformed is transmitted," he told me, and it's a sentence that was very top of mind as I explored my family's past in Norway. A year or so after the trip, former child star Mara Wilson would tell me that she thinks one of the reasons she's struggled with anxiety disorders is her family's Ashkenazi Jewish heritage. Those ancestors, she says, had plenty of reasons to never get too comfortable, and although life in contemporary Burbank, California, does not pose the same threats her forebears faced in central Europe in the '30s, the anxiety remains.

It's a little much to expect to connect all elements of an extended family's mental health history during one sunny midnight whiskey-sipping, and indeed I could not. I didn't need to know the Viking stuff, mind you, but was hoping for a glimpse into events since the traumatic Nazi occupation during World War II. We told stories of suicides and suicide attempts in the family from over the last few decades. We talked about nervous breakdowns and affairs and families falling apart. I knew, and I think we all knew, other more current stories that we chose not to share even in an intimate group.

"And then," said Per, glass of whiskey in hand, "there are the things we don't talk about."

"Yeah?" I asked, leaning a bit closer.

Per took another sip of whiskey and sat quietly while other people talked. Like now, I thought. We are talking about it right now. Fun fact: the Norwegian word for boundaries is *grenser*.

A year and a half earlier, my daughter Margaret—now going by the name "Marge," thus making her the youngest Marge in America by fifty years—had to do a third-grade report about someone famous. She chose Johan Moe, who was not really famous at all except in the northern Norway town of Melbu (population 2,200). Johan was my great-uncle, my dad's uncle, and he died in 1994 at the age of eighty-four after a long career as one of the top singer-songwriters in Melbu. The Bob Dylan of Melbu. Melbu's Johnny Cash.

Johan was so famous and beloved in Melbu that since his death the town has held an annual Johan Moe's Night where a band plays his songs and everyone is invited to sing along. Jill and I had planned our trip around catching this event. Melbu is only a short drive from Sortland, and we drove over with our kids and Metteline. The hall was packed by the time we arrived, but they allowed us to squeeze onto a bench in the back as the band started to play.

At one point, Jill snuck out to use the restroom and, since she's socially comfortable, struck up a conversation with one of the event organizers. Soon word was buzzing through the hall that Johan's relatives were here from America, which was exciting. And in Metteline's case from southern Norway, which wasn't as exciting but perhaps a bit interesting. After intermission, the bandleader made an announcement from the stage in Norwegian, so we had no idea what he was saying aside from the word "Minnesota." Then everyone gasped and oohed, turning around to applaud us. We waved.

After the concert, we found framed photos on the lobby wall of Johan and his guitar, as well as photos of Johan with his brothers Thorvald and Gunnar performing some sort of musical comedy. They had a little musical trio that Conrad, my grandfather, had never been part of. We met two older women who had been sitting in front of us the whole time. Greta and Toril were Johan's daughters, my dad's cousins. There was much hugging and translating and explaining that no, my dad, who had met my mom when he cast her in a play, didn't do much acting after he left Norway. A reporter for the regional newspaper appeared and interviewed us all and took our picture. Toril told us this was the most exciting thing that had ever happened to her.

It was the first family-related encounter I could think of that didn't involve a hint of secrets or sadness lurking below the surface. Apparently you could be related to me and be, God, I'm scared to even type it, just fine.

After we returned to the States, my mom spoke to her sister Aud. Aud said the visit was wonderful for everyone, and it was so nice to see me again and meet my family. "And John was asking a lot of questions," she told Mom.

"Really? What kind of questions?" Mom asked.

"About the family. About all these things in the past," said Aud, clearly a bit alarmed by my actions.

"Well," said Mom, "he's like that." She sounded proud of me.

18

GETTING BETTER BEFORE I DIE

B y now, you're noticing that there aren't a ton of pages left in this book. You might be waiting for the big climactic event. Having read through the protagonist's challenge and journey, you may be expecting me to face a battle that almost kills me and then emerge triumphant.

No such luck.

I went to my first appointment with my new therapist, Julie, a couple of weeks after returning from Norway. She was therapist number twelve. And you know what they say: twelfth time's the charm.

"You have been through more than most people," Julie said after our intake sessions, saying it slowly and cautiously. Water started leaking out of my eyes.

A big part of cognitive behavioral therapy is tackling what are called "cognitive distortions," ways of thinking of the world that aren't true to what is known as "reality." It's not necessarily just depressed people who get into patterns of cognitive distortion, but I've never known any saddie who didn't dip into these, and usually with great frequency. Here are a few:

- All-or-Nothing Thinking: Everything is either the best or worst. You're the greatest or you're a monster. If you get that job or pass that audition, you are a god, but if you don't, you're a failure.
- Overgeneralization: One event is an indicator of all other events past and future. You didn't get into the college of your choice? That means you'll never get into any college.
- Mental Filter: Saddies are great at this one. You screen out anything that doesn't fit a preexisting negative narrative. Twelve nice comments about a presentation at work are obliterated in favor of a single critical one.
- Disqualifying the Positive: This is Mental Filter's jerk cousin. In this one, you recognize the nice things people say, but you find reasons why those people are wrong. Disqualifying the Positive is a key component in many an impostor syndrome.
- Jumping to Conclusions: You see a guy walking down the street with a disgusted look on his face. Naturally, it's because he knows you and hates you. In reality, he ate some bad clams.
- Catastrophizing: Every event is a harbinger of a horrible future. If a catastrophizing baseball player doesn't get a hit in a game, it's a sign he'll never get a hit again.
- Control Fallacy: Things would be different and better, goes the thinking, if the forces and circumstances that control everything didn't make success impossible.
- Emotional Reasoning: The phrase "Trust your gut" is much catchier than "Trust your gut unless it flies in the

face of normal reasoning and logic." And that's too bad. Emotional Reasoning tells us that whatever we feel must be true. For instance, if you feel stupid, then you're stupid. Even though of course you're not, idiot.

When I signed up for cognitive behavioral therapy, or CBT, I fully expected Julie and I would go through these "distortions" one by one and tick off reasons why they aren't true. Then maybe there'd be some sort of hypnosis about catching the stream of thoughts heading toward dark places and redirecting them to a healthier reservoir. I wanted a trick, really. I wanted to work through everything with an eye toward it all turning out fine.

It wasn't that.

Instead, it was the methodical work of taking decades' worth of beliefs and slowly, sympathetically exposing them to the harsh light of reason. It was about understanding where those beliefs actually came from and what trouble they've been causing since.

One of the first issues I wanted to tackle was this habit of converting stress into bleak, goth-eyeliner-wearing despair. Well, it turns out that people who grew up with an addicted parent are more prone to the effects of stress. Normies have a belief that, deep down, everything is basically secure, and therefore stress is merely a passing storm. People who grew up in the unreliable orbit of an addict or in other similarly traumatic situations have no such belief in a grounded universe, so to them that passing storm is likely to destroy everything. To them, the storm is how weather is supposed to be. Add depression, either through brain chemistry or environment, and every stressful period is an existential threat. If I feel like I'm about to be wiped out, well, yeah, despair makes a lot of sense.

Once I was able to understand the pattern my mind was

using, I could hold it up against other patterns. If I'm stressed about getting a podcast episode made, I can remember that I've been making shows for my whole life and they always get done, meaning I know how to get them done, so it's okay. Stress won't ever go away, but after spending a comparatively brief amount of time looking into how I think about it, I can spot the negative patterns and mostly bring them to a halt.

I found myself in a pattern not long ago in which I couldn't seem to get away from members of my own family if things got a little noisy around the house, as happens when there are five humans and two dogs, all of whom can be loud and demonstrative. I had noticed that when I would, say, go to my bedroom to get away from it all, the kids would come into the room, one by one, to join me. As the room filled up, the dogs, intent on being part of the pack, would join as well and, excited by the party they were then attending, would wrestle with each other or whomever they could find. So before long, I would be smothered in three kids and a couple of loud dogs, all in a room where I went, remember, to get away from the noise and chaos. This vexed me.

Julie asked about the idea of setting boundaries, of simply saying, "No, this door is closed. I'll see you all later." And of course that's the right thing to do, and of course I knew that. What's stopping me, I explained, is that if I do that then I'm putting myself ahead of my family, and that's wrong.

"Why does that feel wrong?" she asked.

"Because then I'm a bad dad," I said. I knew it was a distortion, but damn, it felt true. If I'm present for my kids, always looking them in the eyes, able and willing to engage in conversation any time of the day or night, then I'm not a bad dad. If not, then I'm a bad dad. It's of note that there is no clear path here to being a "good dad," only a forestalling of bad-dadness.

I explained to Julie that the right thing for a dad to do is sub-
jugate himself entirely to the service of his children, to sacrifice
everything for their well-being and always, always, always be
present and . . . "Oh boy, this is about MY dad, isn't it?" I asked.

"Is it?"

"Well, my chief issue with him was his mental absence. And
whether that was a result of trauma, depression, alcohol, or all
three, it seems pretty obvious that I've held on to it. I always
bring it up in conversation and quite a bit in the book I'm writing. I think about it all the time."

Julie asked, "Do you think that if you close the door or deny
your kids some attention, you're a bad dad?"

By this point, I was feeling kind of stupid, because, yep, I did
not see the obvious plot twist coming. But I told the truth. "Yes.
There's all sorts of ways I can be a bad dad. And even if I do everything perfectly, I'm still a bad dad, although I know that last bit is
depression chiming in." I could never get attention from my father,
so I'll compensate by flooding my kids with it.

"Maybe you're a good dad and none of these individual decisions affect that," said Julie. "From everything you've told me in
our sessions, it seems to me you're a good dad. And it's good for
kids to see a parent do things for themselves so when they grow
up they can make healthy choices for themselves, too, and not be
dependent on other people and acting compulsively."

After months of these sessions, I felt a fundamental shift beginning to take place, less like a lightning bolt and more like
tectonic plate movement. There emerged the possibility of a belief, unknown throughout my life, that I was okay. (I'm aware
that the previous sentence sounds like trite '70s self-help, but I,
healthier, am likewise allowing the option that it sounds fine.)
Believing I was okay was not as simple as it sounds. It had noth-

ing to do with any accomplishments; it was the concept that I was a valid and acceptable person.

I had always understood this satisfied-to-exist mindset from an intellectual standpoint. What I had never been able to cipher was what that felt like. Without dread, self-shaming, and casual loathing, how did these people fill their days? Smiling for photographs can't take up all that much time.

"It's pretty common," said Julie, "for people from backgrounds like yours to feel like they always need to prove themselves. Because you don't have that solid footing."

"And we're perfectionists," I said, "and because nothing can ever be perfect, we are perpetually frustrated and ashamed. So we think we need to try harder. And when that doesn't fix anything, we despair."

Depression is lonely, in part, because life feels like complete chaos. You could fall apart at any moment in a way disproportionate to the circumstances. It makes no sense to be unable to stop weeping in junior high or to want to die on the way to making e-cards or to tail two guys from the city dump. And if that's the world we live in, there is no reason to believe anything connects to anything else, and therefore nothing matters. At that point, depression has you exactly where it wants you. Remember, this illness is a parasite that wants to destroy its host.

To slow down enough to understand one's mind, even a little better, changes that. It presents a world where there is logic, where A is followed by B, instead of A being followed by F or Q or a shrub or breakdancing. I don't know if something finally took hold because Julie is an outstanding therapist, or because I had spent months writing about my depression, or because I spent years working on a show about depression, or because I spent a lifetime trying to work around depression, or because I just wanted it to work. Probably all of those. And a lot of it, quite honestly, was that I was so sick and tired of nothing working.

Once I saw that I was fundamentally an okay guy, not even a great one, but okay, then I could get a clearer picture of the chaotic parts of my mind, the parts that didn't make sense and were intent on wrecking my life. Those parts emerged from cognitive distortions, from depression, from trauma, from anxiety, from unhealthy thinking. And at that point, they did make sense after all, because I knew what they were up to. I knew not just that depression lies but how depression lies. And now when the really dark depressed thoughts come in, when that distortion flicks on, it is not as scary or as bleak; it's something I can recognize, distance myself from, and try to neutralize.

The healthier understanding is all pretty new to me, and I certainly don't always succeed in recognizing what's reality and what's a deceptive mind. I have so much work to do, so many years of labor to get good at this. But it works more often than I would have thought. I'm mentally healthier than I've been in my entire life.

It hasn't let go. I'm not cured. I've accepted Rick's death even though I'm not over it and never will be. I think about him every day, and I hurt for the pain he had been going through. I hurt a lot for how that pain came to an end. But instead of spinning my mind around the subject and letting depression loose to have its way, I return to my thoughts of the world as it really is.

My brain will always want to go dark. As I write this, that still happens a lot, and it's up to me to lower that recurrence. It's also up to me to be ready when that happens, to know why the thoughts are going in that direction and how to head it off. My mind is an old car that has been in a few wrecks. There's body damage; I had to replace a door. There's rust on the fender, and the seats are all ripped up. It still runs, but on cold days you need to hit the dashboard with a phone book for some reason to get it started.

I can't trade it in, though, so I just have to keep driving.

According to *THWoD* (the Podcast), *THWoD* (the Book), and THWoD (the World)— Nine Things I've Learned

So there it is. I've pried open my brain, poured the contents into my heart, ripped open my heart, and bled it all onto these pages for you. I think we've all had some fun together. But I'd like to give you a little something more. A small gift bag of tips to go with whatever it is you may have gleaned. I hope you find them useful and, if not, I hope you stay quiet about it.

1. People Want to Talk

Jeff Tweedy had no reason to invite me to hang out at the Wilco loft in Chicago where the band rehearses and records. But he did, playing us (me, Kryssy the producer, our engineer Corey, and videographer Nate) some new recordings of Mavis Staples he made there, and opening up about his addiction and depression. We weren't making Wilco any more famous than they were. All we were doing was soaking up the exciting vibe of the place until we were asked to leave. But Jeff found value, for himself and others, in sharing his pain and struggle.

My friend Ben Acker co-created *The Thrilling Adventure Hour*, a stage show in LA and a podcast presented like an old radio program. They get all kinds of super-famous people to participate in their show for free, and I asked him how they do that. "Because it's cool," he said. "People like to be a part of cool things. It feels good."

And obviously, it's not just celebrities who enjoy being part of cool things. It's the guy who held my hand by the oranges in the grocery store. It's the listeners who write in. It's the crowd of people I inevitably accumulate around me after I give a speech, eager to tell me, a stranger, about the struggles with mental illness in their families.

Think of a junior high dance. The gym or cafeteria has been decorated with crepe paper. A DJ has been hired and they brought some swirly disco lights. Some hit song of the day is playing at a semi-loud volume (I usually imagine "Don't Stop Believin'" by Journey but you can use whatever you like), and no one is dancing. Boys pinned against one wall, girls against the other. Then I get out in the middle of that floor and dance like a fool. I lip-sync the Steve Perry vocal, I do an air guitar solo, I pound those invisible drums. The people want to dance, that's why they came, they just need someone to go first. I do and they dance.

Yes, there is discrimination against people with mental illness and, yes, it can be a scary thing to talk about. But the hunger to do so is there, and by being open yourself you can get that conversation out on the dance floor.

2. Everyone's a Fraud

Most people who have accomplished something and have at least a trace of humility will experience the feeling that they are in way over their head. They'll wonder if their achievements are flukes and worry that they will be exposed as frauds. And this is all healthy and fine for the normies. The normies can laugh it off.

For the saddies, it's terrifying. The saddies attach little or no sense of intrinsic value to their person, so accomplishment automatically feels fraudulent. It would be like giving the big promotion to a pile of mud. Eventually, the pile of mud's co-workers will notice that hey, that's just a pile of mud. Why does that pile of mud get the nice office? As a result, the saddie will likely look just a bit more jumpy around the copier because the whole pile-of-mud secret is bound to seep out.

In fact, the more accomplishments the saddie rings up, the better the chance the saddie will have impostor syndrome because they're constantly striving and sharpening their skills in order to get further ahead and throw the authorities off the trail. The normie, meanwhile, will use the term "impostor syndrome" to demonstrate some humility in discussing an accomplishment that they're probably pretty sure they earned.

It's a bit like getting out of bed. A normie will complain about being tired and say, "I did *not* want to get out of bed this morning." The saddie will have desperately wanted to get out of bed but found she could not.

I had a fun exchange with YouTuber and author Hannah Hart on the show about how to trick the depression that plays tricks on you. "I've kind of come up with the idea that I'm a fraud but they haven't caught me yet so they're probably not going to get around to it," I told her. "I must be way down the docket or I'm really good at hiding it."

"Well, okay," Hannah replied. "I have this alternate perspective. How arrogant of *me* to think that they don't know what they're talking about?" This was a rare double-reverse depressive rationalization, a move almost never even attempted except in closely moderated international depression competitions.

The people who never believe themselves to be impostors, the ones who feel completely unreservedly entitled to all their good fortune, those are the freaky bastards you got to look out for.

3. Words Matter

The terminology associated with mental illness is tricky to employ, and we as a society suck at it. We say someone is "schizophrenic" when all they're doing is changing their mind about something. Or we call them schizophrenic because they behave in different ways in different situations, which isn't close to the meaning at all. We say we're "totally OCD" for lining up our pencils in the right place on our desk when in fact all we are is tidy. You're not "in a major depression" when your team loses the big game, you're just sad and disappointed like a normal healthy human gets. One's a mood, the other's a mental illness. If you were really depressed, you'd feel the same thing if your team won or lost, or perhaps feel nothing at all regardless of a game's outcome.

Screwing up words like this isn't just a matter of being linguistically imprecise, however. It has the potential to cause real damage. By applying actual words with significant specific diagnostic meanings to much lighter circumstances, people are robbing and devaluing people with mental illness. OCD can be a debilitating, life-destroying illness, but each time the term is used for pencil tidiness, the general public takes actual sufferers of OCD a little less seriously. That slide then contributes to an already huge understanding gap between the normies and the genuinely mentally ill. The normies wonder what the big deal is with untidy pencil storage, while the mentally ill are made to feel that they're exaggerating their problems. This, in turn, leads to less treatment and worse health.

And I've been one of those jerks using the words in a way that isn't especially good. I have described depression as a disease in the past, but I've been gently corrected that a disease has a specific physical cause like a virus or bacteria, while an illness is anything that makes someone feel unwell. Emily Bulthuis, a psychotherapist, specializes in the issue of mental health language. She takes issue with the word "stigma" (a word we'd been using freely since launching the show), because all it means is discrimination against a minority group. And we already have a word for discrimination. Discrimination.

Our show has also tried to adopt "person first" terminology. This means not saying "Bob is a schizophrenic," but instead "Bob is a person with schizophrenia" or "Bob's a guy who deals with schizophrenia." Bob is many things, and only one of those things is the mental illness he happens to have. Bob is a Cubs fan. Bob is left-handed. Bob is a database administrator and he's married and he collects antique lamps. You wouldn't say, "Bob is a husband" to describe Bob. Bob is fully dimensional. Really, I probably shouldn't be using the terms "saddie" and "normie" throughout this book. I should go with "Jennifer is a woman with saddism" or "Bruce is a person stricken with normism."

And yeah, this is a polite way to talk to people, but it's more than that. It's a way of retraining your own mind to separate the human from his or her illness. This clears the way for a better understanding of the illness and it makes the presence of the illness in society less intimidating. Using person-first terminology means that when you see Bob walking toward you on the street, you don't see six feet of clothed and ambulatory schizophrenia, you see Bob. And then you can just say, "Hey, Bob!" And that's what it's all about: being able to cheerfully say hey to Bob.

4. Privilege Is Real

I'm a straight white man. The last three words of the previous sentence give me three layers of support in this society. Toss in a college education and my status as married with kids, that's a few more. Oh, and a homeowner! Man, I'm piling them up. So it is extremely easy for me to say that everyone should be out talking about their mental illness all the time and everyone should be completely honest about it. No matter what, I have all the mechanisms of society in my favor to back me up. Even if someone has a bias against me for being a person with depression, I have plenty of other widely held biases that work in my favor, like racism, sexism, ableism, and homophobia. I abhor all those things but there's no question that, through no effort of my own, I've benefited from them. It's important to understand how high the stakes are for people in groups that get dumped on.

The late Reggie Osse was an attorney and journalist but was best known as Combat Jack, the host of an influential hip-hop podcast, *The Combat Jack Show*. He was also depressed, a fact he didn't figure out until after age fifty. In his circles, the term wasn't widely used and the vulnerability it indicated was not welcome at all. "I would talk to my peers and I'd be like, 'Dude, I need a vacation,'" he said. "And their response was like, 'We're making good money. Why the hell would you want to take a vacation? Stop being lazy. Man up and snap back.' So the conversation then definitely wasn't welcoming, and after I introduced the fact that I didn't feel well, I said, 'Well, let me keep it to myself.'"

He was skittish about even going to a general practitioner. Not only did he have this inherited idea that all problems could be solved through toughness and persistence, he also knew that the white establishment was responsible for stuff like the Tuskegee syphilis experiment. "From slavery to reconstruction to Jim Crow, we've always been forced to get up and continue to move forward. Our relationship with the medical industry is kind of shaky. I refuse to go to the doctor unless I'm totally incapable," he said. Two months after I interviewed him, Reggie died of a cancer that was detected way too late.

Comedian and actor Baron Vaughn once spent a period of weeks subsisting on Cheerios and washing in Dawn dish soap. It wasn't out of poverty; he was on location filming a television series at the time. He was depressed but just didn't really know what that was. He told me, "When I started thinking about depression and anxiety and all those feelings, I didn't see how much racial baggage I had wrapped around those different things because I was like, 'Depression, you mean the thing that white people do?' I saw depression as something that was for the well-off, that you have the time to sit there and become depressed."

Margaret Cho is Korean-American, and that fact is central to her relationship with her own mental health. "That generation of Koreans coming over to America in the sixties and seventies, they had this incredible identity crisis because they were coming from an extremely rigid culture; everything was regulated. And then they come over to America where, in the height of the seventies, the 'me' era, and all of this crazy stuff going on around them, you know, they were shell-shocked." She says it was crucial in the San Francisco immigrant culture to demonstrate that you could work hard and be productive and that nothing could slow you down.

"I knew of one family. They had done a little bit well for themselves in America. They had gotten a white wall-to-wall carpet, and then the day after they got it one of their brothers who came over with them from Korea shot himself on the carpet. And so the bloodstain was just all the way across the floor. But they didn't want to change the carpet because they'd just gotten it, so they just kind of moved the furniture over the bloodstain and you'd just kind of, you know, see it peeking out from underneath the sofa. And so that's sort of like the way that Koreans deal with suicide or depression: they just kind of try to cover it up."

Margaret gets a lot of attention for how bold and brash her comedy is, especially around issues of sex and gender. And that's true, she is very open, loud, and funny about that. But the very act of talking about it at all goes hard in defiance of her culture and makes her approach even braver.

I talked earlier about how impostor syndrome is much more than an annoyance to people with depression, it's an existential threat. And that's because of the diminished self that they're dealing with. For people of color in America, for people in the LGBTQ community, for any group other than people like me living in their castles high atop Mount Privilege, openly talking about depression is likewise an existential threat. What I've learned, and I had to be taught this because I've never lived it, is that opening up about depression can feel like giving one more weapon to someone who you know can use it against you.

5. It's Not Your Fault

"Depression lies," said Jenny Lawson on a season two episode. "Because every single time, it says, 'You'll never come out of this again. You are absolutely worthless, your family is better off without you.' And then I remind myself depression lies. Those things are lies."

When you take a minute to look at those lies, you can see how patently ridiculous they are. The tricky part is that depression is not just a liar but a tremendous impressionist. Not in the Claude Monet sense but in the Rich Little or Frank Caliendo sense (side note: there really aren't a lot of professional impressionists out there). Depression poses these lies as your own self-generated thoughts and not those of your illness. Depression is good at making you think it's not even there and that you are the problem. Depression wants you to think you made a choice to be this way. When you fall for that, as I did for decades, you hate yourself even more.

As if someone would choose depression. As if you or I or anyone would opt for this kind of life. As if our real problem was a kind of monumental stupidity when it came to lifestyle choices.

Compounding the problem, of course, are the actual stupid people: the jerks who tell you to snap out of it, to smile more, to go for a walk. When this happens, I believe you have two options. Option 1: Give them a look of sudden delight and squeal, "Oooooh! I never thought of that! I bet that'll take care of it lickety-split! Thanks, pal!" and skip away, leaving the jerk in your sarcastic wake. Option 2: Look the jerk square in the face and ask, "Do you think I haven't tried that? Do you think I'd be in this situation if that shit worked?" And then wait for an answer. And then skip away. The important thing is the skipping.

Depression is an illness that happened to you. Maybe it was from the chemicals and inherited genetic traits that appeared in your brain before you were even born. Maybe it was from a trauma that occurred and then festered in your brain. Maybe there were people with power over you who behaved in a way that screwed you up. It wasn't you. You didn't choose this. No one would ever choose this. It's not your fault.

Let's say you're a bank manager and you notice that thousands of dollars are going missing from your bank every day.

It's not because you're absentminded, it's because there's a god-damn bank robber robbing your bank. So the proper response is not to think that you deserve it and it's all your fault. No, you call the cops and review video and you go catch the bastard and lock him up. Then you hire better security guards.

6. You Can't Achieve Your Way Out of This

Depression isn't keeping an eye on your LinkedIn account. It does not care about your success. Getting a big promotion or a sweet new job will not make depression go away. Those things might affect what you have but not what you are. I've covered this a lot in the book, but it tends to shock people when I talk about it on the show or in speeches so I'll say it again.

I suspect that people with depression are fixated on the pos-sibility of ambition being rewarded with happiness. Probably more than most people are. That's because ambition about the future is a way of avoiding looking at a past that's often pretty bleak or a future that is terrifying.

This isn't to say that getting a better job or a pile of money can't be really great. They often are. Achievements or windfalls can often wipe out a particular cause of worry or dread, maybe even wipe out that worry forever. But then you get used to that new version of normal, the novelty wears off, and you're left with the same brain you've always had, and that's when depres-sion emerges from dormancy.

Throughout my life, I looked to the future and figured my mental cloud would disappear if I achieved the next big thing or happened to be valued by the next employer / director / girl / editor. When it didn't, I took it as a sign that I wasn't aiming high enough. Which is crazy! In my defense, I actually am crazy. I wrote a book about that.

7. The Past Matters

For the last several years, I have been marinating in depression as a full-time job (the podcast), second job (giving speeches), third job (writing this book), and chronic mental illness. And it's been good and meaningful work, not least of all because I've ended up getting paid to ask famous people about their darkest moments and then the famous people tell me(!).

In that time, my opinion on where depression comes from has evolved. Before we started the show, I was generally of the mind that, sure, there could be family histories or trauma, but I chalked a lot of it up to being something akin to getting hit by lightning. You're out in an open field, a storm comes along, and zap, you get hit. Could have happened to anyone but it came bursting out of the sky and hit you right in the brain.

But after sifting through all these stories, I've spotted a lot of patterns that point to trauma being a major culprit. I've heard about people getting screwed up in some way early in life, not dealing with the trauma sufficiently or at all, and then being knocked down by depression later on. The musician Ted Leo was molested by a piano teacher at age ten and later became an angry punk rock teen, throwing himself into mosh pits and aggressive music. It was a way for his pain to be expressed even if he couldn't get rid of it. It was only years later, when he gained a better understanding of what had happened, that he could make more sense of his depression and manage it more effectively.

Scott Thompson of the Kids in the Hall, who I talked about earlier, grew up in a family of five kids, all boys. He says there are still holes in the plaster in his childhood home from indoor hockey games that got especially rough. Scott's father had a violent temper, too, which the boys were always having to keep in mind. When Scott grew up, he joined Kids in the Hall, a group of five young men, and became the angriest and meanest person in that group because that's what he had been taught. Scott's brother Dean died by suicide, and that contributed to his depression but so did the fact that the rest of the world isn't nearly so accepting of violence and anger as the Thompsons had been.

I'm like a lot of people in that there is a clear history of depression among my ancestors. But the more I learn about the long-term effects of trauma, the blurrier the line gets between nature and nurture. Sure, I may have had a genetic predisposition, but if that's the case, I probably had some behavioral patterns—addiction, emotional remoteness, anxiety disorders—that went with it.

Because I am over fifty years old now and a dad, I have an interest in history. Didn't always. In high school, I thought it was boring and irrelevant to my boldly innovative MTV young person life. Only now do I realize how fascinating it is because it's how we got here. History is why everything that's happening is happening.

8. There's No Tidy Ending

We live in a story-driven culture. When we get together with other humans, we talk about the shows we're watching, the movies we've seen, and sometimes, if we're lucky, the books we're reading. What we might not realize is that an overwhelming number of these cultural items follow the same formula of "hero goes on a journey." If it's Disney, throw in a sassy animal sidekick and a dead mom.

A few years ago, I was unexpectedly invited to write a screenplay for a movie studio based on a property they had licensed that I knew a lot about. On a phone call, the producer told me to "just go ahead and follow the standard three-act structure."

"Sure," I said, "no problem," while frantically Googling "standard three-act structure." It's the formula of almost every movie you see. The hero is living his life, a crisis happens, the hero must go forth and solve it, they encounter increasingly difficult obstacles, a completely impossible final obstacle appears and is overcome, the task is completed, and the hero returns home. It's most of the entertainment we consume. It gets repeated and resold over and over because audiences crave it.

Depression is not like this. It's just a big hard weird undefinable thing and you don't know what will happen next or when or if it will ever end. And, yes, I'm sorry to break that to you. I've talked with people who were in the depths of an episode and others who haven't thought about it much for years. I've never known what was ahead for anyone or myself. There is reason for optimism when one moves from ignorance to understanding but no guarantees. I'm in a position where I can see more of the obstacles heading my way, and I'm more skilled at overcoming them but that's about it. Our stories will end when we die but the ending won't be satisfying in any kind of cinematic way.

9. Yes

On Labor Day 2019, my son, Charlie, was two days into his first year of college. The dorm room he shared was tiny, so he and his roommate had opted to have their beds "lofted," which meant placing them on long beams suspended over their desks. It's a good use of space, but it does require some means of actually reaching the bed.

The college is a reasonable drive from our house, so I volunteered to buy some ladders and bring them over. When I got to the dorm with the ladders, they were clearly too short, necessitating a return to the nearby huge hardware store where I bought them. Charlie decided to go with me.

As we drove, familiar dark clouds formed in my mind. I worried Charlie was completely unprepared for college, as poorly suited as the too-short ladder. I fretted over his sisters starting their years of high school and middle school the next day. I judged myself a terrible father for all the poor parenting I'd done over the years. I was a failure again just like always.

But then something shifted.

How wonderful, I thought, to be in a minivan right now, driving down this street, trees and birds all around, alive like me. And my son is with me and he is setting off on a tremendous adventure. We get to return a ladder and find a better ladder! What a fun puzzle to solve with my son, whom I love and who loves me. His sisters start school tomorrow and these flowers that are my kids will further bloom. Look at those clouds. The air is perfectly balanced for a human's respiratory system. I'm alive and I get to experience all this.

If I had ever felt this way before, it had been too long ago for me to remember.

My brother Rick left a note behind before he died twelve years before. He said it was all too much. He said he just needed to take a break for a while. He left us to wonder what he meant by this. I never will know the answer.

But in this van, on the way to get a new ladder, I said yes to the world. Yes. Yes. Oh my God yes. Yes, yes, yes! I said yes!

ACKNOWLEDGMENTS

I thank the people who helped me and the people who harmed me. Deliberately or accidentally. With planning or with spontaneity. I thank the events that led me here, be they glorious or disastrous. Together they all formed the world I'm delighted to live in. I am here. Hooray.

More specifically, thanks always go to my loving, twisted, hilarious, and brilliant family. Jill, Charlie, Kate, and Marge, you are always my favorite part of the day. Also, thanks to Sally and Maisy, who, being dogs, are too stupid to read this.

Thanks to my family of origin, who are good humans. Also their spouses and children for helping.

My agent of many years, Jennifer Gates of Aevitas Creative, told me in very clear and urgent terms that I could and should write this. She was correct. Thanks, Jen, for always showing me the hope in my efforts.

Thanks to Elisabeth Dyssegaard and St. Martin's Press for understanding this book right from the start, often in clearer terms than I did. And to Alan Bradshaw and his elite copyediting squadron.

Peter Clowney was always on hand for clear eyes, blunt opinions, and constant encouragement. Thanks also to Thomas Höft and Andrew Beveridge of Math Emergency and Steve Alliston, Sean Farnand, Scott Reed, Joe Seefeldt, Tom Donahue, and the five thousand bassists of Free Range Chickens and Chicken Starship.

I'm fortunate to have befriended people I had previously admired from a distance, and many have become advocates for our podcast and for the cause of mental health awareness. So thank you to Peter Sagal, Andy Richter, Neko Case, Paul F. Tompkins, Patton Oswalt, Maria Bamford, John Green, Gary Gulman, Jonny Sun, Jen Kirkman, Open Mike Eagle, Ted Leo, Aimee Mann, Rhett Miller, Jenny Lawson, Jeff Tweedy, Neal Brennan, Craig Finn, John Darnielle, Ana Marie Cox, and many more.

The podcast, this book, and my general career direction wouldn't be possible without HealthPartners and Make It OK. Thanks to Donna Zimmerman, Andrea Walsh, Marina Olson, Marna Canterbury, and everyone there.

Big thanks to Kryssy Pease and Kate Moos for all the energy and creativity they have invested in *THWoD* the podcast and *THWoD* the book. Thanks, too, to my colleagues Kristina Lopez, Brandon Santos, Mike Reszler, Nancy Cassutt, and everyone at American Public Media and Minnesota Public Radio. Also to Steve Nelson, who advocated for *THWoD* and pushed it through to reality during his time at APM. Katie Sisneros provided valuable assistance with her smart brain. Roger Lindberg gave me excellent genealogical information and insight. John Hodgman and Dave Eggers rule.

~

Albums listened to while in the act of writing this book:

Quadrophenia, The Who
No Depression, Uncle Tupelo
Anodyne, Uncle Tupelo
A Ghost Is Born, Wilco
Run the Jewels 3, Run the Jewels
Robyn Sings, Robyn Hitchcock
Melodrama, Lorde
I Am Easy to Find, The National
Let Go, Nada Surf
The Best of Everything, Tom Petty & the Heartbreakers
Nebraska, Bruce Springsteen
Hell-On, Neko Case
The Sunset Tree, The Mountain Goats
Blue, Joni Mitchell
Rumours, Fleetwood Mac
Fables of the Reconstruction, R.E.M.
The Low End Theory, A Tribe Called Quest

And sky-high towers of thanks to the *THWoD*-balls, our listeners, who make all this work a pleasure.

JOHN MOE is the creator and host of the acclaimed mental health podcast *Depresh Mode with John Moe*; he has served as host of national public radio broadcasts such as *Weekend America, The Hilarious World of Depression,* and *Wits.* His writing and reporting have been heard on *All Things Considered, Morning Edition, Marketplace, Day to Day,* and more. He's the author of four books, and his writing appears in humor anthologies, *The New York Times Magazine, McSweeney's,* and *The Seattle Times.* He's a much-in-demand public speaker.